Kenneth Rexroth

THE ELASTIC RETORT

BOOKS IN PRINT BY KENNETH REXROTH

CONTINUUM BOOKS / HERDER AND HERDER:
The Alternative Society
With Eye and Ear
American Poetry in the Twentieth Century
The Orchid Boat: The Women Poets of China
    with Ling Chung

NEW DIRECTIONS:
The Phoenix and the Tortoise
The Collected Longer Poems of Kenneth Rexroth
The Collected Shorter Poems of Kenneth Rexroth
100 Poems from the Japanese
100 Poems from the Chinese
Love and the Turning Year:
    100 More Poems from the Chinese
Pierre Reverdy: Selected Poems
Love Is an Art of Time: 100 More Japanese Poems
Bird in the Bush
Assays
An Autobiographical Novel

UNICORN PRESS:
Sky Sea Birds Trees Earth House Beasts Flowers

CITY LIGHTS:
Beyond the Mountains
30 Spanish Poems of Love and Exile

PYM RANDALL PRESS:
100 French Poems

UNIVERSITY OF MICHIGAN PRESS:
Poems from the Greek Anthology

AVON BOOKS:
The Classics Revisited

The Elastic Retort

*Essays in Literature
and Ideas*

Kenneth Rexroth

A Continuum Book
THE SEABURY PRESS · NEW YORK

ACKNOWLEDGMENTS

The author extends grateful acknowledgment to the following periodicals, where chapters of this book originally appeared: *San Francisco Magazine* for "Japan and the Second Greater East Asia Co-Prosperity Sphere." *The Nation* for "Six Japanese Novelists," originally published in slightly different form. *Continuum* for "Lamennais," "The Evolution of Anglo-Catholicism," "Some Notes on Newman." *The New York Times* for "20 Plays of the Nō Theatre," © 1971 by The New York Times Company. Reprinted by permission. *The Antioch Review* for "The Surprising Journey of Father Lonergan," © 1970 by The Antioch Review, Inc. First published in *The Antioch Review*, Vol. 30, No. 1; reprinted by permission. *Book Week* for "*The World of the Shining Prince* by Ivan Morris," reprinted, courtesy of the *Chicago Tribune*. *Saturday Review* for the series, "More Classics Revisited."

"Japanese Poetry Now," reprinted by permission of Schocken Books Inc. from *Japanese Poetry Now* by Thomas Fitzsimmons, Introduction Copyright © 1973 by Schocken Books Inc. Yvor Winters, "Hunter," "Sleep" reprinted from *Collected Poems*, © 1960 Yvor Winters, by permission of The Swallow Press, Chicago. "In a Station of the Metro," reprinted from Ezra Pound, *Personae*, © 1926 by Ezra Pound. Reprinted by permission of New Directions Publishing Corporation, and by permission of Faber and Faber Ltd. from *Collected Shorter Poems*. "The Influence of Classical Japanese Poetry on Modern American Poetry" was originally presented at The International Conference on Japanese Studies, sponsored by the Japan P.E.N. Club, in November, 1972.

Copyright © 1973 by Kenneth Rexroth
Design by Paula Wiener
Printed in the United States of America

Library of Congress Cataloging in Publication Data

Rexroth, Kenneth, 1905–
   The elastic retort.

   (A Continuum book)
   1. Literature—Addresses, essays, lectures.
I. Title.
PN511.R58   809   73–6425
ISBN 0-8164-9168-2

For Carol

Contents

JAPAN

RELIGION

More Classics
Revisited

The Song of Songs

To judge from contemporary literature, the easiest books of the Bible for modern man, in his completely secular society, to appreciate are *Job* and *The Song of Songs*. The reason is obvious. They are not what he thinks of as religious. Least of all do they fit into the common notion of the "Judaeo-Christian tradition." From the Talmudists or the unknown authors of the *Kabbalah* to Orthodox rabbis or Hasidic zadiks drunk with holiness, from the Fathers of the Church to the mystics of the Middle Ages, these two books, of all in the Old Testament, have been held central to the meaning of religion. So today's extraordinary reversal of judgment shows only that most men in our predatory thing-bound society have no idea of what religion is.

There are almost as many interpretations of *The Song of Songs* as there are interpreters. Orthodox Christianity has interpreted it as a dramatic hymn celebrating the love of Christ for his Church, the mystics as the love of Christ for the human soul. The compilers of the Propers, the variable parts of the Mass, and the prayer hours of the Breviary, have mined it for antiphons and versicles on feasts of the Blessed Virgin Mary. Only recently has it come to be used for this purpose in underground nuptial masses. Jewish interpreters have often taken it simply literally as a marriage ode for the marriage of Solomon and the Queen of Sheba. Otherwise the Jewish interpretations differ little from the Christian—which they have usually preceded. The Kabbalists and the Hasidim parallel the more extreme mystics of the cultus of adoration of Mary. To them *The Song of Songs* is a collection of hymns showing forth the love of Jehovah for the Shekinah, his per-

3

sonalized Power and Glory, a concept not unlike the shaktis of Shiva, Vishnu and Buddha—Pravati, Lakshmi and Tara. This places *The Song of Songs* in the same class as the *Krishnalila,* the songs of Krishna's love play with Radha. Central to this interpretation in Judaism is the central sacramental concept of Judaism itself—the idea that it is in the consummation of marriage that immanence and transcendence become one.

But what in fact is, or was, when it was put together, *The Song of Songs*? Was it the liturgy of an *hierosgamos,* a dramatic poem accompanying the mystical marriage of one of the many Baals and Ashtoreths of Canaan, acted out by priests and priestesses in a so-called fertility rite? Possibly. We have several dramatic odes and fragments of poems of this kind in Ugarit, in the languages of Mesopotamia, and in Egyptian. Many modern interpreters have tried to put it together as an actual play, just as they have *Job,* but its dramatic continuity is not really very apparent. Then on the other hand neither are the *hierosgamos* dramas of the Near East generally. They were written a long time before Sophocles or Aristotle's *Poetics.*

It is common nowadays to talk about the Bible as a collection of myths. There are even profoundly secularized theologians who want to "de-mythologize" it. The shoe is on the other foot. It is Biblical exegesis which is a collection of myths. Each age constructs the myth it deserves. Only a little while ago both Moses and Jesus were sun myths. A little while after that they were non-existent. The most fashionable myth at the moment is "God is Dead," paralleling exactly the art of Andy Warhol or the politics of our rulers.

The mythic interpretation of *The Song of Songs* that I prefer, and suspect might even be true, greatly resembles Marcel Granet's *Festivals and Songs of Ancient China,* his essential and revolutionary interpretation of the *Shi Ching,*

the Chinese *Book of Odes*. There are several contemporary Biblical critics who share this interpretation.

That is: *The Song of Songs* is a collection of dance lyrics for group marriage which were sung as young men and maidens danced in the fields and vineyards at the corn harvest festival, then when the water was turned from the irrigation ditches into the runnels between the rows of vines, and last at the grape harvest. All of these ancient rites, due to the shifting of the seasons in an inaccurate calendar, eventually came to be concentrated in Succoth, the Feast of Booths, or, as some versions of the Bible call it, the Feast of Tabernacles. The booths themselves, still built in the backyard, or on the roof, on Succoth by Orthodox Jews, are survivals of the little shacks of leaves and sticks that sheltered the grape pickers. The roof is left flimsy, with the sky looking through, so that the Shekinah can descend and cover with her wings of glory the husband and wife as they sleep together under the leaves and stars and moon on the nights of the festival.

So we can think of the separate songs of *The Song of Songs* being sung by a row of girls just come to womanhood and a row of boys just come to manhood, dancing a dance, not unlike a modern hora, on opposite sides of the living waters, while the king and queen of the festival, whom they have chosen from amongst themselves, march to the fulfillment of the marriage of Heaven and Earth.

This is by no means an eccentric or even mystical or Hasidic interpretation. Furthermore, scattered about the Bible are many passages which might refer to the same rite. To conflate: In the shadow of the *lingam* and *yoni,* the *massebah,* on the feast of oil and wine, from the arbors of Asiph, from the embracing lovers, joy spread like a sweet incense in the fire of communion. Then the virgins of Israel, adorned with tabrets, went forth in the dances of them that make merry. Then the winepress was trod with joy and gladness. There was shouting at the vintage. When the daughters of Shiloh came out to dance in dances, the men came from the vineyards and every man took a bride.

Most especially the psalms which culminate in the 84th embody the other aspect of the rites of the harvest, the procession with palm, willow and myrtle branches up to the temple, in memory of the day when Solomon—*Shelemoh*—"Peace"—consecrated the temple to Jehovah—another marriage of Heaven and Earth. It is fascinating to go through the Bible with a good analytical expositor's concordance and look up all the references to tabernacles and the key words like tabrets, vineyards and winepresses. Put together, they form a pretty clear picture of the ancient rite, even down to small details—as for instance the fires of sarments, the dry prunings of the vines—saved from spring—which blazed alongside the channels of new water, and lit the dance and through which the dancers may have leaped.

This is not all dry exegesis. An understanding of the background of *The Song of Songs* not only makes the poems themselves far more thrilling, but it restores to the central place in our conception of the world as holy, the sanctification of the communion of man and woman, of the people in community, of mankind and the earth from which he is made, and of earth and heaven. Last and not least, the songs of *The Song of Songs* are very simply amongst the most beautiful love songs in all the literatures of the world (not to speak of their contemporaneity—"I am black, but comely, O ye daughters of Jerusalem").

Tao Te Ching

The *Tao Te Ching* is one of the more mysterious documents in the history of religion. Nothing is known of its author, called Lao Tzu or Old Master, except a few legends given by the historian Ssu Ma Ch'ien. Its date is the subject of dispute amongst scholars. Even its nature and purpose are ambiguous. What it most resembles is our own *Book of Psalms* as used in Christian monastic orders, a collection of poems and short prose passages to be used for meditation or for chanting in choir by a community of contemplatives. As far as we know there were no monks in China until the introduction of Buddhism hundreds of years after the latest possible date for the *Tao Te Ching*. Nevertheless this is the best way to understand the book—as a collection of subjects for meditation, catalysts for contemplation. It certainly is not a philosophical treatise or a religious one, either, in our sense of the words religion, philosophy or treatise.

Arthur Waley, whose translation is still by far the best, rendered the title as *The Way and Its Power*. Others have called *Tao* "The Way of Nature"—*Te* means something like *virtus* in Latin. ("Lao Tzu" is pronounced "Low Ds;" "Tao Te Ching," "Dow Deh Jing," "ow" as in "bow-wow".)

In the Confucian writings *Tao* usually means either a road or a way of life. It means that in the opening verse of the *Tao Te Ching*, "The way that can be followed (or the road that can be traced or charted) is not the true way. The word that can be spoken is not the true word." Very quickly the text drives home the noumenous significance of both *Tao* and *Te*. *Tao* is described by paradox and contradiction—the Absolute in a world view where absolutes are impossible, the ulti-

7

mate reality which is neither being nor not being, the hidden meaning behind all meaning, the pure act which acts without action and yet the reason and order of the simplest physical occurrence.

It is quite possible—in fact Joseph Needham in his great *Science and Civilization in China* does so—to interpret the *Tao Te Ching* as a treatise of elementary primitive scientific empiricism; certainly it is that. Over and over it says, "learn the way of nature"; "do not try to overcome the forces of nature but use them." On the other hand, Fr. Leo Weiger, S.J. called the *Tao Te Ching* a restatement of the philosophy of the *Upanishads* in Chinese terms. Buddhists, especially Zen Buddhists in Japan and America, have understood and translated the book as a pure statement of Zen doctrine. Even more remarkable, contemporary Chinese, and not all of them Marxists, have interpreted it as an attack on private property and feudal oppression, and as propaganda for communist anarchism. Others have interpreted it as a cryptic work of erotic mysticism and yoga exercises. It is all of these things and more, and not just because of the ambiguity of the ideograms in a highly compressed classical Chinese text; it really is many things to many men—like the Tao itself.

Perhaps the best way to get at the foundations of the philosophy of the *Tao Te Ching* is by means of an historical, anthropological approach which in itself may be mythical. There is little doubt that the organized Taoist religion which came long after the *Tao Te Ching* but which still was based on it, swept up into an occultist system much of the folk religion of the Chinese culture area, much as Japanese Shintō (which means the *Tao* of the Gods) did in Japan. If the later complicated Taoist religion developed from the local cults, ceremonies and superstitions of the pre-civilized folk religion, how could it also develop from the *Tao Te Ching* or from the early Taoist philosophers whose works are collected under the names of Chuang Tzu and Lieh Tzu and who are about as unsuperstitious and anti-ritualistic as any thinkers in history? The connection is to be found I feel in the shamans and shamanesses of a pan-Asiatic culture which stretches from the Baltic far into America, and to the forest philosophers and hermits who appear at the beginnings of history and literature in both India and China and whose prehistoric existence is testified by the yogi in the lotus position on a Mohenjo-Daro seal. The *Tao Te Ching* describes the experiential or existential core of the transcendental experience shared by the visionaries of primitive cultures. The informants of Paul Radin's classic *Primitive Man as Philosopher* say much the same things. It is this which gives it its air of immemorial wisdom, although many passages are demonstrably later than Confucius, and may be later than the "later" Taoists, Chuang Tzu and Lieh Tzu.

There are two kinds of esotericism in oriental religion: the proliferation of spells, chants, rituals, mystical diagrams, cosmologies and cosmogonies, trials of the soul, number mysticism, astrology and alchemy, all of which go to form the corpus of a kind of pan-Gnosticism. Its remarkable similarities are shared by early Christian heretics, Jewish Kabbalists, Tantric worshipers of Shiva, Japanese Shingon Buddhists, and Tibetan lamas. The other occultism (held strangely enough by the most highly developed minds amongst some people) is the exact opposite, a stark religious empiricism shorn of all dogma or cult, an attitude toward life based upon realization of the unqualified religious experience as such. What does the contemplator contemplate? What does the life of illumination illuminate? To these questions there can be no answer—the experience is beyond qualification. So say the Zen documents, a form of late Buddhism originating in China, but so say the Hinayana texts, which are assumed to be as near as we can get to the utterances of the historic Buddha Sakyamuni, but so say also the *Upanishads*—"not this, not this, not that, not that," but so also say some of the highly literate and sophisticated technical philosophers (in our sense of the word) of Sung Dynasty Neo-Confucianism. So says the *Tao Te Ching*.

In terms of Western epistemology, a subject Classical Chinese thought does not even grant existence, the beginning and end of knowledge are the same thing—the intuitive apprehension of reality as a totality, before and behind the data of sense or the constructions of experience and reason. The *Tao Te Ching* insists over and over that this is both a personal, psychological, and a social, moral, even political first principle. At the core of life is a tiny, steady flame of contemplation. If this goes out the person perishes, although the body and its brain may stumble on, and civilization goes rapidly to ruin. The source of life, the source of the order of nature, the source of knowledge, and the source of social order are all identical—the immediate comprehension of the reality beyond being and not being; existence and essence; being and becoming. Contact with this reality is the only kind of power there is. Against that effortless power all self-willed acts and violent attempts to rule self, man, or natural process are delusion and end only in disaster.

The lesson is simple, and once learned, easy to paraphrase. The Tao is like water. Striving is like smoke. The forces of Nature are infinitely more powerful than the strength of men. Toil to the top of the highest peak and you will be swept away in the first storm. Seek the lowest possible point and eventually the whole mountain will descend to you. There are two ways of knowing, under standing and over bearing. The first is called wisdom. The second is called winning arguments. Being as power comes from the still void behind being and not being. The enduring and effective power of the individual, whether hermit or king or householder, comes from the still void at the heart of the contemplative. The wise statesman conquers by the quiet use of his opponents' violence, like the judo and ju jitsu experts.

The *Tao Te Ching* is a most remarkable document, but the most remarkable thing about it is that it has not long since converted all men to its self-evident philosophy. It was called mysterious at the beginning of this essay. It is really simple and obvious; what is mysterious is the complex ignorance and complicated morality of mankind that reject its wisdom.

Euripides' *Hippolytus*

Euripides' *Hippolytus* is distinguished, first off, by its title. During the ages since it was written, the same plot and characters have been used by many authors, most notably Racine, but the central character has always been Phaedra, and the other plays have usually been called by her name. It is hard for us, with our romantic notions of the relations between the sexes, to think of Hippolytus as the hero of the play. Certainly he is not very heroic. Or is he? Phaedra is dead before the play is half over, and her confrontation of Hippolytus is brief indeed. She has all our sympathy. Hippolytus has little or none. As Euripides portrays him, he is one of the most disagreeable characters in classic literature. A great deal of dramatic time that could be put to more telling use is taken up with his priggish monologues. Yet the play is structurally closer to Aristotle's prescription for the perfect classicist drama than any other of Euripides, more Sophoclean than Sophocles—but in structure alone. All of Euripides' plays are odd, but Hippolytus, superficially so conventional, is more odd than most.

The extraordinary cultural telescoping in the evolution of Greek drama has often been remarked. Aeschylus is the dramatist of the newly evolved imperial city-state, Sophocles of its prime, and Euripides of megalopolis, and yet they were almost contemporaries and Sophocles and Euripides died in the same year. Euripides was the most popular through the long centuries of Hellenistic and Roman empires, and rightly so, he is a poet of the great city and its ills and frustrations, quite as much as Baudelaire or Bertolt Brecht. *Hippolytus* is a play about over-civilized and demoralized people.

When Arnold Toynbee wished to give an example of the failure of nerve, the alienation and loss of life aim, characteristic of a megalopolitan civilization entering on its decline, he quoted a famous passage from Lucretius' *On the Nature of Things*. But this is an echo of Phaedra's speech which sets the dramatic situation of the play. It is more appropriate than perhaps even Euripides imagined, although he was a sophisticated philosopher of history himself. Phaedra, after all, is a princess raped away from the old decaying Minoan civilization of Crete by Theseus, the representative of barbaric Athens. According to the mythological demands of the plot, she is only an instrument of Aphrodite's curse on Hippolytus for neglecting her worship. In fact she is a world-weary nymphomaniac, married to an insensitive soldier and hot for her homosexual stepson, just like someone in Proust or Ford Madox Ford.

The situation is quite unlike that of Joseph and Potiphar's wife. Joseph was a clever and lusty slave, Potiphar's wife just another adulterous woman. Phaedra and Hippolytus are personifications of the breakdown of the classical order of Greek culture. For Hippolytus is not what the myth made him, the son of a barbarian war lord and a savage Amazon. He is at least as decadent as his stepmother, and his romantic nature worship and horror of sex are as symptomatic of social decay as Phaedra's *accidie* and eroticism. Aphrodite, Artemis and Poseidon are not the gods of myth, they are symbols of psychological forces. Myths are externalizations of internal social dilemmas, but in Euripides myths are internalizations, like the figures of neurotic dreams. Even the comic figure of the nurse is a function of social disorder, the corruption of the noble by the base. Euripides puts into her mouth all the persuasiveness of a crooked lawyer who has learned from the unscrupulous rhetoricians of the decadence of the sophistic movement to make the better seem the worse case, and evil seem good. Her transvaluation of all values is the crux of the play. Without her, there would have been no tragedy; Phaedra would simply have committed suicide. Or is the play a tragedy? It has noble characters destroyed by tragic flaws, at least that is what it says. Yet they are all lacking in heroic dignity and self-respect. The characters of Aeschylus and Sophocles are always at home in their own doom. Hippolytus, Phaedra and Theseus are lost in their myth, without self-possession. Only the representative of mass man, the nurse, "knows her way around."

Greek philosophy and literature, like American, was peculiarly medical in its outlook. Unlike Americans, Sophocles, Aeschylus, Aristotle, Plato, in ethics, psychology, politics, were health oriented. Human conduct was described and judged ultimately in terms of man at his physical and mental best. Euripides, like American medicine or psychology or literature, was morbidity oriented. He is the most psychological of classic writers, at least in our sense, but only because we define psychology in terms of pathology. "Who is well?" Euripides asks this question again and again in every play. It was a nonsensical question to the classic Greek thinker to whom the traditions of Aesculapian and Hippocratic medicine still determined the understanding of human minds and motives.

Is the play a tragedy? Certainly not if we agree with those eccentrics who hold that King Lear is a black comedy. The latter half of the play is taken up with speeches by Hippolytus and Theseus which reveal them as a prig and a dolt. Hippolytus is mentally ill in a most unpleasant way, and Theseus is the embodiment of the conventional authoritarian. Both are totally self-righteous. It is easier to sympathize with Macbeth. Certainly it is far easier to do so with Phaedra. But Phaedra is gone.

Why has the play remained so popular? Why does it still move us profoundly? First, it contains some of the finest poetry Euripides ever wrote. Although his extraordinary mastery of verse is not translatable, much of the emotional power survives in the meaning alone as long as the translator is careful to convey that meaning. Second, *Hippolytus* is a classically constructed play, true to Aristotle's strict rules, but it is about anti-classical people. During the long war with Sparta Athenian life became widely neurotic. A new type of interpersonal sickness came into being. The organs of reciprocity were crippled. Words for human relationships lost their meanings and turned into their opposites. Thucydides describes this derangement of communication at length in one of his greatest passages, a diagnosis of the internalization of madness of war which sounds like a description of contemporary America. *Hippolytus* is a clear and simple presentation of the price of late megalopolitan civilization, of empire, the loss of the meaning of love. We return to the play down the ages because, down the ages, the characters return to us. They are the archetypes of our own ills.

Aristotle's *Poetics*

Tragedy, then, is the imitation of a good action, which is complete and of a certain length, by means of language made pleasing for each part separately; it relies in its various elements not on narrative but on action; through pity and fear it achieves the purgation of such emotions.

—Poetics

Is Aristotle's *Poetics* a classic? Certainly it is the mother of classicism, or rather neo-classicism, and as a textbook it has begot many a classic. It has probably been printed more often than any Greek book except the Gospels and Plato's *Republic*. Commentaries on it in every civilized language are innumerable. It is the first work in the general field of esthetics in Western literature; yet to class it so is only the roughest of approximations, because what we now call philosophical esthetics scarcely is hinted at. It has provided rules and recipes for countless dramas and other fictions yet the best known of these rules, the famous doctrine of the unities of place, time and action, is not to be found in it, nor, for that matter, are most of the other "laws" of literary construction attributed to Aristotle.

Most critics of the Western world have been influenced either positively or negatively by the *Poetics* and in every generation there has existed a critical school which considered itself Aristotelian. Most of the principles of these schools have not been found in the letter of the *Poetics,* but have been deduced from it, or read into it, by the changing tastes of generations of neo-classicists. The Anti-Aristotelians likewise have attacked the *Poetics* for things that Aristotle never said

16

and often for ideas which, given his time and place, he could never have conceived, and would have found totally incomprehensible if they were presented to him.

Around each of the key words of Aristotle's short definition of tragedy the most violent controversies have raged, and to this day no two translators or commentators agree on the meanings of all of them. If Greek tragedy is the etherialization of myth, Aristotle's little essay—it is not really book length—on tragedy is something like myth itself. It has functioned as a myth of criticism, the subject of innumerable etherializations. There are existentialist, Marxist, Neo-Thomist, pluralist, Hegelian, Neo-Kantian—and so on back to the Arabians and the Alexandrian Greeks—readings of the *Poetics,* all of them quite different. No critical work in Indian or Far Eastern civilization has played so provocative and seminal a role.

This enormous influence is due, first to the great prestige of Aristotle's name; second, to the fact that the *Poetics* is the first extended serious criticism of literature surviving in the West; third, to its great simplicity. This simplicity is not that of the clear, succinct statement of profoundly understood fundamentals. Quite the contrary. There is no evidence in the *Poetics* that Aristotle possessed any sensitivity to the beauties of poetry as such. Although the *Poetics* is concerned almost exclusively with tragedy, Aristotle had less of what we call the tragic sense of life than almost any philosopher who ever lived, less even than Leibniz with his "best of all possible worlds." Aristotle was an optimist. Leibniz' judgment never entered his mind. The world he studied was simply given. It was not only the best, it was the only one possible. There was nothing in the human situation that could not be corrected by the right application of the right principles of ethics, politics, and economics. Even Plato, who banned the poets from the *Republic,* and in the *Laws* permitted only happy,

patriotic plays to be performed by slaves, had a greater awareness of the meaning of tragedy—which is precisely why he
banned it.

It never occurs to Aristotle that the three great tragedians,
Aeschylus, Sophocles, Euripides, are, from his point of view,
themselves philosophers, and that together they form a philosophical school, a body of doctrine with insights into the
meaning and end of life that have never been surpassed. Unlike the notions of the technical philosophers, their "tragic
world view" is not subject to the changes of fashion, but remains true in all times and all societies. Of course Aeschylus,
Sophocles and Euripides are not primarily philosophers. They
are artists. But Aristotle does not consider them as artists
either. He considers them as craftsmen.

The *Poetics* is a textbook of the craft of fiction and as such
it is far more applicable to the commercial fiction of modern
magazines than to Greek tragedies. It has been called a recipe
book for detective story writers. Actually the fictions that
come nearest to meeting Aristotle's specifications are the
standard Western stories of the pulp magazines. These are
not to be despised. Ernst Haycox and Gordon Young raised
the American Western story to a very high level. Year in,
year out, Western movies are better than any other class of
pictures. The great trouble with Haycox and Young is that
they *were* rigorously Aristotelian and therefore ran down into
monotonously repeated formulas. It is hard to think of any
other kinds of fiction, either novels or dramas, which do
exemplify the *Poetics*. The neo-classic theater of Corneille
and Racine or Ben Jonson is governed by rules which are
pseudo-Aristotelianism, the invention of Renaissance critics.

If we are prepared to etherialize the *Poetics* and give the
meanings we like to its key terms, we can make it mean anything and apply it to *The Brothers Karamazov,* Kafka's *The
Trial* or Andre Breton's *Nadja.* This has been done. The one
modern novel it does fit better than almost any other is Joyce's

Ulysses. Joyce was quite well aware of this, but *Ulysses* is neo-classic Aristotle, closer to Corneille than to what Aristotle actually says.

It has been said that the *Poetics* is a pamphlet in praise of Sophocles, and an attack on Euripides, and that the only Greek tragedy which meets Aristotle's prescriptions is Sophocles' *Oedipus the King.* But *Oedipus* does not meet all of Aristotle's prescriptions and violates others. Furthermore Aristotle suddenly reverses himself with the simple sentence, "Euripides is the most tragic of all dramatists." He also says that the best tragedy is one with a happy ending. The primary emphasis of the *Poetics* is on plot, but many of the surviving Greek plays are as plotless as Chekhov or a Japanese Nō play. The notion that the tragic hero possesses a flaw in his otherwise noble character, and that this flaw is usually *hubris,* and that *hubris* means pride, which brings him to disaster, is not found in Aristotle at all. Nor is it a common element in the plot of most of the tragedies we have. Do most tragedies evoke pity and fear or terror in the spectator? Does the witnessing of a tragedy purge the spectator of these socially undesirable emotions? Obviously not for us. It does no good to think up remote meanings for these three Greek words. By *katharsis* Aristotle means the same thing that we mean when we say "cathartic." His attitude toward the arts was not at all that they were the highest expression of mankind, but that they served as a kind of medicine to keep the ordinary man who lived in the world between the machines of meat— the slaves—and the philosophers who spent their time thinking about first principles; free from emotions, and hence motives, that would disrupt the social order. Like Freud after him, Aristotle's esthetics are medical. What the *Poetics* says in the last analysis is, "Timid, sentimental, and emotionally unstable people will feel better, and be better behaved, after a good cry on the stone benches of the theater." This is an esthetics identical with that of the child psychologists who are hired to apologize for lust and murder on television. There is never a hint in Aristotle that tragedy is true.

The *Poetics* could have been written substantially unchanged if Aristotle had never seen a Greek tragedy. The imaginary tragedy which could be deduced from the *Poetics* resembles the commercial fictions of our day for a very simple reason. It is a projection of the ordinary mind, the same then as now. It is the kind of play Aristotle himself would have written if he had possessed, not the genius of Sophocles, but the learned talents of an ordinary craftsman. It is the kind of play that a highly competent academic philosopher, biologist, physicist, or psychologist would write today.

Why did Aristotle write about tragedy at all? Because of its immense social importance in the society in which he lived. We know that the plays of Euripides were performed, on the eve of the Christian era, far away from Athens, on the borders of Afghanistan and on the coasts of Spain. Tragedy was the mass sport of the Greeks as the gladiatorial combats of the circus were of the Romans. It is undoubtedly true that tragedy did perform the functions of social hygiene that Aristotle attributed to it, for many in the way he said, but for others in ways he could not comprehend.

The *Bhagavad-gita*

"Action shall be the sister of dream and thought and deed shall have the same splendor." So said Baudelaire. Sometime around the third century before the Christian era an unknown author inserted into the epic story of *The Mahabharata* a comparatively short religious document, not only small in comparison to the immense size of the epic itself—which was already becoming the gather-all for Hinduism—but shorter far than any of the scriptures of the other world religions. This is the *Bhagavad-gita, The Lord's Song,* one of the three or four most influential writings in the history of man. It is not only influential, it is more profound and more systematic than most religious texts. This statement may sound strange to those who are familiar with nineteenth century rationalist Western European critics who attempted to abstract a logically consistent philosophy from the *Bhagavad-gita,* and who ended up emphasizing its contradictions and ambiguities.

The *Bhagavad-gita* is not a philosophical work, but a religious one, and beside that, a song, a poem. It is not to be compared with Aristotle's *Metaphysics,* or the creed or catechism of the Council of Trent, but with the opening of the *Gospel According to St. John* or to the Magnificat in St. Luke. Its seeming contradictions are resolved in worship. In the words of the great Catholic Modernist, Father George Tyrrell, *Lex credendi, lex orandi,* "the law of faith is the law of prayer." What the unknown author of the *Bhagavad-gita* intended was precisely the resolution and sublimation of the contradictions of the religious life in the great unity of prayer.

The *Bhagavad-gita* is above all else a manual of personal devotion to a personal deity. But to establish this devotion and to give it the widest possible meaning the author subsumes all the major theological and philosophical tendencies of the Hinduism of his time. It is as though the *Summa Theologica* of St. Thomas Aquinas had been dissolved in his prayers and hymns for the feast of Corpus Christi. It so happens that as he lay dying St. Thomas said that that was what he had done. Unless the reader begins by understanding the devotional nature of the *Gita,* its many meanings will always elude him and its over-all meaning will be totally unapproachable.

There are two main strands of thought in the *Gita* which divide and sometimes interweave but which are nonetheless easy to distinguish and follow. First is an exposition of the nature of reality and of the Godhead and its self-unfolding, and second is a description, practically a manual, of the means of communion with the deity.

The poem starts out simply enough and scarcely seems to violate the context of the epic; in fact the first two chapters may largely be part of the original tale. At the major crisis of *The Mahabharata* the warring clans, and their allies numbering uncountable thousands, are marshalled for the crucial battle that will exterminate almost all of them. The Prince Arjuna is sickened by the vision of the coming slaughter and is about to turn away in disgust, and give up the battle. His charioteer Krishna advises him to fight. He tells him that no one really dies, that the myriad dead of the day on the morrow will move on in the wheel of life, and that anyway killer and killed are illusory, and that the warrior's duty is to fight without questioning, but with indifference to gain or glory, dedicating his military virtues to God as a work of prayer.

This advice horrifies modern commentators with their sophisticated ethical sensibility, although it is certainly common enough advice of army chaplains. We forget that the *Bhagavad-gita* begins in the epic context, as though the Sermon on the Mount were to appear in *The Iliad* evolving out of the last fatal conversation between Hector and Andromache. Even

Radhakrishnan, India's leading philosopher of the last generation and spokesman on the highest level for Gandhi's *satya-
graha,* spiritual non-violence, speaks of Arjuna's doubts before the battle as pusillanimous.

Krishna describes briefly the roads to salvation—work,
ritual, learning, or rather, wisdom by learning, contemplation
and devotion. He then describes the metaphysical structure of
being which culminates in what nowadays we would call the
inscrutable ground of being, Brahman, the source of the creative principle of reality. He then goes on to a most extraordinary concept. Behind Brahman, the ultimate reality in all
Western theories of emanationist monism, lies Ishvara, the
ultimate god behind all ultimates, who is a *person.* In answer
to Arjuna's plea, Krishna reveals himself as the incarnation
of the universal form, the embodiment of all the creative
activity of all the universes. That itself is only a kind of mask,
an incarnation, for he, Krishna, is the actual, direct embodiment of Ishvara, the Person who transcends the unknowable
and who can be approached directly by the person Arjuna, as
friend to Friend. The central meaning of *The Lord's Song* is
that being is a conversation of lovers.

Nirvana, as Krishna defines it in the *Gita,* is the joy in
the habitude of illumination, after the dying out of appetite.
It is the medium in which the enlightened live, as in air. As
we of air, they are conscious of it only by an effort of attention. Faith is Shraddha—bliss, the disposition to orient one's
life around the abiding consciousness of spiritual reality. Bad
karma, consequence, drains away in successive lives but good
karma is saved up always, throughout all the thousands of
necessary incarnations, to reach enlightenment. All men
travel toward the eternal Brahman. When we reach the end
of the road no space will have been travelled and no time
spent. You are *sat, cit, ananda*—reality, truth and bliss—and
always have been. Always becomes a meaningless word when
becomes is transformed to *be*. The direct experience of God

is not an act of service or devotion or even of cognition. It is an unqualifiable and unconditioned experience. Who illusions? You are the ultimate Self, but you dream. Work is contemplation. Rite is contemplation. Yoga is contemplation. Learning is contemplation. All are prayer. They are forms of dialogue between two subjects that can never be objects. Insofar as the noblest deed or the most glorified trance is not devotion, it is unreal.

The poem culminates in a hymn of praise to devotion itself—Krishna, speaking for his worshipers, himself to himself. The later sections are a long drawn-out cadence and diminuendo, of recapitulation, instruction and ethical advice. Then we are back, "marshalled for battle on the Field of Law," and Arjuna says, "My delusion is destroyed. Recognition has been obtained by me through Thy grace! I stand firm with my doubts dispelled. I shall act by Thy word."

Reading the *Gita* in a decent translation for the first time is a tremendously thrilling experience. No one who has ever heard it chanted, hour after hour in an Indian temple, before a statue of dark-skinned Krishna, dancing his strange shuffling dance, and playing on his flute, while a cluster of worshipers sat on the floor, silent and entranced, in their white robes, once in a great while someone uttering a short cry, like a Christian amen, is ever likely, no matter how long he lives, to forget it. More commonly of course one hears the chanting of the *Gita Govinda,* the song of Krishna's love adventures with Radha and the milkmaids—but, as any devout Hindu will tell you, the two songs are the same song.

The literature of the *Gita* is enormous. Incomparably the best translation is the recent one by Ann Stanford. Two very free translations are *The Lord's Song* by Sir Edwin Arnold in Victorian verse, and the *Bhagavad-gita* by Swami Prabhavananda and Christopher Isherwood. There are good versions in Penguin, Mentor and the Modern Library, and modern scholarly editions by Franklin Edgerton, and S. Radhakrishnan.

For readers unfamiliar with Hindu thought there are books by Eliot Deutsch, Sri Aurobindo, Radhakrishnan, B. G. Tilak and S. N. Dasgupta. Good introductions to Hindu thought generally are the histories of Indian philosophy by Dasgupta and Radhakrishnan and *Sources of the Indian Tradition,* an omnibus volume edited by William Theodore de Bary for Columbia University Press. In a field so beset with unreliable guides it is essential that the novice get started off with the best authorities. Even so, the most reliable people, for instance, Dasgupta, Radhakrishnan, Aurobindo and Tilak, often contradict one another and are best read together.

Catullus

Tennyson called Catullus the tenderest of Roman poets. He probably gave a considerable amount of thought to that epithet. It could not be better chosen. Gaius Valerius Catullus is distinguished from all the other writers of antiquity by his vulnerability. He is the most personal of Latin poets, and more personal than any Greek poet including Sappho. There is a kind of ceremonial ecstasy about the surviving love poems of Sappho. Catullus translates one, but he adds a stanza which personalizes and gives an intimacy and a wistfulness not in the original. It is this quality that has led critics to speak of his complete spontaneity of utterance as though he dashed off his poetry on the spur of the moment, in the immediate situation of emotional reaction.

Other critics have pointed out that he was called *doctus,* "learned," that his poetry is immensely so in fact, that he was the leader of the group known as the New Poets, disciples of the most scholarly and artificial Greek poets who had written in Alexandria after the end of the Classic period. One of his poems is a translation of the courtier poet of the Ptolemies, Callimachus. People have spoken of his poetry as being colloquial, based on the common speech. Others have pointed out that it is nothing of the sort but a highly artificial literary convention, a kind of pseudo-colloquialism based on decadent Greek models. Both sides are right. Both err because they are laymen. They do not understand the nature of the poet's job. There was no question but that Catullus was deeply involved in the subject matter of his poetry, in a way Virgil, Horace, and even Propertius were not. The small body of intimate love poems and snarling satirical epigrams on which his great reputation is based are not set pieces.

We are never convinced that Horace cared much one way
or another about the curly haired slave girls and other minxes
in his erotic poems. His satires are almost as impersonal as
political pamphlets. Even the elegies of Propertius are far too
world-weary and sophisticated. His subject matter is his ironic
refusal to capitulate to his emotions. The poems of Catullus
are convincing cries of rapture, pain, disgust or wrath, or,
above all, tenderness. Later antiquity was baffled by Catullus.
His limpid speech was still appreciated but the kind of man
he was had become incomprehensible.

Catullus' works dropped from sight and were not recovered
until profound changes in civilization had brought round his
type again at the Renaissance, and the appreciation of his
poetry grew in time as that type became more common.

He was born in Verona, a city of Gauls and Etruscans, and
his character, and his music, have been attributed to his
imagined Celtic blood. Catullus has often been compared to
Burns. The comparison is just if its limitations are understood.
Burns was a poor man, a political radical. His social pleasures
were taken in a world which was exclusively male or male
dominated. The society in which he lived was as hypocritical
as any in history. He was a provincial and his poetry owed
everything to a profound feeling for folk speech and folk
music.

Catullus was the exact opposite. He was exceptionally rich
in an age of irresponsible millionaires. His father was able
to entertain Julius Caesar and his entourage when he visited
Verona. Catullus accompanied the proconsul C. Memmius to
his job in Asia Minor in his own yacht, which he was later
able to bring up the Po and overland to his villa at Lago di
Garda. His friends and enemies were the most wealthy and
most powerful people in Rome, the men and women whose

savage feuds over the loot of Asia and the subjection of Italy and Gaul were responsible for the death of the Republic. His mistress almost certainly was Claudia, the most depraved member of the aristocratic Claudian *gens* and the wife of the political opportunist Metullus Celer.

The social circle in which Catullus flourished was dominated by rapacious, lustful but highly cultivated women. Evidence of his connection with the common people whether of Verona, Bithynia or Rome is non-existent in his poetry, which is as remote as could conceivably be from common speech. Its rhythms, which are so musical that they are overpowering, are foreign, deliberately adapted, to show off his virtuosity, from the widest variety of Greek meters. It is this the Latin critics referred to when they called him *doctus*. *Doctus* is also a word used for women naturally learned in all the ways of love and in this sense too it applies to Catullus.

There is one specific characteristic shared by the poetry of Catullus and Burns—a peculiarly caressing delicate intimacy. This is natural in Scotch speech. So it may have been in the Roman speech of Catullus' day, as it became again in the Latin of the Middle Ages. Catullus' skillful use of this petting language enormously intensifies the conviction of purely personal utterance. The famous poem on Lesbia's sparrow can be paralleled with many epigrams in the *Greek Anthology* which are only literary exercises. In Catullus' poem we feel that we are admitted to the most secret intimacies of affection, to the wistful play of the bed of love. Lesbia always seems to be in negligée when Catullus gives her a poem, even when, broken-hearted, he sees her, debauched with treacheries, stumbling in the arms of ruffians in the alleys of the slums of Rome.

Catullus may well have been the richest poet of any importance in the history of literature. He was certainly one of the most skilled and most cultivated. The naturalness coupled with the seemingly spontaneous splendid music is certainly the work of consummate craftsmanship and almost certainly of painstaking revision and long consideration. This does not mean that it is not spontaneous in the sense that the greatest poetry is spontaneous. It takes great labor to uncover the convincing simple speech of the heart. Poetic candor comes with hard labor, so even does impetuosity and impudence.

The society in which Catullus lived at the end of the Republic was not only sophisticated but it was unbridled. That high living, highly educated, High Society in which anything was permitted and all was understood, even if little was ever forgiven, passed with the Republic. It was succeeded by the social rigidity of the reign of Augustus, which could be described as specifically designed to stamp out the Catullian world. People would go on being rich and wicked; the glad, confident morning of grande luxe bohemianism was over, not to return until the Renaissance.

Today the special ethos in which Catullus lived has been democratized. If the bohemian is he who would enjoy the luxuries, both physical and emotional, of the rich without being able to afford the necessities—the society of Catullus is all about us. He did not believe in the Social Lie because he lived amongst the liars. He could afford to be completely honest with his emotions. He and his Claudia could afford anything.

Today if his love poems could only be duplicated in English they would be popular at every level of society and might be sung in night clubs or by rock groups. If we consider this for a moment we realize the immense change in society. The degree of emotional liberation which exists today was in his time confined to a tiny handful of the most privileged caste in the Western world. Today his sensibility is the material of the lyrics of Bob Dylan.

This is what makes Catullus great. He speaks with accents of complete emotional liberty. It also makes him possibly untranslatable. There are no first-rate translations in any modern language. They all make him sound frivolous, and no poet has ever been more piercingly in earnest. There are not even good imitations, like the poems of Herrick or Ben Jonson that imitate other Latin poets. A whole literature has grown up of imitations of the million kisses that he proposed to exchange with Lesbia. They are dusty kisses indeed. Most of them are really imitations of the *Basiae* of Johannus Secundus, a Renaissance German scholar who expanded Catullus' poem into a whole book of osculations, very *doctus*.

The *Aeneid*

After Augustus had consolidated his empire both internally and externally, and the long, savage civil wars and the brutal wars of conquest had receded into the past, and a long peace had settled down over the Roman world, the Emperor let it be known that he would appreciate an epic poem celebrating his achievements, most especially his victory over Antony and Cleopatra in the Battle of Actium.

The poets in the circle patronized by his multimillionaire friend, Mycaenas, were approached with subtle invitations. Horace and Propertius even more subtly suggested in verse that the Emperor employ a hack. After a long period of diffident refusal the most pacific of the group accepted.

For years intellectual Rome gossiped about the great Augustan epic which was occupying so much of Virgil's time. At last sections of it were read, first to Mycaenas' literary circle, and then to Augustus. But Virgil died before it was completely published and his epic is generally considered to be incomplete. It is not about Augustus. He is celebrated briefly three times in prophecies. The Battle of Actium is reduced to the description of a detail on a piece of martial jewelry—one of the panels of bas relief on a shield. It shares this honor with, amongst many others, Augustus' enemy, Cleopatra. Even in the description of the Battle of Actium itself, Augustus takes second place to his admiral Agrippa. Truth is, Rome was sick of war and glory, and the intellectuals of the court, at least those whose writings have survived, did not find Augustus a very likeable person. Rightly so. Augustus was the archetype of the mildly but definitely self-righteous and hypocritical reformer, the kind of man whose children become shocking delinquents but who programmatically is the most dedicated first citizen of the community.

What is the *Aeneid* about? The plot is simple enough—the Fall of Troy, the escape of the noble Trojan Aeneas with a small band of men, their adventurous journey westward across the Mediterranean, their layover in Carthage, Aeneas' love affair with Dido, Queen of Carthage, his rejection of her and her suicide, and his struggle to obtain mastery of the lower Tiber valley. Virgil's contemporaries accepted this story as fairly close to historical fact. In modern times it has been considered purely legendary. In recent years archaeological evidence has turned up for at least the existence of the legend far back in Etruscan times. The story may well be truer than most accounts of the Folk Wanderings at the end of the first Bronze Age civilizations on the Eastern Mediterranean.

This of course is the material of Heroic Age epic, whether Homer, the Arthuriad, or the *Nibelungenlied*. The *Aeneid* is an epic, but an anti-heroic epic. Strategically placed throughout the narrative are a number of heroic deaths, from Priam's useless throwing away of his life to Turnus' wrathful and wasteful duel at the end. In every instance the civil conscience argues against heroic virtue—Hecuba tries to calm Priam; the family of Turnus try to hold him back; Anna tries to restrain her sister Dido. All of these glorious deaths are not mocked but are described with quiet, unobtrusive irony. Virgil is not interested in celebrating, in the guise of ancient history, the heroics of the Civil War. He is interested in revealing the necessary virtues for the Augustan peace.

"Arms and the man I sing," the poem begins. The arms are subordinated to the story of a man. The book is an epic quest, the quest for *pietas*. Over and over Virgil calls his hero "pius Aeneas." Piety in the Roman sense was a kind of etherialized civil etiquette, not unlike the moral principle of Confucianism, "human heartedness." Virgil tries to answer by the example of a biography the questions, "How does the warrior become spiritually the citizen? How does the leader of a heroic war band become the founder of a civilization?"

Homer, writing in a still barbaric time about an age of trouble hundreds of years gone, a poet by the fire and a clerk in bloody halls, sees only malevolent frivolity outside the circle of comradeship. Virgil sees about him the possibility of the fulfillment of civil community. *Pietas* is polity individualized. Homer is archaic Greek. Virgil is incorrigibly Roman. His tone derives from the optimism of a youthful imperialism. Home, farm, garden, conversations with friends, dinner with fine wine served by pretty slave girls, the care of orchards and vineyards—all the pastoral and convivial experiences immortalized by Horace and by Virgil in his shorter poems, are so poignant and memorable because they were so precious. There had been little enough of such amenity in the long years of Civil War, delation, proscription, and betrayal. "'Tis well an old age is out and time to begin a new."

The *Aeneid* is full of allusion, echoes, competition with Homer, yet how vastly different it is from James Joyce's parody of the *Odyssey*. What each author makes of Homer provides an exercise in social, historical criticism more fundamental than was dreamed of in Marx's philosophy. The *Aeneid* is not only the *Iliad* turned inside out, with many episodes and personalities repeated but given a contrary significance; it is also a counter-*Odyssey*, the last and most transcendent of the *Homecomings*, the tales of what happened afterwards to the heroes of the Trojan War. Aeneas does many of the things that Odysseus does. He leaves his Calypso. He raises the dead. He defies the Cyclops. But for quite different reasons. Odysseus' guardian is the wily Athena, the mistress of traders on the archaic sea. Aeneas' mother was Venus, but Venus Pandemos, Venus of the *Agape,* the communion of the civic community. Aeneas resolves in himself all the figures of the Civil War—he is Pompey at Troy, Julius by the Tiber, Antony in the arms of Dido, and always Augustus, who grows from a handsome young adventurer, to an astute general, to the father of his country.

Virgil was not what Tennyson called him, "Wielder of the stateliest measure ever moulded by the lips of man," but he was certainly one of the most accomplished stylists in all the world's poetry. Unfortunately one of his greatest virtues is his extraordinary skill in manipulating the highly inflected and sonorous Latin language in ways that cannot be transmitted to English. Of all his translators, Dryden understood him best, and brings across something of the heroic character of his verse, where heroic means "fully conscious of one's responsibilities." Gavin Douglas' translation in late Medieval Scotch is a spectacular poem, but it bears little relationship to the spirit of Virgil.

The Early Irish Epic

Can something be a classic when strictly speaking it does not exist? On the face of it the question is absurd, yet the Ulster Cycle—the stories of King Conchubar, the Knights of the Red Branch, Cuchulain, the tragedy of Deirdre, and the other tales now so familiar—certainly functions as a classic. There is only one trouble. No single integral text embodies the whole epic. The separate books are not accessible to the general public, not even in Irish. Most of the translations in scholarly works are of small literary merit. If the translations are good, the style of the originals is extremely remote to modern taste. For most of their history the Irish common people have known little or nothing of the Ulster Cycle. Only sporadic episodes survive in popular folklore, quite unlike the story of the Fenians—Finn MacCool and his band, a brotherhood of warriors something like the free companies of Medieval and Renaissance Italy. The Ulster Cycle is concerned only with Ulster, little bigger then than now, isolated from the rest of Ireland, and almost continuously at war with its neighbors, but especially with Munster. The court of the High King, what there was of Ireland as an imperium in those days, is scarcely mentioned.

In spite of all these objections the Ulster Cycle does function, not only as a classic, but as the fundamental mythic expression of Celtic civilization. More than the Welsh *Mabinogion,* much more than the late Medieval French versions of the lost Breton *lais,* or the immense mass of literature connected with King Arthur and the Quest of the Holy Grail, the Irish tales give symbolic and dramatic substance to the archetypes of a culture. Reading even a children's book of

"Cuchulain stories," you are soon aware that you are dealing with a special sensibility, a way of life, a way of viewing life, that led Arnold Toynbee to separate off Celtic civilization as distinct from the rest of Western Europe. These are myths, not legends.

Although the manuscripts are all late, and written by Christian monks, and although the originals of the manuscripts come long after the epic itself had taken what final form it possesses, the civilization portrayed is, after Homer, the oldest in European literature. Only partly due to our familiarity with Homer does he seem more modern—the Ulster heroes live in a world of literally "immemorial antiquity," an environment as strange as the inventions of science fiction. Not only that, but the esthetic values are different from our own, as different say, as those that create the values of the Japanese Nō play, with its tensions and resolutions of a kind unknown to Western drama from the Greeks to the twentieth century. Mystery, ritual, and tragedy and a special, unearthly glamor that envelops even the subsidiary characters—there is something of this in the Arthurian legends, especially those of the Grail Quest, but in the stories of Cuchulain and Deirdre these qualities appear in a uniquely pure form. The characters are like the celebrants in the rite of some mystery religion that we cannot understand, but that we know to be overwhelmingly powerful, magicians of an effective magic. Simply as plots the stories themselves are ritualistic. Step by step from birth to death the life of Cuchulain follows the rubrics of the most ancient sacrificial rites. Behind the love story of Deirdre and Naoise and his brothers Ainlee and Ardan, quite sufficiently a heart-tearing tragedy in itself, and reaching its culmination in perhaps the most beautiful lament in any language, lies another factor, the memory of the struggle of an ancient polyandrous culture against the patriarchal monogamy of the warrior band. This of course is also the germ of the plot of the *Mahabharata*, the Indian epic, and is its most ancient element.

It is impossible to date the evolution of the Ulster Cycle earlier than the long period from the first to the eighth century A.D. This was certainly the Iron Age. The Celtic invasion of Ireland was long over, yet King Conchubar and his warriors have all the characteristics of Bronze Age civilization. They fight in chariots. They live in ring houses with a communal hearth in the middle, apartments around the side, protected by a wall and ditch. Agriculture is scarcely mentioned. They are the warrior aristocrats of a herdsman society, but they seem to spend more time stealing other people's pigs and cattle than raising their own. Their morality is that of modern gangsters or at least of gangster movies. The ties of loyalty between a war lord and his warrior band with no roots in the community of common people, an especially foolhardy and violent courage, and an overmastering irrational romantic love are the principle values of this society. As tragedies the stories are more concerned with the violation of the first two values, usually due to the third, than to their observance. The Norse sagas, the *Nibelungenlied*, Homer, all presume social order. Their tragedies result from its disruption. The violation of social order is inherent in the early Irish epic. It seems more normal than anything else.

Some of the minor elements are extraordinarily primitive— headhunting as well developed as in Borneo, ritual cannibalism, battles prefaced by personal combat of the most bloodthirsty character, followed by general mutual destruction, taboos and curses afflicting whole peoples. At Cuchulain's final battle the Knights of the Red Branch lie under "a bad cess." They are periodically sick and incapacitated—"like women"— while Cuchulain himself is doomed by a whole nest of curses. There is no trace of Christianity. The religion is Druidism. The Druids march with the armies and fight with their magic. For instance, they can raise dense clouds of darkness. Over the Druids are priests whose functions are not very clear. Beside them are poets whose role is prophetic and whose songs have magical powers. Underneath the four castes, warriors,

priests, druids, poets, there is a whole assortment of witches
and warlocks, shamanesses and shamans. Maeve, the enemy
queen of Munster, is a royal witch like Arthur's relative Mor-
gana le Fay. Underfoot are all sorts of magic boars, white
hounds with one red ear, talking birds, talking horses, and
people who turn into swans. Even the weapons, like Cuchulain's mysterious whirling *gaebolg,* are magical. Behind all this
uncanny activity the ancient gods, the Sidhe, come and go un-
announced from their homes in the grave mounds and are
practically indistinguishable from common men and women
who are not common but magical. Not least every episode of
the myth has a ceremonial structure as well defined as Solemn
High Mass. There is no other world like this accessible to us,
no literature which takes us so far back to our own beginnings,
and no other as deeply rooted in the unconscious. Not even
the Finnish *Kalevala* is as much like a collection of real
dreams. This is the final significance of the Ulster Cycle for
modern man. It raises more sharply than any other literature
the questions, "What is dream? What is reality?"

"For one cycle of creation Shiva dances. For the next cycle
he dreams. We think we are living in the real world and Shiva
is dancing. We are not. He is dreaming." "Chuang-tsu dreamed
he was a butterfly and woke and asked, 'Am I man dreaming
I was a butterfly, or am I a butterfly dreaming I am a man?' "
Like the Hindu and Chinese philosophers, the mythic world of
early Ireland questions the very nature of the sensibility and
reason at the foundation of modern civilization. It does so
more effectively by far than the deliberate subversion of the
mind of Rimbaud or the Surrealists.

The best introduction to the Irish mythology is Lady Au-
gusta Gregory's *Cuchulain of Muirthemne,* perhaps the finest
prose to come out of the Irish Renaissance of the first years of
this century. From there the reader can go on to the immense
literature of retellings and translations of widely varying merit
in which he can get lost for years.

Abelard and Héloise

Few people in all history have been permitted to live lives which acted out in reality the archetypal dramas of the imagination. The *Letters of Héloise and Abelard,* his *Story of My Misfortunes (Historia Calamitatem),* and his *Plaints,* the hymns that he wrote for Héloise and her nuns, taken together form one of the very greatest love romances in all literature. Not only are the protagonists cast in molds more heroic than almost any creatures of fiction, not only are the motivations and issues of tragic love probed more deeply and exposed more candidly, but simply as a literary work the documents in the case of these two lovers surpass the talents of Flaubert, Stendhal or Choderlos de Laclos.

It is with the last perhaps that their correspondence can best be compared. *Dangerous Acquaintances (Les Liaisons dangereuses)* is in the form of an imaginary exchange of letters and Laclos' purpose is the definition and description in action, of conscious, purposive evil. He attempts to describe actors who defy Socrates' rule, and, perfectly conscious of the good, choose evil. Unless one is an incorrigible optimist, this is not really a difficult task. Life provides the novelist with plenty of examples. Héloise and Abelard struggle with a far deeper problem. They are equipped with more powerful intelligences than are common amongst the writers of literature. They have a capacity for analytical psychology and insight into their own motives unknown until modern times, and then certainly practiced largely in reference to others and seldom on oneself. Driving them from sentence to sentence is actual, not fictional, passion—the memory, but the living reality in memory, of an insuperable physical and spiritual love. It is this which gives

39

to their words a terrible impetuosity and glamour so that each sentence partakes of a dramatic intensity, like the most tragic moments of the lovers of Racine.

We have no other actual record of the tragedy of two personalities of such stature. Abelard was not only the greatest philosopher of his time but a crucial moment in the evolution of the human mind. Had he not lived, philosophy would not be the same. He lived at the very dawn of the high Middle Ages and was responsible, almost single-handedly, for opening up the universe of discourse which for the next two hundred years forms that great body of philosophical analysis we call Scholasticism. His prose is amongst the finest of the Middle Ages, whatever he is writing about. It is surpassed only by Héloise's in the then unique subject matter of their letters. He is also one of the four or five greatest Medieval Latin poets.

In personality Abelard was not really a philosopher. In another age or born into another class he would have been a man of combined intellect and action, a great engineer or entrepreneur, or a revolutionary like Lenin or Trotsky. Reading him one always feels a certain impatience with his confinement to ideas and therefore his ideas take on the character of actions. His philosophical notions are always designed to have serious consequences in the real world. They certainly did. He was the most hated and feared and loved and respected personality of his day. His students and disciples made up a mass movement of enthusiasts like that which attaches to entertainers and movie stars in our time.

At sixteen Héloise was famous throughout the scholarly community of Paris. Today she would be called still a child. Her contemporaries thought of her as a most learned woman. Our only record of her intelligence is her letters, where she is patently the superior of Abelard.

They had need of their great minds, considering the problems they chose to confront themselves with in their correspondence. In the first place there was Abelard's own corruption. He had tasted a full measure of that power which always corrupts, and that in its most subtle form, the unarmed power of a superior mind. He had, as he says, not only power, but luxury and apparent security in the highest place. Kings may be murdered or overthrown but world philosophers usually die in peace untroubled by their challengers. Héloise had the opposite quality, an incorrigible innocence. She always sees all the issues quite simply from her unalterable point of view and always in their starkest purity. This may be a virtue, as an Abelard's may be a vice, but neither qualities make for the ordinary compromises that quiet life into commonplace.

These are their ordinary disabilities, but Abelard and Héloise take upon themselves to give flesh to the combat of two impossibilist ethics—the life of perfection, the strict following of all the injunctions of the most intransigent interpretation of the Christian calling, and against it the claims of an absolute Romantic love. Certainly this is the issue of innumerable fictions, both magnificent and tawdry, and the source of countless miseries in individual lives, but hardly ever has such a spiritual struggle been worked out in such remorseless detail and with such nobility.

The extraordinary thing is that Abelard does not embody one antithesis and Héloise another. Héloise speaks for both. Christ for Abelard and Abelard for her—a heart-rending objectification of that silly Victorian phrase—"He for God and she for the god in him." Against her relentless logic of the passions Abelard can only struggle in the coils.

Life of course is lived by compromising an impossibilist ethic. Such constructs exist for the purpose of being compromised, usually as much as possible. Worldly prelates and flirtatious spouses worry little about the hard commandments of the gospels of either Christ or romantic love. So life is lived. The other thing we leave to art. Héloise and Abelard refuse the compromises that would have enabled them to conjure away their tragedy.

Abelard struggles with his conscience over memories of his carnality and his greed that drove him to insist on a disastrous marriage which he hoped would save his job but which ruined both of them. Even his present relations with her as they write to one another from their respective convents torture him. Héloise remains single-minded. For her Abelard owes his great talents to God and to the glorification of God to man. While as for herself her aim always is the fulfillment of Abelard's highest potential. Abelard is constantly entangled in destructive commonplace whether within himself or with his rascally monks in far off Brittany. Héloise paraphrases St. Paul, "God forbid that I should glory save in the name of lover." She yields, she marries, they separate, she enters a convent, in obedience to Abelard, that he might be fulfilled. To the end it is Abelard she loves first, not God. To his dying day she never ceases to struggle to make a Christian saint out of him and in so doing she becomes herself a saint of romantic love. Abelard dies in trouble and contention. Héloise outlives him for many long years with a manifest saintliness of character, loved by all about her for her wisdom, charity, and kindliness. The demands of the Christian life lived without compromise may have crucified him. But of Héloise and her religion it was said, "In my Father's house there are many mansions."

We badly need a new English translation of the *Historia Calamitatem* and the *Letters* and this should include a literal translation of the poetry of Abelard, because in all of it, behind the disguise of Biblical characters, are the apparent faces of Abelard and Héloise stricken with their great heartbreak. Etienne Gilson's *Héloise and Abelard* and Helen Waddell's *Peter Abelard* are good introductions, sounder by far than George Moore's *Héloise and Abelard*, which is a bit overwritten, superficial and distorted. The translation of the *Letters* by Scott Moncrieff is none too accurate but at least it is in decent English.

St. Thomas Aquinas

There are circles, and not small ones, in the Catholic Church today where Aquinas has become a seven-letter bad word. This is a passing phase, the result of almost a century of enforced Thomism, and that of a Counter Reformation Spanish cardinal. During the last generation it was as though the Church had forgotten that Thomism had not existed for the first twelve centuries of her life and had been a confused minority movement for three centuries after the end of the saint's own life. The breakdown of a rigidly enforced Thomism, like the breakdown of a rigidly enforced Marxism, makes it possible to discuss St. Thomas with Catholics or non-Catholics, with a new, refreshing, equanimity.

Men whom life has taught wisdom are by definition pretty good judges of their own lives. Before his death St. Thomas dismissed his lifelong work in philosophy and theology and said that his greatest achievement was his poetry, his hymns and antiphons and prayers and arrangement of psalms and lessons that make up the prayer offices and Mass for the Feast of Corpus Christi, the celebration of the gift of the flesh and blood of the creative heart of the universe—one of the Catholic feasts clustered around the summer solstice. There is a legend that St. Thomas in his young days, growing up in the ambience of the pagan court of the Emperor Frederick II, where Jewish Kabbalists and Muslim mystics mingled with late born Gnostics and heretical troubadours, himself wrote songs like those of Cavalcanti or Sordello, poems of mystic love of the kind that would reach their ultimate perfection in Dante's *Vita Nuova.* Certainly Aquinas' greatest hymns, *Pange lingua* (*tantum ergo*), *Adora te devote, Verbum supernum* (*O salutaris hos-*

tia), and the rest are amongst the very greatest poems of the West from the age of Augustus to Dante in any language, equalled only by Abelard and perhaps a scattered handful of secular poems—two or three troubadours, Wolfgang von Eschenbach, Walter von der Vogelweide, St. Mechtild of Magdeburg. They are essentially prayer of the highest sort, the utterance of complete spiritual rapture. Out of these mystical utterances, rather than out of the philosophized theology of the sacraments in the *Summa Theologica,* would grow the cultus of the Blessed Sacrament, central still to the devotional life of most Catholics—poetry and prayer was followed, rather than preceded, by doctrinal definitions. Belief is the vesture of prayer as prayer is the vestment of vision, and vision is pure and ultimate act. In the beginning is the act.

St. Thomas Aquinas spent his life carefully defining his terms. The philosophy called Scholasticism in its perfected form greatly resembles symbolic logic or the ideal of logical positivism. It is an immense structure, like the greatest computers, capable of absorbing all experience, if only the experience is programmed into its own terms, and producing satisfactory answers—satisfactory within the terms. We speak of systematic philosophy, but no one, certainly not Aristotle or Plato, actually produced a completely systematic philosophy until St. Thomas, St. Bonaventura and Duns Scotus, each in their own way. Purely as system their achievements would never be equalled, not by Leibniz or Spinoza or Kant or Hegel. If we take the works of Aquinas as a whole, grouped around the comprehensive but incomplete *Summa Theologica,* there are practically no loose ends, and there are plenty of them in the most systematic philosophers since. We can find any number of contradictions in Leibniz or Marx that threaten the very integrity of their systems. The flaws in Aquinas are the flaws of the age before rigorous experimentation and before the development of an acutely sensitive humanitarianism. He may have believed that vultures were only female and fertilized by the wind, and that one of the minor joys of the blessed is the contemplation, from the walls of Heaven, of God's Justice inflicting suffering on the damned in Hell, but quaint notions like these, painlessly expurgated by most of his modern editors, have nothing to do with the integrity of his system. If they had, it would not be possible for a thoroughly modern man like Etienne Gilson to find Thomism a completely satisfactory world-view.

Or is this false? The computer works only on what is programmed into it. If the programming itself becomes irrelevant, the machine falls silent. "What is the answer?" said Gertrude Stein, as she lay dying. And then, "What is the question?" There is a remarkable similarity between these last words and those of St. Thomas. So this immensely elaborate, almost flawless, logical structure with all the answers built in, survives like Dante's *Divine Comedy,* as what after all it is, and can only be, a vast architecture of symbols. Reason put the symbols together, but the work survives as a work of art, a great poem, and only in those terms is it permanently relevant. It cannot provide every imaginable answer, because the questions man asks, in his long career from Stone Age to conflagration, may be always the same questions, but they vary infinitely through history in their inflections. And it is the inflections that make the difference. So men are content with inadequate or evasive or dusty answers that meet the inflection, not the question.

One of the great souls of our time, Teilhard de Chardin, has never struck me as much of a systematic philosopher. His ideas, when formularized, bear an uncomfortable resemblance to a baptized Herbert Spencer. Teilhard owes his power to his vision as a contemplative, to his aesthetic realization of the sacramentalization of all being, and of history as the slow divinization of man. His life and his work make a great poem culminating in his most significant act. When on an expedition deep in the Gobi Desert, hundreds of miles from bread or wine, he celebrated Mass and offered up the world instead. There is no difference here with St. Thomas' prayer offices and Mass for the feast of the Body of the Logos. Catholicism, or even Christianity as we know them, could vanish from the face of the earth, but these visions in their ultimate meanings would remain.

Today all the world is in revolt against a civilization busy with both the left hand and the right emptying life of transcendent meaning. *"Tout passe. — L'art robuste/ Seul a l'éternité. . . ."* All passes. Only the most powerful art possesses eternity. As an incidental increment—St. Thomas is very entertaining reading—Aquinas was a favorite author of skeptics like Sainte-Beuve, Renan, and James Gibbons Huneker.

The English and Scottish Popular Ballad

At the height of the Age of Enlightenment, of Rationalism and the worship of classical order, men grew weary of the neat, domesticated universe they had constructed for themselves and began to seek in older times, and remote places, and in the lower classes, uncorrupted by the narrow discipline of their superiors, the values which were so conspicuously lacking in eighteenth-century culture. The most sensitive organisms discovered that the society was suffering from spiritual malnutrition. Once new elements of the diet were discovered, the hunger of the public made them immensely popular. We call this movement the beginnings of Romanticism. In English it centers around the discovery of folklore, the return to nature, the idealization of the common people, the poetry of Burns and Blake, of the young Wordsworth and Coleridge. Crucial in this development was the popularization of folk song amongst a cultivated audience. The values of a preliterate or illiterate society became suddenly popular amongst the highly literate. Percy's *Reliques of Antient English Poetry* and Scott's *Border Minstrelry* were not only best sellers in their own day, but both are still in print, at least in Great Britain.

The "problem of the ballad" has usually been considered one of origins. On the contrary, the important question is its ever-increasing popularity. Why today should a singer be able to fill an auditorium with thousands of people, come to hear her sing the songs of herdsmen and peasants and cattle rustlers five hundred years gone, and this not only in Great Britain and America, but in Berlin or Tokyo?

The ballad has been defined as a folk song which tells a story, concentrating on the dramatic situation of the climax,

47

rather than long narrative unfolding action and reaction. The tale is presented directly in act and speech with little or no comment by the narrator. Although the most violent passions may be shown by the characters, the maker of the ballad remained austerely unmoved. So does the performer. Emotional comment, where it occurs, comes through a special kind of rhetoric peculiar to the ballad, often, especially in some of the refrains, dependent upon the use of rather remote metaphors to intensify the psychological situation. Most ballads are in "ballad measure," four lines of alternating eight and six syllables—really fourteen syllables or seven stressed syllables with a strong pause after the eighth—rhyming usually at the end of each fourteen syllables. However this pattern varies constantly even within the same song. What varies it is the fluency of the music clustered around a simple melodic pattern, which a good ballad singer seldom, stanza for stanza, exactly repeats.

The English and Scottish ballads, so far as they can be dated from internal evidence, seem to have reached their highest development in the troubled times of the War of the Roses and the consolidation of the Tudor monarchy, the fifteenth and sixteenth centuries. They have been called collectively the folk epic of a minor Heroic Age or Time of Troubles. It is true that the long drawn-out struggle over the emerging wool economy of northern England and the Scottish Border had many of the elements of a Heroic Age, but contrary to Arnold Toynbee's hypothesis, ballads of the same type were collected in stable, agricultural, untroubled parts of England. Ballads of the Scottish and English type are found from Mongolia to Spain, and they are still being made from the Appalachians to Yugoslavia. The greatest collection is that of S. Grundtvig and A. Olrik, made in Denmark in the middle of the nineteenth century. Many of the Danish ballads give the—false—impression of being direct translations from the classic English collection of F. J. Child made at the end of the century. This is sometimes the case even when both the Danish and the British ballads concern known historical figures in their respective countries and are, within the limits of dramatic license, both approximately true. In other words many ballads are archetypal dramatic situations that wander through space and time seeking body in history.

What are these situations? They are rigorously personal. Battles of the Scottish Border, cattle and sheep raids, sieges of castles, family feuds, are shorn of the complications and ramifications of history. They are reduced to the starkest relations between human beings, presented at their moments of greatest intensity. This is equally true of the few religious ballads with a Christian story and of the ballads of the supernatural, many of which contain elements of pre-Christian belief or ritual. People come back from the dead unable to rest because they are bound by the sorrow of their survivors. Men are rapt away into fairyland or saved from thralldom there in the world that is entered through the fairy mounds, where the people of the Sidhe, the old Celtic gods, live under, or rather, beyond, in a kind of fourth dimension, the grass-grown grave mounds and ruins of an older race. Long stories, for instance of Orpheus who survives as King Orfeo, are reduced to a crystalline dramatic moment. There is a remarkable similarity between the earlier ballads, especially those of the supernatural, and the Japanese Nō plays. In both dramatic realization comes not as the culmination of a process, but as the precipitate of a situation. Most of the great British ballads could be turned into Nō plays and vice versa. Some have identical plots.

Perhaps this comparison reveals the secret of the ballads' ever increasing popularity until today, when enormously popular folk singers have become determinants, not just of contemporary poetry and song, but of an ever growing new sensibility—a new culture. The classic ballads deal with human lives which have been taken out of the tangle of grasping and using of an acquisitive and exploitative social system by the sheer intensity of the ultimate meaning of human relationships.

The ballads deal with people who have been opted out by circumstance. They are living, or dying, or have died, in realms where motives are as pure as they can be. They have the unearthly glamour of beings acting beyond the world, like the demigods of Sophocles. The Russian students sing *"Stenka Razin"* and American students sing "Lord Thomas and Fair Eleanor" for the same reason. Their values are utterly incompatible with society as now organized, here or there. The world of the ballads may not be the ideal society of Marx or Plato, but it is a supernatural realm where nothing is important but the things that really matter. Of course this is Romanticism pushed to its ultimate, but it is also the morality of classical drama, a terrible intensity of life pushed to its limits, beyond all responsibilities of the getting and spending that lay waste our time.

So the great ballads of the common people at the end of the Middle Ages are more popular today than they have ever been because we are witnessing the evolution of a counter culture, antagonistic to the dominant one, whose principal characteristic might well be defined as the taking seriously of the ethics and morality of the dramas of folksong.

The literature of balladry is enormous. Child's great collection is in paperback, five volumes. The melodies most commonly sung are in Cecil Sharp's *One Hundred English Folksongs* and *English Folksongs from the Southern Appalachians.* Much of Grundtvig is available in translation. There are many state and regional collections. B. H. Bronson, *The Traditional Tunes of the Child Ballads,* when complete, will gather all variants of text and music. He gives, in volume two, 198 versions of "Barbara Allen!" There are collections, in English, of ballads from Mongolian, Yugoslavian and dozens of other peoples. H. C. Sargent and G. L. Kittredge, *English and Scottish Ballads, Edited from the Collections of Francis James Child,* Boston, 1904, is still the standard one volume edition. The Penguin book and *The Oxford Book of Ballads* are overedited.

Racine's *Phèdre*

Racine's difference with Euripides is obvious. His play is named *Phèdre,* and she dominates the play from beginning to end. It is not just about her, it takes place within her. It is indisputably a tragedy, with none of the ambiguity of Euripides, but it is a different kind of tragedy than any either the classic dramatists or Aristotle could have conceived. Between Euripides and Racine lies not just Christianity, but a specific Christian tradition that begins in St. Paul, is given definitive statement by St. Augustine, and reduced to absurdity—the "absurd" of the contemporary existentialists—during the Reformation and Counter Reformation. Phèdre is not doomed by the old Greek Fate, or Chance, or Destiny. She is damned, and predestined to damnation.

Macbeth is lost because he is impenitent. He cannot believe in forgiveness because he cannot forgive himself. Phèdre is a model of penitence. Almost every speech exemplifies contrition, confession, desire for amendment of life. It does her no good. Each time she moves towards salvation she is remorselessly struck down. Succeeding generations have never ceased to marvel at the construction of the play. Racine has built it with the precision of one of those mathematical machines with which the *philosophes* amused the great courtesans of the French court. Each scene is a trap and they are all wired in series, each one sets off the next. The action clicks like the clicking jaws of some omnivorous and omnipotent cacodaemon —The Ruler of the World. Doom can be moral. Predestination is necessarily evil.

Racine was brought up in the Counter Reformation Catholic puritanism of Port Royal—Jansenism. But Jansenism was not only precisionist in morals and pietist, verging on hysterical, in devotion; it was relentlessly logical. Logic could find no reconciliation between an omnipotent and omniscient Deity and human free will and salvation by good works. The absolute power and foreknowledge of God predestined some men to salvation, some to damnation. True, the theologians of Port Royal dodged the issue in their long controversy with the Jesuits, and major thinkers like Pascal were only semi-Jansenists. In *Phèdre* Racine works out the logic of the Jansenist moral universe to its terrible conclusion, and objectifies it in the torture of one soul who above all else desires innocence.

What is the intention of this play, one of the most harrowing experiences in all literature? It is usually said that it marks the beginning of the turn of Racine from his courtly, worldly ways back to the religion of his youth. He cannot have been blind to the nature of the Deity he portrays. He is certainly not the Father in Heaven of the Gospels, but the absolute evil personified of the Manichaeans and Gnostics. Euripides, like Homer, is fundamentally secular. His gods and goddesses are the symbols of the amoral forces of nature, whether thunderstorms or the biological drives of men. The conflicts and motives of his *Hippolytus* are generated from within his characters, they are, as we would say, psychological. The doom in which they move as in a cloud is impersonal, neuter, indifferent. The corruption that taints them is socially derived, the sickness of a decaying imperial society. What snaps the traps, what interposes a pawn to each move of Phèdre's, what shuts down in the final damnation is something personal, active, malevolent, the Prince of Darkness, to whom, in the ultimate logic of Racine's philosophy, has been given the rule of this world.

We are in the "absurd" universe of modern atheist existentialism, but Racine's absurdity is far more horrifying than Sartre's. *No Exit* (*Huis clos*) is a picture of the triviality of mankind shut in by the impassivity of *néant*—Not Being. It is a Being that closes all the exits for Phèdre, an all-powerful, positive Evil. There is no exit, not even into nonbeing. There is no solution and no negation. The only exit, the only solution, is grace—but grace is given gratuitously. There is no necessity, no logical reason, why anyone should be lifted out of the net of fire. Grace in this universe is as frivolous as the gods of Homer and Euripides, but grace does not operate this universe; malevolence does.

Doubtless *Phèdre* does represent Racine's turn back to the Church. To most of us today who hold to a more humane ethic it seems a strange entrance, a sub-basement door through Hell. But again, *Phèdre* does not mean to us what the play meant to Racine. We watch it without theology and to us Phèdre is simply a guilt-tortured woman, though a greatly noble one. But Racine intended this also. Central to the philosophy of Jansenism is its doctrine of the imperceptibility of the supernatural. The world is put together in such a way that miracle and grace can be explained by any mechanist or atheist. Divine intervention is perceptible only to faith aided by grace.

There is one flaw in this philosophy and it is the flaw in the play. Most people are simply obviously not worth the operation of such monstrous ontological or metaphysical forces. So Hippolytus, his "love interest" Aricie, Theseus, and the servants and messengers are all bystanders. They watch Phèdre's damnation from outside, from a different, very ordinary universe, and Theseus is little better than a clown, and is often so played. If all men are predestined, then most men are predestined not to salvation or damnation, but to mediocrity. Only the privileged, the most noble souls, are worthy of the tortures of Phèdre.

The role is perhaps the greatest ever written for an actress. It was a farewell gift to Racine's mistress when he left the theater, returned to the Church and married, prudently and not for love.

It is a commonplace that Racine is untranslatable. This is

not because his verse is difficult, but because it is not. No one, except possibly the Greek Simonides, has ever been able to achieve such profound effects with such starkly simple language. The problems and conflicts of his plays have baffled philosophers and saints since the beginning of literature. The words were comprehensible to his cook. If they weren't he crossed them out and found simpler. Yet these words have an unearthly, soul shaking beauty more subtle than the subtlest rhythms of Baudelaire or Mallarmé or the most ambitious of Hugo. Only the plot, the basic issues and motives, and some of the prose meaning has ever been brought across into English. What escapes with the beauty of the verse is the ultimate profundity of meaning. Yet it all seems so easy. Here are the pivot lines of Phèdre, which she says after she has revealed her love to Hippolytus:

> *Un fil n'eût point assez rassuré votre amant:*
> *Compagne du péril qu'il vous falloit chercher,*
> *Moi-même devant vous j'aurois voulu marcher;*
> *Et Phèdre au labyrinthe avec vous descendue*
> *Se seroit avec vous retrouvée ou perdue.*

Here is Kenneth Muir in the Mermaid Dramabook:

>   I would not have trusted
> To that weak thread alone, but walked before you,
> Companion in the peril which you chose:
> And going down into the labyrinth,
> Phaedra would have returned with you, or else
> Been lost with you.

What has been lost in translation? Nothing except an aweful glory.

Gulliver's Travels

The critical literature on *Gulliver's Travels* is immense, contradictory, and exhausting. It is as though Swift had written an additional "Voyage to the Land of Pihsralohcs," a land governed by the iron rule of Publish or Die. In all this vast mass of paper to which beautiful trees have been sacrificed, there is scarcely a mention of the greatest mystery attending *Gulliver's Travels*. Why has it been for over two hundred years one of the most popular of all children's books? If the critics are right, especially about the fourth book, it is an obscene and immoral rejection of the weak but striving, falling but trying, human race, the work of a psychotic who hated all men, especially women, who was impotent, paranoid, and fixed in a clinging and cloying anal eroticism. This, it would seem, is reading matter for adults only. Even if the critics are wrong, the fact that they can make such deductions would make the book dangerous, or incomprehensible, or both, to children. Yet children love it, quite innocently, and see nothing bad or even nasty about it. So likewise do very common people. A good measure of this was the immense popularity amongst peasants and simple workers of the classic Russian motion picture made of *Gulliver's Travels* long years ago.

On his voyage to the island of Balnibarbi and the flying island of Laputa, Gulliver learned, long before they were ever seen by real astronomers, that Mars had two moons. Swift describes them with considerable accuracy. This has fascinated many a science fiction writer. There are stories which describe Swift's visit to Mars or the Martians' visit to him, but the best is one based on the hypothesis that Swift himself was a Martian—an engineer who had planned to put two large satellites in orbit about Mars (the moons were not discovered until later because they were not there), but had been swept away in his space ship, and forced to land on earth. The science fiction writers are sounder critics than the scholars. Like the children who love *Gulliver's Travels,* Swift is an Outsider, one of the first and greatest. He was horrified by the condition of humanity and dumbfounded that he was a human being.

Superficially there is nothing extraordinary about the satire of *Gulliver's Travels.* Swift uses the standard classical formula that goes back to Aristophanes, Menander, and Plautus, and survives to this day in all plays based on the Italian Comedy. In his own day, in Molière, or Aphra Behn, or the disciples of Ben Jonson, the formula dominated the popular stage. Each character in the classic comedy is assigned one of the vices or follies of mankind and acts out its consequences in absurdities or incongruities which follow logically from a given situation. What Swift did was simply use whole peoples, instead of individuals, as personifications. Starting with an assumption, men six inches or sixty feet high, the roles of horses and humans reversed, literal physical immortality, he deduced all the consequences he could think of, with relentless logic and realism, from an initial absurdity. But the absurdity is the only vesture of a vice, or folly, or major defect of ordinary people. The Lilliputians are petty; the Brobdingnagians are gross, the Struldbruggs are senile, the Houyhnhnms are endowed only with rationality, the Yahoos lack it. Taken altogether the nations of *Gulliver's Travels* make up a well-rounded human character—seen from the outside.

So children, like Martians, see the adult world. Who did not dream as a child that some day, after he was grown up, he would meet the real adults, so unlike those he saw about him—rational, just, and large of vision—who keep the world from collapse. Somewhere they must exist, a little conspiratorial committee of the sane in ice caves in Tibet or the undersea palaces in Atlantis or The Land of Oz. Certainly the world a child sees about him, and judges by the simple values of innocence, or the equally simple ones he has been taught—"Don't do as I do, do as I say"—could not endure overnight unless somewhere the responsibles were keeping it going. The perspective of Swift is no different. His "savage indignation" is just outraged innocence. The point of view assumed by all satirists with him was not an assumption or a pose; it was congenital and incorrigible.

It is his innocence that distinguishes Swift from Franz Kafka and those who have come after him in the Theater of the Absurd or the novels of the blackest Black Comedy. The squeamish and sheltered academicians of an older generation like the critics of earlier times from Sam Johnson on, have been outraged and nauseated by the fourth voyage. In our day it seems mild indeed. The Houyhnhnms, except for their rationalism, differ little from horses. In fact, the only difference is that they can take care of themselves at the standard of living of rather pampered racehorses. The conclusion that this was in fact the status of the philosophers of the Enlightenment is easily drawn. As for the terrible Yahoos, they behave pretty much like human beings unable to think up excuses for their behavior. Neither species is evil. Swift was himself a man of the first half of the eighteenth century in this—or an Outsider. He did not know what evil was. Nowhere does he give any indication of comprehending that human beings of the greatest intelligence can deliberately live out a rationally organized evil or that whole societies can operate in decency and order for the most vicious ends. To Swift, as to Aristophanes, war, treachery, exploitation are follies. Vice may be disgusting, but it is never reasonable. So Swift is outside the human condition in a way that Choderlos de Laclos, or Balzac, or Proust are not. This is innocence.

It is his innocence that endears Swift to children. As he logically draws out the details of Lilliputian or Houyhnhnm behavior, he is inexhaustibly playful; he is never whimsical. Uncorrupted children loathe whimsy because it is one of the final manifestations of corruption. *Gulliver's Travels* is at the opposite esthetic pole to *Winnie the Pooh*.

Robinson Crusoe

Daniel Defoe is perhaps the only writer of fiction whom critics have honored by calling him a liar. He is rightly distinguished from other novelists because he is not a novelist in the usual sense of the word at all, but an utterer of false documents, a kind of literary forger. It is not true, as some modern critics have said, that he did not know what he was doing, that the novel was so primitive in his day that the dramatic and as it were, abstract, nature of the art of fiction was unknown to him. It is true that his tales are real autobiographies with imaginary narrators, as Samuel Richardson was to write novels of real letters from imaginary correspondents.

Neither writers were primitive or naive. The modern novel had already come into existence. Defoe had plenty of examples if he wished to take them. The art of prose fiction goes back to the beginning of literature. How many medieval romances are novels? Surely *Le Morte D'Arthur* is an elaborately constructed dramatic novel, even if the romances on which it is based are not admitted to the category. No. Defoe was very well aware of what he was doing. He wrote his novels like an enormously skilled criminal testifying under oath and throwing his prosecutors off the track. He was a master of imaginary evidence not unlike the great detective novelists, Conan Doyle, R. Austin Freeman and Simenon, and he surpassed them in the verisimilitude of his testimonies. In the opening paragraph of *Robinson Crusoe* he begins to throw the reader off the track. There is no dramatic structural reason whatsoever why Crusoe's father should be a naturalized German from Bremen or why his name should be Kreutznaer mispronounced. There is a structural reason—the demands of an elaborate structure of verity. So the central artistic meaning, the bull's-eye of the esthetic impact of Defoe's fictions, is quite different from that of "the novel as a work of art."

Unless we are romantic adolescents or barbarians, we never think of Ivan Karamazov or Emma Bovary as real people, not anyway when we have escaped from the delusion of the hypnotism of immediate reading. Most novels provide their greatest satisfaction when they are finished and we look back over them, or rather, through them. The novel as a whole, not any character, is an artistic structure that reorganizes experience. The narratives of Crusoe, Moll Flanders and Roxana are intended to affect us as though we had discovered them in an old trunk in the attic that had come down through the family, a bundle of papers that cracked as we opened them, written in a long out-of-date hand and tied with ribbons that disintegrated at our touch. We are supposed to be put in direct encounter with persons, a specific man, two specific women. Everything is stripped to the bare, narrative substance and it is this that reveals the psychology or morality of the individual. The most significant details are purely objective, exterior. The interiority of the characters is revealed by their elaborately presented outside. When they talk about their own motives, their psychology, their morals, their self-analyses and self-justifications are to be read backwards, as of course is true of most people, certainly of any bundle of letters we might find in the attic. This is true even of autobiographers who are famous for their sincerity. If we believe everything that Amiel and Marie Bashkirtsiev say about themselves, we are going to start off in life with misleading and sentimental ideas of human nature. It is the naïveté of his critics that has led to Defoe's reputation for superficial or non-existent psychology.

It is very fashionable nowadays—or was at least in the heyday of the faddist exegesis of Kafka, Kierkegaard and Henry James—all confused together as though they were one author—to write of *Robinson Crusoe* as though it were written by San Juan de la Cruz, an allegorical spiritual autobiography with dark nights of the soul and ladders of illumination. Defoe as a matter of fact states quite plainly that Crusoe's vision of an avenging archangel was due to a surfeit of turtle eggs. His terrors and panics of which so much has been made are no more than would be engendered in the most normal of men by simple loneliness, and they die out as he becomes habituated to his total isolation. The psychology of a man in solitary confinement is accurate. Crusoe is afraid of what men might do to him because year after year men do nothing to him whatsoever. He is terrified by an inexplicable footprint, but master of himself when the real cannibals finally show up.

The sense of sin that haunts the early part of his narrative is no more than what would be expected of a man of his time brooding on the reasons for his predicament. As time goes on, it ceases to be a predicament. It is fruitless to search for an allegorical original sin in Crusoe's opening pages. He says what it was. He didn't want to go into business. He least of all wanted to be a member of the middle class, that "best of all states" in his father's words, and he ran away to sea. "Of man's first disobedience and the fruit"—indeed. If this is original sin no boat would ever have been invented and put out to sea.

What is *Robinson Crusoe* about? The best way to answer is to begin with *Moll Flanders, Roxana,* and the stories of highwaymen and pirates. Moll and Roxana are businesswomen, a wise and a foolish whore. Like all of Defoe's heroes except the cavalier and the explorer of Africa, their lives are dominated by money. *Moll Flanders* is a kind of audit, a drama of double entry bookkeeping. Crusoe runs away from the business ethic and finds on shipboard, with its companionate isolation, and in those days its constant mortal danger, the withering of self-alienation. It never withers quite enough.

The voyages end and the cash nexus takes over. Crusoe on his island, as he says of himself, is a man without money. He has plenty but it molds in a drawer in his cave, the most meaningless thing on his island. There is nothing to connect it to. It is cash but not a nexus. If we believe that money is the root of all evil then presumably it is the apple of original sin. Crusoe is Adam with an inedible apple. So he gradually grows back into a state of original grace.

Crusoe has been called a kind of Protestant monk and it is true that he turns the chance of his isolation into an anchorite's career. The story is one of spiritual realization—almost half a lifetime spent in contemplation works profound changes, whatever the subject's religion. We can watch Crusoe become, year by year, a better, wiser man. He writes little about his interior development and when he does his vocabulary is mostly inappropriate. We see it happen behavioristically. Defoe has been accused of insensitivity because Crusoe shows little compassion for Friday or sorrow at his death. But Defoe is portraying a true-born Englishman whose vocabulary cannot cope with the deepest personal emotions if they cannot be translated into the symbolical language of Dissenting piety.

At the end of the story as it first stood we watch Crusoe grow foolish again. He is back in the world of men and their commerce. It is only when human relationships escape from commerce that the spiritual wisdom he spent so many years acquiring as a hermit has a chance to show itself. Of course he has considerable worldly wisdom and the sequel is largely the story of a Ulysses of many devices who happened to have spent a few years by accident in a Zen monastery.

Samuel Johnson said that *Don Quixote, The Pilgrim's Progress* and *Robinson Crusoe* were the only three books a mature man wished were longer. In his time he was close to being right. *Robinson Crusoe* may still be the greatest English novel. Surely it is written with a mastery that has never been surpassed. It is not only as convincing as real life. It is as deep and as superficial as direct experience itself. The learned but incorrigibly immature will never see in it anything but a well written boys' story interspersed with out-of-date moralizing, best cut out when it is published as an illustrated juvenile. Others will believe that Defoe placed himself on record just this once as an unneurotic Kierkegaard, others as a critic beforehand of Montesquieu and Rousseau, others will see Crusoe as the archetype of Economic Man. The book is all these things and more. It is what Defoe intended, a true life narrative.

Dangerous Acquaintances

The editor of a jazz magazine once answered an inquirer, "The term 'square,' as used by musicians and the underworld, was invented by La Rochefoucauld and popularized by Choderlos de Laclos, who commonly referred to people as *carré*." It was a joke, but an apposite one. It was not until the eve of the French Revolution that serious secular writers in any numbers began to believe, much less say, that organized society was based on and saturated with fraud, that the moral facade was a Potemkin Village, a Social Lie. Most effective, and most damning was Choderlos de Laclos. He is saner far than Sade or Restif, and he is also a very great artist. *Les Liaisons dangereuses* is not only a terrifying portrayal of high society, of a ruling class who have ceased to rule, it is one of the world's finest novels, as well as a dramatic presentation of a mature and analytic philosophy of the nature of evil and the interactions of human motivations. After this one book, a pivot in the history of the novel, things could never be the same again, not at least for any novelist who read and understood it.

Blake, Hölderlin, Baudelaire, Stendhal, all are prophets of the coming generations, when, at least outside the English-speaking world, rejection of the values of the dominant society would be the first assumption of the significant artists of that society, whether painters, poets, novelists, dramatists or musicians. The disaffiliation of the intellectuals from the reigning predatory elite would be a secession in favor of a humane value system, a profound moral revolution. They would become enemies of a society which was the enemy of man. Then too, the intellectuals, the caste of clerks, of responsibles, would be already outcasts, unwanted and feared by the new ruling class with its business ethic.

The people in Choderlos de Laclos' novel are the ruling class of the old regime and they are alienated from all values whatever. They live in a world of total moral night, of triumphant nihilism. The good people are all dupes, the middle sort are fools and rascals, and the two persons capable of acting are demonic creatures of positive evil, motivated only by the desire to destroy others. Each character has a place in a scale of values, of negative values preceded by a minus sign. With the planning of an architect and the precision of a watchmaker, Laclos assigns each a place in a dynamic tableau, a systematic exposition of the nature of evil unsurpassed by any professional moral philosopher. Most of the subsidiary characters in the novel are morally inert, as incapable of good or evil as animals. Evil to them is simply privative, the slow waste of fact. They never had any innocence, and therefore cannot be corrupted. They do not know what is happening although it takes place before their eyes. The victims, the innocent and passionate, know evil as something that befalls them. Their own values are corrupted and ultimately their selves are destroyed. In the process they are essentially passive. The two devils of the novel, the Marquise de Merteuil and the Vicomte de Valmont, are active agents, the only ones in the book, who have put a "not" in front of each of the ten commandments, "Thou shalt not not commit murder." They are thoroughly convincing demonstrations of the Socratic Dilemma. It is not true that rational men, presented with all the alternatives, infallibly must choose the good. They choose evil quite deliberately. The others may be trapped because they choose the lesser immediate rather than the greater ultimate good. The Marquise and Valmont, presented with alternatives, choose no good at all, but always the greater evil.

Dostoyevsky, writing of purposive malevolence, casts his dramas in a *mise en scène* of politics and philosophy. Choderlos de Laclos is not writing of Russian intellectuals, but of French aristocrats. They are exhibited in a solution of eroticism like fish in an aquarium. In the end the motivations and the results are the same, the destruction of the integrity of others. These adulteries are simply forms of murder. The seduction of a child is only a means to her spiritual evisceration, the inner core of her being is enucleated, like the lens cut from the eye.

The story is told in letters, mostly between the Marquise and the Vicomte, but all the others write letters too. This is usually the most artificial and flaccid form a novel can take. Not in this instance. It is the ideal method for Laclos' purposes because it permits him to present each character in her and his own terms, with the result that irony piles up until its weight is almost unbearable. Then too, he can introduce as many aspects and as much time shift as he wishes without seeming unrealistic, again, with maximum ironic effect. This shift back and forth is one of the causes of the whipsawing of the reader that, as the narrative draws to a climax, leaves any sensitive person torn and exhausted. *Les Liaisons dangereuses* is one of the world's greatest novels, but it is also one of the world's most painful works of art in any medium —Euripides in satins and powdered wigs.

It is all so elegant. Even the priests and nuns are elegant, but of course the devils are the most elegant of all. In the end they have nothing else, and then that is destroyed. What destroys them is their rivalry in evil. Unlike Milton's Hell, there is hierarchy in this human one, Lucifer and Beelzebub, male and female, ex-lovers who have already violated each other's pride, are enemies, each hiding hate from the other. The instrument of their destruction is their reason. They are Socrates' or Diderot's fully rational human beings. They use their reason to destroy others and are at last destroyed by their own irrationality—something they did not believe existed. In a sense the book is a polemic against the assumptions of the Enlightenment, against Leibniz' "best of all possible worlds" but equally, perhaps more so, against Voltaire's *Candide* as well.

Rule, as distinguished from government, is a mystical notion. Prescientific peoples believed that good kings and chiefs made the rain fall and the crops grow and families increase. *Les Liaisons dangereuses* is an analysis of a ruling class from whom the mandate of Heaven has passed. They have no function. They are in fact far more outcast than the caste of clerks whose alienation is conscious. Their alienation is circumstantial and one and all they inhabit a moral vacuum. This is why the purposive malevolence of the Marquise and the Vicomte can take on the character of positive evil—everything takes place on the far side of zero.

Was the *ancien régime* really like this? Were characters like Merteuil and Valmont common? They were not common, but only possible. That is all they are in the book. The majority are indifferent in fiction as in life. Sade is not shocking, but silly, because he assumes universal malevolence. Laclos only assumes a world like our celebrities, our international Jet Sets. Nothing holds society together except the solution of sex in which they swim, and so all things are possible. In the two centuries since Laclos wrote we have considerably democratized the possibilities of Merteuil and Valmont. Once only the aristocracy was redundant. Now it is a privilege of both rich and poor. So *Les Liaisons dangereuses* is not, for us, a political tract directed against a dying class; it is a description of people we know.

Gilbert White's
Natural History of Selbourne

There are a number of books scattered over the long history of literature in English which owe their reputation to their avoidance of greatness, to their modesty. Roper's *Life of Thomas More,* Walton's *Compleat Angler,* Jeremy Taylor's *Holy Living and Holy Dying,* William Law's *Devout Call,* Woolman's *Journal,* Walton's *Lives,* Bunyan's *Pilgrim's Progress*—except for the *Compleat Angler* the six that occur most readily to mind out of many are religious in intent, but what distinguishes the whole group is a tone that can only be called religious—and that of a specific character. Outstanding in any such list is Gilbert White's *Natural History of Selbourne,* a collection of seemingly random field observations, by an amateur, at the beginning of the systematic study of nature.

From 1789 to 1901 the book went through ninety editions in the British Isles alone, as well as others in the United States, and translations on the Continent. Since then every few years has seen a new edition, illustrated, lavishly produced, or in cheap pocket book form. Meanwhile the entire scientific age has gone by and Gilbert White's observations have been superseded, some of this theories proven wrong, and his taxonomy, his naming and classification of species, has been out of date almost since the year the book was first published. Yet his book holds its own. No other work of early science is still so widely read for its own sake, not Newton, not Galileo, not Clerk Maxwell. Only Audubon can compare with Gilbert White in popularity.

The reason is precisely the tone of the book, a reflection of the character of the man. We think of Gilbert White not as religious, although he was a priest of the Church of England, but as a learner in the kindergarten of science. The special modesty which is his distinguishing virtue may have found its expression before him in overtly religious works concerned with the arts of living, of dying, and of meditation. As we read his simple observations of missel thrushes, tortoises and earthworms, we realize that it is the same virtue that characterizes the greatest science—of the art of science, which is one aspect of the art of life.

With the corruption of language, humility, like charity, has become the name of a vice rather than a virtue. With Gilbert White, as with Izaak Walton or John Woolman, it is a special form of natural grace—or of graciousness towards nature— from which flows a whole hierarchy of virtues, both literary and personal, which make up the foundation stones of a profound reverence for life, the basis of both religious and scientific devotion. The style of the man is the style of the prose, simplicity, strict honesty, lack of all pretension, careful objectivity, the rhythms of plain and quiet utterance, and plain and quiet being.

If anyone had told Gilbert White he was one of the greatest masters of English prose style he would have gently doubted his flatterer's sanity. He did not even consider himself a scientist, but just a country clergyman making observations in one small village and its surrounding countryside in letters to his real scientist friends, now long forgotten, whom he thought incomparably more important than himself. Even today many who write enthusiastically of the book as literature do not realize its scientific importance.

True, Gilbert White anticipated Darwin in describing the role of earthworms in fertilizing the soil. True, he first understood protective coloration and mimicry. True, he was wrong, or almost wrong, in believing that swallows hibernate in secret nooks and crannies rather than migrate south for the winter. (In recent years a rare few dormant swallows have been found sleeping away the winter in crevices.) What is of far greater importance is his attitude towards natural history itself; that same tone which gives him style also gives him a philosophy of living things, a philosophy we now call ecology, and practice as a science.

As we follow White's patient, day-by-day chronicle of the drama of living beings played on the tiny stage of a small section of eighteenth-century Hampshire, we are in fact witnesses to a major drama in the life of mankind, the birth of natural science itself, and the exciting practice of a new-found virtue, the scientific method. The very lack of specialization gives White his enduring significance. Since he saw, within his limited perspective, all things together, all the time, through the months and years, his book is permeated with an unobtrusive emphasis on the interrelatedness of life. Where a later biology, under the influence of economists apologizing for unbridled competition, for a world where the war of each against all would result in the greatest good of the greatest number, would emphasize the competitive and combative struggle for existence and survival of the fittest, Gilbert White, seeing his little biological province whole, emphasized mutual aid and interdependence. Even in this, however, he is never polemical, the conclusions of Piotr Kropotkin's *Mutual Aid* or of twentieth-century ecologists are immanent rather than explicit, they are the inherent, distinguishing characteristic of his own life style, and so of his literary style.

There are few other books that so well communicate the first law of scientific research, the practice of a humility from which springs both personal integrity and the discovery of facts and laws which are revelations of the integrity of nature. "The day of the country parson naturalist, strolling about, and jotting down observations in his notebook, is gone forever, to be replaced by teams in great research institutes, financed by millions of dollars." Is this true? We should never forget that Karl von Frisch, using means which were available to any amateur, now or in Gilbert White's day, and working with his methods and his style, made one of the most important discoveries of our time—that bees "talk" by dancing, and are able to communicate highly complex and variable information, a discovery as revolutionary as any in cosmology, and made only a few years ago.

On the *Natural History of Selbourne* is formed the whole very English tradition of amateur natural history, the bird watching and botanizing and passionate devotion to hedgehogs in the hedgerows which gives the letters columns of the British press a unique charm quite unlike any other papers in the world.

Finally, Gilbert White communicates the beauty and quiet drama of the English countryside through the seasons, one of the two most beautiful, with Japan, of the thickly populated parts of the world. He does this of course by careful, concrete, accurate description in the first instance, but secondly by intimacy—by a special talent for unobtrusive companionship. He takes us with him, person with person. There is something very Japanese, or Buddhist, about this that links him with the masters of meditative notebooks, Chōmei's *Hōjōki,* or Kenkō's *Tsurezuregusa,* or the wanderings of the poet Bashō. It is the simple love of all sentient beings, the Bodhisattva heart. It is also the tone of the "Collect for Peace" that ends Evening Prayer in the Book of Common Prayer— that Gilbert White may have said every night of his adult life.

Robert Burns

Robert Burns is a special case in the literature of the British Isles. He is one of the few writers prior to the twentieth century who was a working man. True, he was not a member of the proletariat, but a farmer. He has often been called a peasant poet. In fact his father was a yeoman who went bankrupt trying to establish himself as a moderately large-scale independent farmer. This is a very different background from that of the traditional highland Scottish shepherd or peasant songster. Nonetheless Robert Burns worked hard with his hands most of his life. He was one of the few writers at the end of the eighteenth century to hold fast to the principles of the French Revolution. Liberty, equality and fraternity are warp and woof of the fabric from which all his poems were cut. He was incapable of thinking in any other terms. The reason of course is that in Scotland the small independent proprietor was a decisive influence on the form of the culture and was also, in the tremendous changes at the dawn of the Industrial Revolution, being subject to a process of internal colonization both by the English and by the Scots aristocracy. Burns' father's long struggle and final bankruptcy were not isolated phenomena, but part of a social movement. Far more than the English, the Scottish farmers caught in this historical process were rebellious. They were rebellious because many of them were comparatively well educated.

Burns was taught by a country schoolmaster and learned even the elements of Latin and a smattering of French. Since the mid-eighteenth century was the low point of English secondary and higher education, he was probably a little better educated than the average member of the upper class

to the south. It is this conflict between his situation and his
potential that made him, like thousands of other Scots, an
incorrigible rebel. In France itself the Revolution was not
productive of a literature of its own—at least of a very high
quality. It has been said that Robert Burns is the only major
Jacobin poet. "Jacobin" is easily confused with "Jacobite"
and with reason. Scotland is a separate country with its own
traditions, and at least back before James the First of England
and Sixth of Scotland, its own great literature in its own language. After the final extinction of hopes for a Stuart Restoration, or an autonomous Scotland, in 1745, with the failure of
the romantic Bonnie Prince Charlie, and the enforced total
union with England, there was a great upsurge of Scottish
cultural nationalism. For centuries Scottish writers had thought
in one language and written in another. Burns, to preserve his
integrity—a vague word, better say the efficient functioning
of his sensibility and intelligence—was forced back into the
arms of the common people from whom he came. His verse
in English is mediocre and sometimes silly. It was so obviously
written for the provincial belles of Scottish salons, young ladies
who prided themselves on their southern accents and their
familiarity with sentimental English novels. For all his efforts
to captivate, however, when it came to decision, Burns' love
affairs were with women of his own class or classes, daughters
of farmers and declassé intellectuals.

Their Scottish language should not mislead one in understanding Burns' longer poems, the great satires, "The Holy
Fair," "Holy Willie's Prayer," and his one comic narrative,
"Tam o' Shanter." They are not folkloristic but like so much
Jacobin poetry, Roman in inspiration. But they differ de-
cidedly from eighteenth-century satirical verse in England or
France. Like their Roman models, the English and French
wrote about "the Town." Samuel Johnson's satires are scarcely
altered translations from the Roman poet Juvenal. Burns
satirized the middle class of people, whether farmers, crafts-

men, or small merchants. In France the Revolution was struggling to capture power for the middle class. Scotland had evolved a well-organized middle class society almost unnoticed. Its social upheavals had come from outside, from struggle with England. With the exception of Thomas Dekker, who greatly resembles Burns, the English city comedies of the early seventeenth century are written from outside by declassed intellectuals whose sympathies were with the *ancien régime*. Burns, like Dickens, wrote of the commonality from inside and so his satire had an authenticity and an accuracy which makes it still appropriate.

The long poems are not much read today—few long poems by anybody are. It is for his songs that Burns is famous throughout the world. More than any other one factor they have sustained the cultural consciousness of Scotland. The literary mind is a dangerous thing to turn loose on folklore. The educated editor and adaptor usually spoils whatever he touches. Walter Scott's improvements of the ballads of the Scottish Border, with only one or two exceptions, lessen their sources and rob them of their peculiar wonder. William Morris' adaptations of folklore, ballads and sagas can be read today only with the grimmest effort. Except Burns, only the Finn Elias Lönnrot was able to gather the fragmentary songs and legends of his people and transmute them into something both more wonderful and more socially powerful than the originals. Lönnrot's *Kalevala* is a different thing than its sources, a haunting, dreamlike, fragmentary epic, really meaningful only to modern Finns. Their ancestors, could they read it, would be vastly puzzled. Burns did something different. He wrote songs in his youth, some of them adaptations of folk songs. In his later years, at the height of his poetic powers, he gathered, edited, altered, expanded, combined hundreds of folk songs. Where he changed, he not only changed for the better, but he changed entirely within the folkloristic context, and intensified the specific glamour and wonder of his sources. Sometimes the song is completely rewritten. "John Anderson, My Jo" is changed from a bawdy song to one of long, enduring married love. "Ca' the Yowes tae the Knowes" is subtly altered line for line—literally glamorized—but always within the context. This is the same context that produced the scalp tingling lines of balladry, "About the mid houre of the nicht she heard the bridles ring," "Half ower Half ower tae Aberdower tis fiftie fathoms deep." Lines like these give the great ballads their stunning impact and their haunting permanence.

Burns is the only literary poet working on folk material who could do anything like this. He did it hundreds of times, so that his poems are not just the only Scottish folksong most people know, even in Scotland, but they establish a sensibility which remains characteristic of the best Scottish poetry to this day. "Yestreen, when tae the tremblin string / The dance gaed thro' the lighted ha'," "While waters wimple tae the sea; / While day blinks in the lift sae hie," "Aft hae I roved by bonnie Doon, / To see the woodbine twine; / And ilka bird sang o' its luve, / And sae did I o' mine," "Had we never loved sae kindly, / Had we never loved sae blindly, / Never met— or never parted, / We had ne'er been broken-hearted." . . . these lines are not only bathed in the uncanny light of folk song at its best, but they establish the specific tradition we think of as Scottish. The poetry of Hugh MacDiarmid (Scotland's greatest poet since Burns, and now with the passing of all the heroic generation of Modernist poetry in America and Great Britain, one of the two greatest living poets, I was going to say in Britain or America, but actually I suppose in any country) owes everything to this exact glamour, this vein of phosphorescent precious metal first opened up by Burns.

And finally MacDiarmid, the revolutionary nationalist, raises one last point. Burns took the folk songs of Scottish nationalism, of Stuart legitimism, and subtly altered them into something quite different. Jacobite becomes Jacobin

"Had Bonnie Prince Charlie won, a regime of barbarism, superstition, and incurable civil war, dominated by a mindless and decayed aristocracy, would have been fastened on Scotland." Nobody believes that today, largely due to the myth established by Burns' subtle rewriting of Jacobite folksongs. The Stuarts certainly did not believe in freedom of any kind. The songs of their partisans, filtered through the mind of Burns, become battle songs of freedom, hymns to the integrity and independence of the individual—the individual, middle kind of man who is educated, cultivated and yet works for a living—for example, the Scottish engineers who built bridges and railroads and factories, and spread the Industrial Revolution across the world, and who relaxed over a bottle of uisquebaugh in the evening, singing "Scots Wha Hae Wi' Wallace Bled."

William Blake

One of the most extraordinary ideas in the history of literary criticism is the notion, popular a generation or more ago, that William Blake was a naive, uneducated man, a kind of literary and artistic douanier Rousseau, unable to grasp the refinements and complexities of any orthodox world view or any "tradition," and so forced to make up a cranky system out of his own head. Since then the literature on Blake has grown to enormous proportions and threatens to overtake and surpass that on the more difficult books of the Bible. The old point of view, shared by critics and editors as widely disparate as Dante Gabriel Rossetti and T. S. Eliot, by almost everyone except William Butler Yeats, is completely discredited, and is held now by no serious person.

Blake was for his day an exceptionally learned man, and he was the most impressive and most durable eighteenth-century representative of a tradition older than any orthodoxy —the main line of the orthodoxy of heterodoxy. Blake survives and is read all over the world; the great French Illuminist, St. Martin, is forgotten by all but specialists and learned occultists. It is apposite to compare the ever-growing exegesis of Blake with that of Second Isaiah or the eighth chapter of the Epistle to the Romans, to apocalypse and mystical cosmology. This is where Blake belongs. He speaks the same language, uses the same kind of symbols, deals with the same realities. It is his grasp of this tradition which gives him his power and which makes him ever more meaningful as time passes.

Blake belongs to the very small group of founders of the subculture of secession which has accompanied industrial, commercial civilization since its beginnings. He differs, how-

ever, from Hölderlin, Baudelaire, Stendhal and other purely
literary figures, in that he was able to develop a completely
worked-out world view, a philosophy of nature and of human
relations which could provide answers to the questions asked
at the deepest—or the most superficial—levels. As the cash
nexus shut down over humane culture like a net, strangling
all other values but profit, the poets and novelists reacted—
Blake understood.

Sade, Hegel, Kierkegaard, Marx, the philosophers of alienation, all to a greater or lesser degree fail where Blake succeeds.
In one way or another they themselves become absorbed by
the civilization they attack, and then it turns out, as their
ideas are accepted, that they only caricatured the system of
values they attempted to subvert. Their philosophies are each
the philosophy of business enterprise hypertrophied, each after
his fashion. Blake is indigestible, although I remember long
ago his "Ancient of Days" was used as an advertisement for
a public utility company. That bygone advertising man chose
more wisely than he knew. Blake's famous picture is not of
God creating, with his compass, order out of chaos, but Blake's
diabolical principle of lifeless rationalism reducing reality to
empty quantity.

Herein lies the difference. Blake knew that his age was
faced with a major crisis or climacteric of the interior life.
He could diagnose the early symptoms of the world ill because he saw them as signs that man was being deprived of
literally half his being. His Prophetic Books may be full of
cosmological powers derived from the long Gnostic tradition
of the emanation and fall of creation, but he is in fact concerned with the epic tragedy of mankind as it enters an epoch
of depersonalization unequalled in history. It is not surprising
that the followers of Carl Jung have been amongst the most
revelatory expositors of Blake. He anticipates most of Jung's
diagnosis and prescription, and shares with him the same
archetypal pattern or Olympiad of key symbolic figures. The
reason is not to be found in some mysterious universal over-

soul or undersoul. It is simply that human brains like human bodies are much alike, and men cope with those factors of the mind, or those powers and relationships in life, that cannot be handled by a quantitative rationalism, in much the same way in all times and places, and most especially in crises of the society or the individual.

Blake was not only right about the spiritual, intangible factors, the Guardians of the Soul, or the testers and judges of the Trials of the Soul in ancient mythologies, that are symbols of the struggles of the interior life and the achievement of true integration of the personality. He was also right about the external factors—the evils of the new factory system, of forced pauperism, of wage slavery, of child labor, and of the elevation of covetousness from the sin of the Tenth Commandment to the Golden Rule of a society founded on the cash nexus. A generation before the birth of Marx, and before Hegel, he put his finger unerringly on the source of human self-alienation and he analyzed its process and consequences in a way not to be matched until the mid-twentieth century.

Blake certainly thought of himself primarily as a prophet, because he thought of the artist and the poet as so, and the poet who turned away from such a role as a traitor to mankind. Many Romantic poets since his day have claimed to be *nabis,* descendants of the ecstatic prophets of early Israel and uncrowned legislators of mankind. Most of them have really been concerned with themselves, with the destruction of the clerkly class in a middle class civilization, and the loss of both privilege and responsibility by the age-old open conspiracy of the scribes . . . the disappearance of benefit of clergy. Most of them have also been quite bad poets. For one Baudelaire or Nerval or Rimbaud there have been thousands of extravagant poetasters, cheap occultists and hypnotizers of silly girls. Blake is also a very great poet.

The Prophetic Books are certainly the greatest, the most comprehensive and profound group of philosophical poems in the English language. Only Milton's *Paradise Lost* can be compared with them. Milton may be the greater poet, although that is disputable, but Blake is certainly the deeper seer. There is no question though, but that they are difficult reading, are best accompanied with a reliable commentary, or even preceded by extensive reading in modern Blake criticism. They are an acquired taste. The best way to acquire that taste is to read thoroughly the superficially simpler poems of the *Songs of Innocence and Experience* and the early poems.

Blake's songs are amongst the most lyrical in the language, and they are distinguished by their uncanny lucidity. They are modeled on Shakespeare's songs, and at first sight share their simplicity, but, rather like Shakespeare's plays, on examination they reveal an ever unfolding complexity of meaning. It is amusing that the Age of Reason thought Blake mad, for he is distinguished by an extraordinary sanity in a world in which men like him were being driven to the wall. No other poet of the main tradition of secession from modern civilization is so lucid or so conscious of his own logic of purpose. First things come first, and second, second. Blake has a clearly defined scale of values, something Baudelaire or Hölderlin certainly did not have. This is why his simplest lyrics have levels of lucidity, like an ever deeper and deeper gaze into a clear depth which finds revealed greater content at each new level, and with each discovery enters a new qualitative realm. The Prophetic Books only spell out in action and discourse the progressive revelation of the *Songs of Innocence and Experience*. An ear for the subtlest music of language and an eye for the ultimate meanings of minute particulars combine to make Blake one of the greatest of all lyric poets. But what this means is seeing plainly into the clear depths of the soul—hence the inexhaustibility of these simple poems.

Goethe

The leading German poet of the first quarter of the twentieth century, Rainer Maria Rilke, was once leaning gracefully against the mantelpiece in a castle in Switzerland while his devoted duchesses and countesses and other disciples were passionately discussing Goethe's *Faust,* a discussion in which he was taking no part whatever. One of them turned to him and asked, "How do you feel about *Faust,* Master?" He answered, "I have never been able to read more than a page of it." On the other hand, Thomas Mann wrote several very long essays, which he repeated again and again as speeches before enraptured audiences all over the world, which can only be characterized as manifestoes of Goethe-worship—and for all the wrong reasons. One, "Goethe as a Representative of the Bourgeois Age," reads like a parody, but it is in deadly earnest and the deadliest thing about it is that it was delivered on the Goethe Centenary, in Berlin in 1932, as the reign of death, and the death of an age, was overwhelming Germany.

If Baudelaire was the greatest poet of the capitalist epoch, what was Goethe? He was the opposite, the greatest bourgeois ever to write poetry. Or perhaps the greatest poet of the business ethic. In English he is read only out of a grim sense of duty or for a grade in a class in world literature. This is due to the appallingly bad—without exception—English translations. The nineteenth century translated the unearthly beauty of the verse of Aristophanes or Euripides into doggerel because the donnish translators were incapable of either appreciating the Greek or of writing even passable verse. Goethe presents the translator with the opposite problem. Goethe wrote deliberate highbrow doggerel rhythms like

81

the old Sunday Morning Staten Island Ferry Brass Band playing "Ach du lieber Augustin." The point is, for both poet and
reader—"we know better." His verse is often compared to
the naive late medieval poet Hans Sachs, who, for one, didn't
know better, and two, is genuinely simple and singing, like the
finest nursery rhymes or folk ballads. W. H. Auden in our
time has written false naive doggerel deriving directly from
Goethe, as have most of Auden's disciples, the poets of the
old weekend stately home soviets of the English Thirties.
Sachs and his kind were never self-conscious. Goethe was
never anything else. Yet he was capable at rare intervals of
lyric music of a kind not heard in Germany since the end of
the Middle Ages, the complete antithesis of the sterile, neo-
classic formulas of the Enlightenment, truly classic and musical as the best songs of Horace or Catullus.

Faust for our day resembles nothing so much as *Paradise
Lost*. Goethe's devil, like Milton's, seems to us far more, not
just the hero, but a more moral individual than Faust, or
Milton's God. Who today "believes in" Faust? Untold thousands since the first book appeared have gone to masquerades
dressed as Mephistopheles. Who ever went dressed as Faust?
The new ethics personified by Faust are evil and destructive,
and the human organism rejects them with that hidden sense
St. Thomas Aquinas said preserved cows from eating poison
herbs.

"The love interest" in Faust is much like that in the plays
and novels of England's recent Angry Young Men, whose
heroes are torn between marrying a rich, gorgeous, decadent
nymphomaniac of the sort readily available to all fascinating
literary upstarts, or a *Hausfrau* of their own renounced caste,
pretty, not yet too plump, smelling of fresh milk and soap,
an artist at needlework and a devoted slave. Whichever the
new recruit to the bourgeoisie marries, it makes him angry.
The millionairess usually vanishes amidst fires of destruction;
the sweet and the simple wife or mistress is destroyed.

Goethe spent his life trying to re-establish the declassed clerkly caste as essential to the bourgeoisie as it had once been to the aristocracy. He was under the absurd impression that this made him an aristocrat. What it made him was a bureaucrat quite content to sign the death warrants of Gretchens guilty of adultery and infanticide. Small wonder that the tradition of Baudelaire, Blake, Hölderlin, the representatives of the clerkly class who repudiated the middle class from their beginning, loathed Goethe. Richard Dehmel, Stefan George, Rainer Rilke, and most post-war German poets have abominated him. Only would-be Social Democratic *Kultur Kommissars* like Günter Grass admire Goethe. Bertolt Brecht thought he was just hilariously funny.

Yet Goethe is not all bad. He is the only major poet produced by the business ethic. Above all else he was, like Leonardo da Vinci and Marcel Duchamp, interested in making a work of art of himself. It is his autobiographical work which is not only most meaningful today and still readable, but which is his best—*Conversations with Eckermann, Dichtung und Wahrheit,* the writings of his Italian journey, and especially his erotic poems—the more erotic, the better. Perhaps Goethe's sex life in Italy was a little like somebody on a Kiwanis or Rotary charter flight, but he felt it, and the verse is superlatively beautiful. *"Über allen Gipfeln," "Kennst du das Land," "Marienbader Elegie"* are still the greatest German lyrics after the Middle Ages.

Goethe, who seemed so Olympian, was in fact much like Zeus. He was crippled for life by an early betrayal of love. Like Wordsworth, it sterilized him. "Better injustice than disorder" became his life motto, like Wordsworth, and for the same guilty reason. But *Faust* is a kind of immense psychoanalytic session. It is on the pure Idea of Order and the personification of love, the budding German *Hausfrau,* that injustice descends with its beautifully polished axe. Preaching the gospel of the middle class in its early youth, Goethe knew subconsciously a truth quite contrary to Lenin's famous dictum—A ruling class can no longer rule when it can no longer love. Mephistopheles, the pure aristocrat of the *ancien régime,* may tirelessly preach Nietzsche's *gaia scienza,* the ecstatic love of "Life," but when Faust discovers that he is totally, hopelessly lovelost, he begins his escape. So today in the papers Faust's class is distinguished by its terrifying lovelostness, whether at a party of Andy Warhol's or a custody fight in a divorce court. Finally Mephistopheles emerges as really the Devil, for what characterizes the Devil, so busily working away in hell, is his infinite frivolity.

But what is there on the other side? Notice, all through both parts of *Faust,* Mephistopheles' and Faust's mutual contempt for black magic, witches and warlocks, and even for Mephistopheles' chic and sinister haberdashery, but most of all for the pact signed in blood. Says Mephistopheles, "He insists." God is satirized as The Great Accountant. As one ruling class gave way to another, The Lord's Prayer changed, not "forgive us our trespasses" or "our sins," but "Forgive us our debts as we forgive our debtors." Not for nothing did Spengler, that vastly rhetorical spellbinder for Faustian man, say that the *Zeitgeist* of the capitalist epoch would be impossible without double-entry bookkeeping.

Yet Goethe did become outwardly a self-made aristocrat and nobleman of the cloth, the hero of all German burghers to come after him. He really was in Weimar what Anselm had been to Charlemagne. He succeeded, he alone. Future Goethes would be PR men, venal journalists and money writers, even though the day would come when it would be they who would not only manipulate, but who would create, their rulers.

Although Goethe was a rancorous anti-democrat devoted to putting the new class directly into the hieratic vestments of the old, he never managed to be anything else but just middle class. After he has destroyed young love, Faust finds salvation in draining marshes at the sacrifice of the lifelong old love of Baucis and Philemon. "Work! Work! Work!" runs like a refrain throughout *Faust*. Submission to the joy of the passing moment is the irredeemable sin. Today we realize that this ethic is on the verge of destroying the species. *Faust,* as a moral tract, is as dangerous as the hydrogen bomb.

The intensely personal love poems based on folklore—as of course is *Faust* itself—lack one thing—"There is no wonder in those eyes." Just as German romantic music used folk song but got rid of the *mana,* the supernatural glamour, by mechanically measuring time, so Goethe, modeling his verse on ballads and Mother Goose, and his plots on fairy tales, empties them of the effulgence of the uncanny foundations of being. The aristocrat and the peasant are rooted deep, not in the tillable earth, but in the chthonic underworld. Johann Wolfgang von Goethe, certified public accountant of Weimar, could not understand that the manners of the peasant and the chivalrous etiquette of the aristocrat were only the devices of a truce with chaos—not social disorder, but the chaos before Time, over which the Spirit brooded.

My mother used to say, "A snob is a person who mimics the manners of the class above him."

Balzac

Balzac was Karl Marx's favorite author. In the few paragraphs in all his books and correspondence devoted to literature most space is given to Balzac. On these short discussions has been reared a whole Marxist esthetic, in fact, several competitive ones. Every Marxist literary critic has felt it incumbent upon him at least once in his career to write a full dress essay on Balzac. Well he might. It is hard to say whether the *Communist Manifesto* is an ideological reduction of Balzac's *Comedie humaine*—the immense panorama of France of the first third of the nineteenth century, the unified and interconnected series that Balzac made out of almost all the novels of his maturity—or whether the fictions of Balzac are both an allegory and an objectification of the work of Marx.

Balzac is the epic poet of the barbarous age of industrial commercial civilization, what Marx called the period of primitive accumulation. They even have certain emotional and personality traits in common. Both are daemonic writers driven by prophetic fury into rebellion against the human condition. This is overt in Marx but is always there, just below the surface, in Balzac, ready to erupt in caustic analysis of human motivation. It acts as a kind of corrosive medium in his descriptions of dramatic settings—streets, houses, furniture, costumes—an electric charge that makes all his objects glow with a quality beyond realism—Surrealism if you will.

The Surrealists talked a great deal about willed paranoia. The characters of Balzac, insofar as they are creatures of will —his good people are almost always will-less and usually witless—are driven by demons, by lust, greed and black magic. We see them as we would see monstrous creatures in an aquarium, floating in a solution of objective paranoia. The kind of world that tortures the mad with its unreality is the real world of Balzac's human comedy. Louis Aragon, when he broke with the Surrealists said, "Why should we invent insanities? We can never compete with the daily newspaper." Aragon became a Marxist and went back to the methods and the vision of Balzac.

The method is simplicity itself. With few exceptions Balzac's novels are hung on a monomania. Pere Goriot is mad with paternal love for his daughters. Eugenie Grandet's father is mad with greed. They are examples of Ben Jonson's theory of humors pushed to its extreme in derangement. The subsidiary characters are humors, too. Each represents the dominance of one human characteristic—vice, sin, folly, a virtue or a psychological peculiarity or a physiological type. This man is sanguine; this woman melancholic; this one lewd; that one angry; another treacherous; all these qualities could just as well be capitalized and applied as proper names as in *Pilgrim's Progress*. Bunyan intends to portray the complex interactions of the spiritual world. Balzac sees objective reality in this fashion. If this is realism it is madness. Or else it is a special tradition of classical drama, like Jonson or Molière, a development of the commedia dell'arte. Balzac was quite well aware of the parallel—*Comédie humaine—commedia dell'arte*.

Taken altogether the interacting characters of a Balzacian novel should analyze out and then dramatically sum up the entirety of the whole human character, a sort of generalized man, who is himself the Human Comedy. This, however, is not the case. The good people do not have determinative roles. They are examples of that slavish passivity that Nietzsche attributed to Christianity. They are always powerless and they are pious rather than religious. There are no complex spiritual issues forming the threads of the texture of any of Balzac's novels, as there are in Dostoyevsky or Tolstoy, who owed so much to Balzac, but even in Turgenev or Chekhov, or in *Moby Dick* or *Huckleberry Finn* for that matter.

Balzac, like many extreme materialists, was by way of being something of a religious crank. Several of his novels are direct expositions of his beliefs of the moment. Their protagonists do not have an interior life, a spiritual life. They are gnostics and magicians, daemonic characters who assault and coerce reality. Their motives are little different than the robber barons and queens of the salons in the world of France before 1846, where man was wolf to man and the lambs had gone underground or were exterminated. There is no question but that the Western world was like that then. It still is, for that matter, if you choose to see it that way. Tolstoy saw it differently. The major difference of course is charity. Tolstoy's charity was possible because he was at home in that world and yet had no desire to gain from it. Tolstoy was a rich aristocrat. Balzac was a self-made man if ever there was one. This is an apposite term. His novels are all tales of would-be self-made men in a society of all-out competition, where no one except pious sisters back home in some lost provincial village are going to help you to make yourself, and where modern terms like self-realization or integration of the personality would be incomprehensible.

Balzac started out a romantic of the romantics, imitating the Gothic novels of Mrs. Radcliffe and Walpole, and Walter Scott remained his favorite novelist. The novels of his maturity, the *Comédie humaine,* are just as romantic. What Balzac did, and he was quite well aware that he did this, was to take Scott from the barbarous world of the Scotch border and apply him to the far more barbarous slums and salons of Paris, and to the stifling, small town houses of the provincial middle class. It is this romantic vision which gives Balzac's novels their melodramatic and cinematographic character. As he starts down a street at the opening of a novel describing the houses, the pavement, the shops, the passersby, constantly sharpening his focus detail by detail, each one significant, until he has revealed the cast who will be the subject of the book, his descriptions have the hyper-reality of the finest costume movie. Even in their time, and describing their own time, his novels are no more realistic than Scott's. They are infinitely more convincing. They certainly enabled his contemporaries to see themselves with a stereoscopic vision, sharper than reality, every detail in focus, players in a costume drama whose clothes were the ones they wore themselves.

It is Balzac's daemonic possession which distinguishes him from all other novelists. In the twenty years of his productivity he wrote more than any other major writer in history. Very little of it is hasty or slipshod, but it is all driven, and it drives the reader. His narrative method takes possession of you in a way that would not be seen again until the full development of the cinema. A novel by Balzac is an obsession which you are at liberty to adopt for a few hours.

He was driven and obsessed by debt, status, the overturn of all old values, and the horror of the empty world. He himself was a man of profound interior struggle, but it is his work as a whole as it reveals himself that shows this. His characters move in his plots like molecules and atoms in fields of force. Tragedy on such a stage is impossible. The tragic drama goes on behind the scenes and between the lines, in the interior of the author, as it does in the materialistic mathematics of Marx's *Capital*.

The Journal of John Woolman

The first volume of the Harvard Classics, the immensely popular "Hundred Best Books" of a previous generation, contains William Penn's *Fruits of Solitude,* Woolman's *Journal,* and Ben Franklin's *Autobiography.* The implication was that an ethic derived from Quakerism was a fundamental or primary component of American culture. True, it was one form of the business ethic, but it was devoid of covetousness and luxury. Even in Franklin the main emphasis was on social responsibility, and in Penn and Woolman the source of responsibility was found in contemplation, the highest form of prayer.

It has been said that a life of prayer presents an exterior, best called unlimited liability, the outward manifestation of its interior gaze at the absolute, or the ultimate, or the ground of being, or God, or even Nirvana. Nirvana originally seems to have meant "unruffled," as the surface of a pool, and those whose minds have achieved that vision of peace are unable to violate it by violence or the exploitation of other living creatures. Conversely, the way to contemplative calm is by the path of kindness and love and respect for the integrity of other creatures.

John Woolman was a simple clerk in a small store and yet his acting upon his "concern," as Quakers call it, was historically as significant as anything done by either Penn or Franklin—each of whom in his own way is considered a very important historical figure indeed. Woolman's assumption of social responsibility in himself for the deeds of other men was most specifically a "fruit of solitude," of a profound interior life. It was an act which was an outward and visible sign of an inward and spiritual grace. So the Anglican catechism defines a sacrament, and the meaning of John Woolman's Quaker ethic was, and still is, that all the significant acts of man's life can be made sacramental in nature. Standing on the corner of 42nd and Broadway on a Saturday evening, or walking down the streets of Las Vegas, it is hard to believe that such a philosophy of life, by no means a monopoly of Quakerism, was once considered the very essence of what meretricious editorial and advertising writers call "The American Way of Life."

Yet insofar as the United States of America, at this summit of historically unparalleled power and wealth, does not disintegrate into chaos within the hour, it is this vision that holds it together—however debauched its language may be by dishonest rhetoric.

Until Woolman's day many members of the Society of Friends had owned slaves and considered their responsibility discharged by their comparative kindness in their treatment of them. George Fox, the founder of the Society, had seen slavery on his visit to the Barbados in 1671 and had realized that slave holding and the principles of Quakerism were incompatible. An anti-slavery movement began within the Society of Friends itself, but it did not result either in many Quakers freeing their slaves or in agitation by Quakers outside the Society.

One day in 1742 the young merchant John Woolman, recently admitted to the Quaker ministry, was making out a bill of sale for a Negro woman for his employer, who was selling her to another Quaker. Woolman, already a man advanced in the contemplative life, had an "opening"—an illumination of that Inner Light which Friends look to for guidance. From then on he travelled up and down the thirteen colonies and eventually over to England, rising in First Day Meetings and voicing his concern. That is all. Meditative prayer and endless travel, a simple speech in Meeting, conversations with many hosts in their homes, work betimes to make a living, and, not to be forgotten, along with this simple activity a physical witness in life and person.

Eventually Woolman ceased to eat sugar, wear cotton or indigo-dyed woolens, because these were products of slave labor. Out of modesty and a disdain of luxury, Friends dressed plain and looked outlandish to their satin-breeched contemporaries, yet in the long run their witness told. Woolman looked outlandish to Friends. Within his own lifetime, cut short far away in England by the rigor of his travels, Woolman's witness told on Friends. The Society not only renounced slavery in Meeting after Meeting but became the earliest, most powerful single force in the anti-slavery movement.

Woolman's *Journal* is the simplest possible record of his ever widening travels and his ever deepening interior life, two aspects of one reality. He came, he spoke, he conquered, solely by the power of an achieved spiritual peace, a perfectly clear personality through which that Quaker Inner Light shone unimpeded from Friend to Friend. It is this moral quality, once called humility in days before our terminology of the virtues became hopelessly confused, that elevates Woolman's writing to the level of great prose. It is a greatness that can never be analyzed or taught in a course in English prose composition, but it can still be communicated to those willing to meditate on Woolman's words, and who try to share his experience. Not of storm-bound roads and Indians and contentious slaveholders, but his experience of an interior reality, a focus, one amongst many millions, of a universe of meaning.

All that Woolman needed to achieve greatness of style in language and life was perfect candor. That of course is not easy to come by at 42nd and Broadway, or Las Vegas, or on Madison Avenue—but it wasn't easy to come by in eighteenth-century England either, in gambling halls or courts or literary coffee shops.

Is Woolman's *Journal* taught in school? Is it one of the hundred best books? It certainly should be. Social action and a resurrection of spiritual values—these the troubled youth of America are teaching themselves today. If a people can be said to have a soul, Woolman like Whitman and Whittier after him, was an avatar of that soul. It is the soul that keeps the body, even the body politic, alive. When the Inner Light goes out, the body is only an unstable mixture of complicated molecules and soon rots way.

Francis Parkman's
France and England in North America

It has never been possible to write an American epic, at least not an affirmative one. The reason a synthetic epic like Lönnrot's *Kalevala* has been so enormously successful in Finland is that the Finns believe in themselves, whether dairy farmers, machinists, or poets. What can we put in the place of Homer or Virgil in America? *The Adventures of Huckleberry Finn*? *Moby Dick*? Both books repudiate the values of the society that produced them. Those who would provide America with a mythic embodiment of American values and who possessed the necessary skills arrived too late on the scene. Toynbee's schism in the soul had already opened up and become unbridgeable.

Francis Parkman deliberately set out to accomplish such a task. His many-volumed history of the struggle of France and England in America purports to provide a true myth of the victory of a business civilization over an un-businesslike culture, and of the conquest of an inchoate and disorderly wilderness and its savage denizens by Puritan discipline. Back in the days when people had more time to read, Parkman's long history was a bestseller, but nobody read it for the message he hoped to convey.

Parkman was not a very good writer. His set pieces on the beauties of the forest primeval, the savagery of an Indian war dance, or the debauchery of the wilderness high society at Montreal, are rather comic reading today. Although he wished to deflate the legend of the noble savage and certainly knew his Indians, most of his descriptions of Indian life are as over-colored and romantic as anything in Chateaubriand's *Atala* or Cooper's *Leatherstocking Tales*. It is only when he is caught up in the circumstantial rush of a narrative that excites him that he writes well. And what excites him is seldom the heroic virtues of his New England warriors.

The thesis of *France and England in North America* is that drinking, running around with women, rising late and loafing in the woods must go down to disaster before the righteous onslaught of the forty-eight-hour day, the well-kept savings account, patriarchal domesticity, well-shined shoes and cold baths. During the nineteenth century this was probably true, but the nineteenth century is a very brief period in the long history of man. It is doubtful if this moral struggle had much to do with the defeat of France in the New World. French America was lost in Europe.

The subjection of the wilderness of the old Northwest by red-coated soldiers and land speculators has moved few boyish hearts, even in New England. But the story of the boats of Champlain poking their way into the dark leafy wilderness, the pathetic death of LaSalle, the joyful portages of Marquette and Joliet, the cognac, riot, and abandoned women in beseiged Montreal are as moving as the defiance of Milton's Satan. Certainly the moral and dramatic climax of the fourteen volumes is the story of the Jesuit missionaries to the Iroquois with their implacable passion for martyrdom and the remorseless systematic cruelty of the Indians. The North American *Jesuit Relations* that Parkman substantially reproduces are amongst the noblest documents in the history of Christianity, singularly evangelical for their time, and saturated with all the graces of the Beatitudes. As the Gospel says in French, but not in English, *"Bienheureux sont les débonnaires."* St. Isaac Jogues and his companions, tortured and burned alive, may not have inherited the earth, but their tradition is still far stronger in the land than those who know only the culture of the Northeastern seaboard can ever imagine. The land held in the vast network of the canoe-ways of the drainage of the

Mississippi and the Great Lakes still possesses a kind of occult tradition, French, Indian, and Negro, that gives it what health and strength it has.

The memory of the Indians connects us with the soil and the waters and the non-human life about us. They take the place for us of nymphs and satyrs and dryads—the spirits of the places. To talk jargon, they are our ecological link with our biota, the organic environment which we strive to repudiate and destroy. And the deerskin-clothed explorers and trappers, the black-robed priests, and red-coated soldiers are all the Greeks and Trojans we have.

Parkman's history is the story of our heroic age, and like the *Iliad* it is the story of the war between two basic types of personality. It is from this archetypal struggle that it derives its epic power. As Parkman works it out in detail, the personal conflicts of its actors give it the intricacy and ambiguity of a psychological novel. That this struggle is echoed in the spiritual conflict of the author gives the book intimacy and depth beyond that of factual history. Blazing council fires in savage villages, long marches through the autumn wilderness beset with snipers and ambushes, and the last formal, purely European chess-like battle on the Plains of Abraham, redcoats, redskins and chevaliers, all this pomp and circumstance give history the fanfare of high romance or grand opera, *Aida* and *Siegfried* together in the wilderness.

Parkman is far from being Homer, or even Walter Scott, but what virtues he has are Homeric. Unlike other great Romantic writers, the bare facts of his subject matter were so romantic that he was usually prevented from being silly and was permitted, again and again, to be actually noble. Underneath the heroic narrative, as in true epic, lies the flooding tide, full of turmoil and whirlpools, of the Unconscious, or the Id, or the "dark forces of the blood," the actual, savage environment that reason and order and humane relationships can penetrate but cannot control. This again is the ethical and psychological assumption of the *Iliad* and the *Odyssey*.

In his youth contact with the dark roots of life, traveling in Italy or vacationing as a guest of the Sioux at the headwaters of the Missouri so shocked the theocratic mind of Francis Parkman that he never recovered. He spent the rest of his life as a valetudinarian in a state of mild nervous prostration that he attributed to his sinful youth. However he might approve of the Business Ethic of his Puritan fellow citizens, he could not act it out. He was incapable of becoming a promoter or business executive or commercialized politician or business-like general or academician. All he could do was write the history of that ethic and its contradiction, thesis and antithesis, struggling on the frontier, the whole fourteen volumes erected on the foundation stone of *The Oregon Trail,* the story of his own brief freedom from control.

Near the end of the last volume, *The Conspiracy of Pontiac,* in lines that echo Melville, Parkman sums up the real moral of his life's work:

. . . To him who has once tasted the reckless independence, the haughty self-reliance, the sense of irresponsible freedom, which the forest life engenders, civilization thenceforth seems flat and stale. Its pleasures are insipid, its pursuits wearisome, its conventionalities, duties, and mutual dependence alike tedious and disgusting. The entrapped wanderer grows fierce and restless, and pants for breathing-room. His path, it is true, was choked with difficulties, but his body and soul were hardened to meet them; it was beset with dangers, but these were the very spice of his life, gladdening his heart with exulting self-confidence, and sending the blood through his veins with a livelier current. The wilderness, rough, harsh, and inexorable, has charms more potent in their seductive influence than all the lures of luxury and sloth. And often he on whom it has cast its magic finds no heart to dissolve the spell, and remains a wanderer and an Ishmaelite to the hour of his death.

Pickwick Papers

The characters of the dialogue in Plato's *Republic* say that what they are doing is trying to create a theoretical environment which will perfectly enable the Just Man and so define him. *Pickwick Papers* starts with the good man, not just, rather benign, as its initial assumption and tells the story of his interaction with the world, in the sense of St. Paul's "the World, the Flesh, and the Devil." Although the two books are superficially very unlike, we have Dostoyevsky's word that it was from Pickwick that he got the idea for his own good man, Prince Mishkin in *The Idiot*. Since that day few novels have had benign heroes. Where they have existed they have been a good deal more idiotic than Dostoyevsky's idiot—The Good Soldier Schweik, for instance, or Franz Biberkopf of *Alexanderplatz Berlin* by Alfred Döblin.

Mr. Pickwick is a synthesis of Don Quixote, Sancho Panza, Tom Jones, and most of the characters in *Tristram Shandy*. He is not only more rational, but more self-conscious and more intelligent, in the ordinary sense, than his fictional ancestors. So likewise his man of common sense, his Sancho Panza, Sam Weller, is not a "natural" whose wisdom is that of the simple appetitive peasant. There is nothing really earthy about Sam Weller. He is thoroughly urban. His wisdom is derived from an adequate sense of the meaning of all the strains and stresses in a complex web of unending human relationships, the acquisitive society. Mr. Pickwick and Sam live in a more densely populated world than their predecessors, where good and evil are never simple, but complicated in each person like the traffic of a great city. Unlike Don Quixote and Sancho, they are essentially equals.

Interpolated in the main story are a number of tales told by the characters. They are the exact opposite of the main narrative. Each is a portrayal of the world as a place of moral horror, and their contrast with the story of Mr. Pickwick and Sam and their friends intensifies the impression that their world is not just a utopia but a Garden before the Fall. Although Sam Weller serves Mr. Pickwick as rudder and anchor and keeps him attached to the planet by his mocking realization of universal self-interest, this self-interest is never judged to be evil as such.

From Dostoievsky's day the assumption has always been that the environment of the nineteenth and twentieth centuries would always not enable, but destroy, the benign man. The good people in Balzac are ground up in the wheels of life as in the chopper of a garbage disposal. The good people in Samuel Beckett are what emerges at the other end of the garbage disposal. Modern civilization is assumed to be the exact opposite of Plato's *Republic,* not the optimum environment, but the worst, for a man entirely virtuous. The situation of Mr. Pickwick, if it were described in the abstract, would be taken for granted by almost anyone to be a tragic situation, or at least, a black comedy.

Does Mr. Pickwick meet with tragedy? He does not—he meets with adventures. Almost all of them to a greater or lesser degree are comic, but with a comedy that is more funny than black. He and Sam Weller and a few of their friends and companions in their journey through life carry their utopia with them. Whatever misadventures befall, it remains intact. So in a sense nothing happens in the book to raise it to the level of dramatic art. Complicated situations come and go. At the end a few people are better, and better off, because of Mr. Pickwick's benevolence, and he has grown old. Perhaps this is really what happens in life to most good men. They are not crucified. They simply pass through life and then die and their passing influences just a few people to make them just a little happy. Mr. Pickwick offers himself to the Great Beast of Things as They Are as a scapegoat in atonement for others but the result is a resurrection without a crucifixion.

Pickwick is a most extraordinary production. It occurs, so to speak, backwards in the author's life. It was his first real book, preceded only by the heterogeneous *Sketches by Boz*. It was written in 1836; Dickens was only twenty-four. The kind of wisdom exhibited by *Pickwick* is usually assumed to come only in old age. Dickens grew backwards. The dark and bitter and perverse tales of his later life are the sort of thing written by young men. It took a long time for life to tell on him. It is extraordinary that a youth subjected to the toil and trouble, insecurity and shame of Dickens' young days should have emerged with one of the most benevolent tales in literature, utterly devoid of the characteristic paranoias of youth— the attribution of deliberate intention and duplicity to almost all human behavior. The young suffer terribly from the belief that the people they encounter are most of them up to something and that something has some relation to themselves. Actually of course, most people just bobble along like apples on a stream. Usually it takes many years of experience to realize this. Dickens knew it at twenty-four. Life, instead of convincing him of his initial judgment, slowly persuaded him otherwise. The motivations of the characters in his last novels are as disingenuous as any in Henry James.

Dickens has been a favorite of those literary nuisances, the psychoanalytic critics. For once they found a patient whose problems do reflect their formulas. The weakness in the Pickwickian utopia is the same as that in Whitman's. It is a brotherhood, a community of affection confined to males. The monstrous regimen of women is there. Later it would grow across the world of Dickens' dramatis personae like a great black cloud. In *Pickwick,* although there are several women of the Dickensian villainess stamp, they are powerless. Life just bobbles along and defeats them. Freudian symbol-hunting is usually absurd, but notice the constant use of milk factually and metaphorically throughout *Pickwick*. What might have been the black comedy crisis of the novel where Dickens directly models his story on the most disgraceful episode in *Don Quixote,* it is milk punch that Mr. Pickwick drinks to excess. Overexcited in the heat of his benevolence and thirsty, he becomes tipsy. He babbles. He tumbles over into a wheelbarrow. He falls blissfully asleep. The evil world pelts him with vegetables and ordure. He sleeps on smiling like an infant who had been nursed to satiety. The utopia of *Pickwick* is a self-sufficient nursery of males, a little like the moving picture of Laurel and Hardy, dressed as babies, in a giant crib. The women in the novel, who are the bad people, are so essentially because they withhold the nourishment that women can give. However nobody really seems to mind. The milk of human kindness flowing from Mr. Pickwick is sufficient.

Unlike Whitman, Dickens by no manner of means avoided women. His life was full of them. He lived in a kind of harem of emotional turmoil all his days. His relations with women were far deeper than those with men. Women play a determinative role in many of his later novels while men tend to become monsters, whether Fagin or Mr. Micawber.

Both Dickens' life and novels reflect back on *Pickwick* and would be expected to make it seem unreal. Quite the contrary. It is the most real of all his books. As he was writing it in his twenty-fourth year he knew that it would be, that his first judgment of life would be his soundest, that he would never write another *Pickwick.* That for once he had written a great classic. The infantile elements in the book can easily be overemphasized. Its virtues are those we attribute sentimentally to infancy—perfect clarity of vision, innocent candor, utter simplicity of judgment and the result of the operation of these factors—jollity. Like Blake, Dickens knew that the song of innocence was the true judgment of life but it was 1836, the dawn of the Victorian and the Industrial Age, and the dark Satanic mills of *Bleak House* and *Edwin Drood* were waiting to gobble him up. Thomas Seccombe in the eleventh edition of the *Encyclopaedia Britannica* article sums up Dickens' career with the sentence: "Dickens had no artistic ideals worth speaking about." If *Pickwick Papers* does not embody the highest artistic ideals, nothing does. It is an accomplishment of untortured artistic lucidity of the sort we attribute to Mozart and Raphael—a kind of angelism.

Uncle Tom's Cabin

In the first half of the nineteenth century, American writing made its first large-scale appearance on the stage of world literature. Benjamin Franklin, Thomas Jefferson, and others like them had been international writers or thinkers with considerable influence abroad, but they were essentially Physiocrats or Girondins or Jacobins—in other terms, radical Whigs. The sources of their inspiration were in France and secondarily in England, even though in those countries they were accepted, not as bright provincials, but as full equals in the international community of the Enlightenment that stretched from the court of Catherine the Great to the discussion clubs of Philadelphia. Two or three generations later American writers were playing a determinative if minor role in international literature. Yet it is almost unbelievable that the picture they were presenting to the European community of Romanticism and revolt included a huge percentage of America's population only rarely and then, even with the best intentions, as comic stereotypes. The point of Ralph Ellison's novel lies in the absence of the article. It is not "An" or "The" but just *Invisible Man*. The American Negro in Ralph Ellison's day, as in Hawthorne's, was invisible to most of the rest of society, and more important, man was invisible in the Negro. His full humanity was simply not seen.

Harriet Beecher Stowe made the moral horror of slavery visible to all the world, but she also made the Negro, slave or free, visible as an essential member of American society, and she made the full humanity of the Negro visible to all, black or white, all over the world. It is possible to disagree with her idea of what a fully human being should be, but she did the best according to her lights. Her lights were, as a matter of fact, just as illuminating as any that have been lit in a more cynical and rationalistic age, by writers with a different kind of sentimentality.

Uncle Tom's Cabin, like Mark Twain's weather, is talked about by millions who do nothing about it—that is, "Uncle Tom" is a term of contempt used by everybody today and yet hardly anybody bothers to read the book anymore. The picture of the humble and obedient slave is derived not from the novel but from the "Tom Shows" that toured America for a generation before the First War. Uncle Tom is in no sense an "Uncle Tom." He is by far the strongest person in the book. Although he is whipped to death by the psychotic Simon Legree, his end is not only a tragedy in Aristotle's sense, the doom of a great man brought low by a kind of holy *hubris,* but like Samson, he destroys his destroyer.

Is Harriet Beecher Stowe sentimental? And rhetorical? Indeed she is. So is Norman Mailer, or for that matter much greater writers, Thomas Hardy or D. H. Lawrence. It is true that we must adjust to changes of fashion when we read her novel. We are willing to do this when we read or see Shakespeare's early plays with their euphuistic rhetoric—the fad of a moment—or the prose of Sir Thomas Browne or the stately rhetoric of Gibbon's *Decline and Fall of the Roman Empire.* The early nineteenth-century rhetoric of Harriet Beecher Stowe takes a little getting used to, but it survives the test of the first twenty pages. Once the reader has accepted it, it soon becomes unnoticeable. The sentimental scenes in the novel, almost the only ones that survived in the Tom Show—Eliza on the ice, the death of Augustine St. Clare, the death of Little Eva—are deliberate devices to hold and shock the popular audience of the time. They drive home, to sentimental readers who gave at least lip service to an evangelical Christianity, the overwhelming reality of the rest of the book. How real, how convincing, this huge cast—as large as any novel of Balzac's or Dostoyevsky's—is. True, the Negroes are seen from the point of view of a white person, but any attempt to "think black" would have been a falsification. Mrs. Stowe simply tries to think human. And human they all are, even at their most Dickensian. Little Eva is not a plaster statue of the Little Flower. The evangelical early nineteenth century produced plenty of saintly little girls just like her. They occur in all the novels of the time, though not in such abnormal circumstances as the Little Missie-devoted slave relationship. When they appear in Dickens they are usually less believable. Mrs. Stowe's sentimentality lacks the subtle lewdness that invalidates Little Nell and other girls of Dickens, because Mrs. Stowe was a far more emancipated and radical person than Dickens, politically and sexually. Tom, of course, does not function as a slave but literally as an "uncle" to Eva. He takes the place of her neurotic and inadequate father, as he substitutes for so many others who are inadequate, and finally atones for all.

Simon Legree may be a monster but he is a human monster, more human for instance than Dickens' Fagin or even Mr. Micawber. No one in *Uncle Tom's Cabin* is completely a villain. Even at their worst Mrs. Stowe's characters are battlegrounds of conflicting motives, of Beelzebub and Michael. Simon Legree is not a devil. Devils and angels struggle within him. The slave trader Haley knows the good, but to him it is reduced to the cash nexus. Uncle Tom in his eyes is worth more money than an "ornery" slave.

Uncle Tom's Cabin is not only an attack on slavery, the greatest and most effective ever written, it is a book of considerable philosophical or religious and social importance. Its immense popularity was a significant factor in the change in the dominant American philosophy, dominant in the sense of "shared by most ordinary people." Mrs. Stowe came out of Puritan New England. In her immediate background was the rigid predestination of strict Calvinism and the literal interpretation of Scripture. *Uncle Tom's Cabin* is far more tendentious in its constant insistence on a kind of secularized evangelical deism than in its forthright, realistic portrayal of the horror of slavery. The book says, "Slavery denies the integrity of the person of the slave; in doing so it cripples the integrity of the person of the master, but it cannot destroy the humanity of either master or slave." This is or should be self-evidently true, and it is presented by a dramatic narrative which is convincing as a marshalling of fact. The philosophy of the good life as expounded by Mrs. Stowe through her various spokesmen and spokeswomen in the novel is disputable, but there is no denying that it was the faith by which most of white—and black—Protestant America lived until recently, a faith by which possibly even a scant majority continues to live today.

It is absurd that in American universities there are countless courses in rhetorical, sentimental and unreal novelists like James Fenimore Cooper or worse, and this book, which played no small role in changing the history of the world, is passed over and misrepresented. Hawthorne, Cooper, Washington Irving ignore the reality of slavery. If one or two Negroes appear in their writings, they are only animal clowns. Yet slavery was the great fact of American life. Harriet Beecher Stowe alone of the major novelists faced that fact and worked out its consequences in the humanity of those involved in it, master or slave or remote beneficiary. She knew that her New England was almost as dependent on the "peculiar institution" as any plantation owner. And what were the final consequences? They are not yet. Of the immediate ones President Lincoln said when he received her, "So you're the little lady who started this great war." As for her literary influence, it is one of the best kept secrets of criticism. Most of the characters of William Faulkner and Tennessee Williams, and many of their situations, can be found at least in embryo in *Uncle Tom's Cabin,* and the old rhetoric is still theirs. It seems to be necessary in describing Southern life. As for Uncle Tom, he was assassinated in Memphis, and has been before, and will be again, until something like Mrs. Stowe's secular, evangelical humanism, or Whittier's, or Whitman's wins out at last, or the Republic perishes.

Frederick Douglass

If the function of a classic is to provide archetypes of human motives and relationships that will form myths for a usable past, the early literature of black America suffers from a limitation which might well be assumed to be crippling. It is conditioned by slavery, and therefore by the highly abnormal relationship between white and black people in a slave society. This is true whether the subject is a Southern plantation or the Abolitionist movement in the North. The slave is forced to live a fundamentally perverted life as though an ant were forced by his colleagues to behave like an aphid. The Abolitionist is engaged in the struggle against an absurdity, an ant protesting against being treated as an aphid. So those earliest works of black Americans are of greatest value when their subject is not simply escape from slavery, but the achievement of true freedom. This is the essence of the program of the radical exponents of black culture today. They point out most correctly that as long as black literature concerns itself with racial conflict in terms that appeal primarily to a white audience it is not a free literature. A classic of black literature would transcend racial conflict and exist in a realm of the fully human. Its terms would be self-sufficient, self-determining and black. This is a subtle matter and has nothing to do with overt subject matter, which, as long as racial conflict exists, must include it.

Frederick Douglass was born free. His servile status was a juridical delusion of his owner. His race, his existence as a Negro, was the "custom of the country." It was also his deliberate choice. His mother was a house servant and not fully black. His father was white. In more civilized countries than the United States he would have been considered, if anyone bothered to think about it, a white man with some mixture of Negro ancestry, no more a black than Pushkin or the elder Dumas. Although his adult life was spent almost entirely with white people, Frederick Douglass chose to think as a black man. This in itself was no small accomplishment. It is more difficult to avoid becoming an assimilado than, for Douglass at least, to escape from slavery.

The most remarkable thing about Frederick Douglass' story of his childhood and youth, the thing that gives the narrative its simple and yet overwhelming power, is his total inability to think with servility. Aristotle said that it was impossible for a slave to be the subject of tragedy because a slave had no will of his own and could not determine his own conduct. Aristotle probably meant this as a permanent, indelible condition conferred by servile status. So that, for instance, the rise and fall of Spartacus, the leader of the great Roman slave revolt, could not be a tragedy, because it was conditioned entirely by his relationship to slavery. Aristotle's is a false assumption. It does not apply to Douglass. He does not escape from slavery, he does not revolt against it, he simply walks away from it, as soon as he gets a chance, as from an absurdity which has nothing to do with him.

We accept the preconditions of Frederick Douglass' life far too easily. We forget how extraordinary it is to witness the growth and ultimate victory of a truly autonomous man in such a situation. The details are amazing enough, his struggle to obtain an education, to learn a trade, his adventures with cruel, or kind, or indifferent owners. Most amazing is the indestructible total humanity of one whom society called a thing, a chattel to be bought and sold.

Douglass' fame in his own day was primarily as an orator, and that of course to audiences mostly of white people. He was the most powerful speaker of a fairly large number of ex-slaves who were professional agitators in the Abolitionist movement. So his writing is colored by the oratorical rhetoric of the first half of the nineteenth century, yet this has singularly little effect upon the present cogency of his style. We find similar rhetoric on the part of white men unreadable today. Douglass' is as effective as ever. It's not just that he is in fact simpler and more direct than his white contemporaries. It is that his rhetoric is true. He believes and means what he says. He is not trying to seduce the reader with the false promises of a flowery style. A hard, true rhetoric is not rhetoric in the pejorative sense. So today his autobiography is completely meaningful. His poetry and quotations from his speeches are being recited in churches and meetings all over America.

One of the great values of Frederick Douglass to us is that he makes it abundantly clear that not all white people, even in the slave states, partook of the collective guilt of mastership. Most of his early education was due to the sister-in-law of one of his owners, Mrs. Thomas Auld. The Aulds later took him back from an owner who had imprisoned him for "suspicion of planning an escape," and apprenticed him to a ship caulker, and thus gave him a trade which enabled him at last to get away.

In these days when people go about shouting indiscriminately, "You kept me in slavery for four hundred years!" many white Americans forget that amongst their own ancestry were people who spent their time and substance in the Abolitionist movement, or risked and sometimes lost their lives on the Underground Railway. We all forget that, although the economic interpreters of history tell us that the Civil War was a quarrel between the industrialists of the North and the great land owners of the South, the thousands of young men who died in the bloodiest battles in history to that date were under the impression they were fighting to free the slaves.

It is horrifying to think that this great man with his indomitable, massive mind was eventually able to purchase his own freedom for 150 pounds subscribed by the anti-slavery movement. It is as though Michelangelo or Thomas Jefferson had price tags of $500 hung about their necks. The autobiography of Frederick Douglass is a "Great Book," a classic —not because it is the story of a Negro escaped from slavery, but because it is the story of a human being who always knew he was free and who devoted his life to helping men realize freedom.

The original edition, *Narrative of Frederick Douglass, an American Slave,* and *The Life and Times of Frederick Douglass,* and selections from his poems and speeches are all available in paperback.

Fathers and Sons

Turgenev's *Fathers and Sons* is the first major work of literature in the nineteenth century to deal with the problem of
alienation in specific and explicit social and ideological terms.
In spite of this, it is generally misunderstood. The tragic hero
Bazarov may call himself a Nihilist, but he is not in fact a
member of any Russian revolutionary group, nor do the things
he says correspond to the program of any organized group in
mid-century Russia. The story takes place on the eve of the
Emancipation of serfs. The forces of social change in Russia
were in a period of temporary disorganization, waiting for the
Emancipation to determine new lines of development.

It is not true that the fathers are more conservative than
the sons, Bazarov and Arkady. Both parents are typical representatives of the professional and land-owning class, not
unlike the Chinese scholar gentry, who from the Napoleonic
Era to the Emancipation had quite clear ideas of the changes
necessary to make over Russia into a healthy modern society.
They were certainly engaged and, however fumbling, in contact with the people. The relations of both parents to their
serfs were as radical as could be in those days. The sons,
Bazarov and Arkady, have no contact with the people and
certainly no program. They have emotional attitudes. Bazarov
has often been compared to totally intransigent revolutionaries like Nechaeyev or Tkachev, or even to Lenin. He bears
no resemblance to such men. They were programmatic with a
vengeance.

The significant thing about both Bazarov and Arkady is
that they take over from their fathers. The countryside
absorbs them. Arkady becomes an enlightened landowner and

Bazarov dies from an infection acquired doing an autopsy on a peasant dead of typhus. Turgenev does not say, as usually quoted, that Bazarov is born out of his time, but that he is doomed to perish because he is in "advance of the future," an ironic statement which exactly describes Bazarov's historical and social isolation. Out of Bazarov's alienation would come the vengeance, but not the program of the future irreconcilables. Bazarov's tragedy is the tragedy of a suspended man—*l'homme pendu.*

Tragedy the book certainly is, with an ordonnance worthy of Sophocles or even of Sophocles as interpreted by the rigor of Aristotle. Few novels march with greater sense of inevitability, an inevitability which becomes apparent in the opening pages. From the very beginning the reader has the sense something is going to happen. All of Turgenev's greater novels belong to—in fact, create—a special genre. They are what might be called ecological tragedies. There are no landscapes, birds, or beasts in Dostoievsky. Even though he may describe them, we really deduce the surroundings from the interactions of the people. Chekhov has told us in his letters, his criticism, and the famous passage in "The Seagull," how he builds his scenes—moonlight on a broken bottle and the cry of a bird. Chekhov's scenes are exactly that—settings. Turgenev's heroes die in the midst of their biota. In the final analysis that is why they die, not because they are political outcasts, impotent rebels, or superfluous men, but because something has gone wrong with their interconnectedness with the living world. Turgenev has been praised again and again for his wonderful descriptions of nature. That is not the point. The actions of men reverberate through the living world. A fumbling declaration of love—"Arkady made no answer and turned away, while Katya searched for a few more crumbs in the basket and began throwing them to the sparrows; but she moved her arm too jerkily and the birds flew away without stopping to pick up the bread." The sexually self-sufficient, autonomous woman with whom Bazarov is incurably out of phase—"Here, in the cool shade, she read and did her embroidery, or abandoned herself to that sensation of absolute peace with which we are probably all familiar and the charm of which lies in a half-conscious, hushed contemplation of the vast current of life that is forever swirling in and around us." This is the ecology of the emotions. Alienated and truculent, Bazarov does not sterilize soon enough a cut from his own scalpel and the biota in the form of a typhus organism overwhelms him. The ecology swallows him up.

Poised in this incoherent moment of history, both fathers and sons seem to us incredibly innocent, yet remarkably civilized for gentry, unlike the country British they admire. They are not less revolutionary than the sons; quite the contrary, but they are more humane. Bazarov is not humane at all. He is an anti-humanist, but his anti-humanism is still innocent. After the Emancipation anti-humanism would become sophisticated and begin the long march to the Winter Palace. Alienation would pass to act—Nachaeyev, Tkachev, Lenin. Dostoievsky would see it as diabolism, but his devil would be a hero to later generations. Artsybashev's Sanine is the thoroughly vulgarized descendant of Dostoievsky's Stavrogin, and certainly a hero to his author and his readers, but it is absurd to say that Bazarov is the direct progenitor of either. "The future was closed to him."

Turgenev is one of the few authors whose prose style survives all but the most wretched translators. Of course, the oral qualities of the Russian do not come through, but the style is dependent far more on objective materials and their careful ordering. Sentence by sentence the opening of *Fathers and Sons* marshals the cast on a stage where every necessary detail has been painted in with immense skill. First Arkady's parents; then Arkady indirectly; then Arkady; then Bazarov; all done with the greatest speed, no words wasted, all with a sense of inevitability and urgency—the opening of the tragedy of the speedy end of a slow and redundant man.

The years since *Fathers and Sons* have been years of revolutionary change and search for the meaning of life. The critics of each generation have concluded by saying, "*Fathers and Sons* is peculiarly appropriate to our time." Today we live at a moment of history of unparalleled incoherence, with an "old world dead and a new powerless to be born." We are all to a greater or lesser degree redundant. We are out of phase with the living world around us. We are all Bazarovs. Unlike him, few are innocent.

Sherlock Holmes

The average literate person if asked to respond with the name of a fictional character to the figures 1885–1905 without pausing for the thought, would almost be sure to answer, "Sherlock Holmes!" From George Meredith to George Gissing, from Samuel Butler to H. G. Wells, the late Victorian Age has been elaborately documented. Above all other periods, it has been most fertile in historical and critical social documents disguised as fiction. Some of these novels are great works of art too, beautifully constructed and with new and profound insights into the human mind, and written in differing but superlative prose. Yet the time lives for us most clearly in our literary memories in a collection of tales, often poorly constructed, hastily written for money, the best ones wildly improbable, peopled with stereotypes, devoid of any insights into human character, profound or otherwise, and regarded by their author, at least so he claimed, as a burden in the writing.

Are these charges true? If so, how can "Sherlock Holmes" be a classic? Are the Greek Romances, like Heliodorus' *Ethiopian History,* classics? Did Walter Scott write classics? Did the elder Dumas? If the *consensus orbis terrarum,* that which is held by all, at all times, everywhere, is the test of faith in literature as in religion, a considerable number of the great works of entertainment, originally commercial fiction, will find their way to places not far below the lofty regions occupied by Sophocles or Dante or Shakespeare. There are probably twice or three times as many devotees of the cult of Sherlock Holmes, from the Argentine to Japan, as there are of William Blake and D. H. Lawrence put together, and

Blake and Lawrence are very great writers indeed, however much their admirers may tend to band into cults.

The most famous lines in Sherlock Holmes are unquestionably:

"The curious incident of the dog in the night-time."
"The dog did nothing in the night-time."
"That was the curious incident," remarked Sherlock Holmes.

Ronnie Knox called that the perfect example of Sherlockismus, and right he was. An undertone of mockery, sometimes subtle, sometimes not so subtle, usually benign, sometimes malicious, runs through all the sixty adventures of Sherlock Holmes and gives them their peculiar style. Holmes himself is as wild a caricature as Dicken's Mr. Micawber. Yet like Mr. Micawber, we are convinced of his reality, precisely because he is an ironic caricature, like so many of the people we have known in real life, who are more outrageous than any character of fiction. Landladies, page boys, countesses in distress, August Personages in trouble, adventurers home from the seven seas, gentry, merchants, clerks, and not least the Archetypal Old India Army Man, Dr. Watson, all are seen slightly askew, distorted by irony and garbed in stereotype like an immense cast of the *commedia dell'arte* of the glory of empire.

This does not mean that Conan Doyle was another Samuel Butler or H. G. Wells, and that "Sherlock Holmes" is an anti-Victorian onslaught like *The Way of All Flesh* or *Tono Bungay*. Quite the contrary. Conan Doyle would not have been so successful if he had not believed almost all of the myths of Victorianism. A Sherlock Holmes who was an admirer of Kier Hardy, founder of the Labour Party, or of Oscar Wilde, would be an embarrassing absurdity. The official Sherlock Holmes societies, like the Baker Street Irregulars, amuse themselves at their dinners by reading papers proving just such possibilities with elaborate parade of scholarship, that Holmes was the Stuart Pretender, or a defrocked Anglo-Catholic priest, or the head of an anarchist conspiracy, or that Dr. Watson was Jack the Ripper, or a woman in man's clothing, or that the entire Sherlockian corpus is a cryptic exposition of Marxism. The secret of the fascination of the world of Sherlock Holmes is its terrifying normality, that dangerous normality an American president was, after all its consequences had been worked out, to call "normalcy," and that, alas, we have never been able to get back to.

Yet it was a more normal world than ours and its glories were real, if a little sooty. The present fashion for all things Victorian and Edwardian is not just put-on and high camp. Now that we are no longer immeshed in modern orthodoxy, it is apparent that the tradition of naturalistic English painting from Ford Madox Brown to James Tissot produced some of the greatest pictures of modern times, that the age was one of the three great ages of British poetry, that there was an intellectual explosion, not just scientific but spiritual as well, unparalleled in history, that the architects produced some of the noblest as well as by far the most domestic buildings ever built, and that even the grand British hotels turned out a service, and even a cuisine—what the British thought was French high cuisine—the like of which there'll never be again. The hotels, alas, are all being torn down or homogenized by the chains, and therein lies the secret. Victorian society was homogeneous without being homogenized. It was, to paraphrase the epigram about Parliament, a society of extreme eccentrics who agreed so well they could afford to differ. And this is why the adventures of Sherlock Holmes form a great comic epic of Victorianism. Conan Doyle, himself an Irishman and an outsider, catches and transmits the intense individualism and the universal consent, and instinctively emphasizes the source of this vast unstable, dynamic balance—empire.

India, China, the South Seas, the Far West, his characters

come home from the ends of the earth to blackmail and murder each other, while heavily veiled noblewomen and frightened governesses and ladies of the proletariat and absconding brokers and hoodwinked royalty drive up through the rain and fog under the gas lamps to the rooms at Baker Street seeking salvation. Holmes is Justice, neurotic, capricious, but humane. The erring escape the vengeance of their own misdeeds, the evil go to dooms they have prepared for themselves. If Sherlock Holmes' adventures truly reflect life between 1885 and 1905, it was haunted by a dangerous insecurity. But so in fact it was. And the symbolic detective is natural law finding out and healing that insecurity—solving the mysteries and absolving the anxiety. The eccentric Holmes, a total personal exceptionalist, is the exception that both proves and suspends The Rule.

The plots are by no manner of means models of the ratiocinative detective story. Even Poe does better. Conan Doyle's favorite stories, "The Speckled Band" and "The Hound of the Baskervilles," are not merely implausible, they are impossible, and the Sherlockian societies have had immense fun correcting or accounting for their errors with much heavy scholarship. R. Austin Freeman's Dr. Thorndike tales are infinitely more logical expositions of criminal induction—which Holmes and Watson persist in calling "deduction." But not until Simenon's Maigret comes on the scene will Law, not police law, but natural law, treat the foolish and evil with such humanity.

There are no better records of the profoundly normal oddity of Victorian England and early twentieth-century France, nor more humane ones, than the detective tales of Conan Doyle and Simenon. And they are possessions like unto pearls of great price, for alas, we will never be as odd again.

H. G. Wells

For the generation of responsible intellectuals who grew up in England and America between 1900 and the First World War, the most important writer was not Thomas Hardy or Henry James, but H. G. Wells. His influence was not only, or mostly, literary; he was a moral guide and spokesman. It is impossible to understand British Suffragism, socialism, the British Labor Party leaders, the middle generation of American Progressives, even movements of greater social responsibility in the established Church, unless it is realized that the English Left, and Progressives of the type of the elder La-Follette, were formed by a tradition, going back to the beginning of the nineteenth century, with William Godwin and Robert Owen, and coming down through Ruskin, William Morris, Kropotkin, and others, that stressed economic and political change as the essential preliminary for a moral and spiritual revolution which would restore meaning to social life, which a predatory society was destroying. They didn't call it alienation, they simply called it intolerable—and ultimately, deadly.

During the long period of formal estheticism from which we have only recently escaped, respectable critics dismissed Wells as a social reformer with a foolishly optimistic view of progress, whose novels were tracts. The orthodox Left dismissed him as a "Utopian," the dirtiest seven-letter word in the vocabulary of Marx and Engels. He wasn't supposed to be able to really write. He was supposed to lack Flaubert's and James' devotion to *le mot juste*. Nothing could be more false than this critical picture, and it is hard to believe that the people who abused him had ever read any of his novels

or science fiction in the period of his greatest accomplishment, from *The Time Machine,* published in 1895, to the
First War.

In the first place he was very far from being an optimist.
The early scientific romances, *The Time Machine, The War
of the Worlds, The Island of Doctor Moreau, The Invisible
Man, When the Sleeper Wakes, In the Days of the Comet,
The War in the Air, The World Set Free,* are not only still
the most adult science fiction ever written, but they are also
peculiarly haunted books. Wells, like Swift, was puzzled by
the species into which he had been born. He believed there
was something wrong with man, something which prevented
realization of the spiritual potential of the human race.

In the period before August 1914, when practically everybody believed in Progress, Wells was saying in his romances,
"Brethren, by the bowels of compassion, I beseech you, be-
think you you may be mistaken." Perhaps the human race
would fail. Extrapolating from the present human situation,
it looked as though it almost certainly would. The heroes, or
in most cases, simply the narrators, of the scientific romances
are as corrupt, every bit, as ever Augustine, Calvin or Luther
judged mankind to be. The difference is that Wells was compassionate, sympathetic, and even amused, where they were
horrified and denunciatory. His heroes were the ordinary sort
of Englishmen bumbling along and muddling through, capable of heroism and love if opportunity offered, which it seldom did, mostly living a life of daily compromise in all the
little things which, when added up over the centuries ahead,
in the grand total of human weaknesses, would spell disaster.
They were starved for love, even for recognition as persons—
like Wells' invisible man, and when panicked, like the narrator of *The First Men on the Moon,* capable of irresponsible
flight and murderous selfishness.

Most of the science fiction since Wells' day seems to be
written by precocious schoolboys. It is Wells' profound in-

sight into small men, making the best they can of the vast
human condition which has been thrust unasked upon them,
that gives him his maturity, and which also accounts for the
fact that, even amongst the juvenile audience of science fiction, his romances still sell, year after year, while later practitioners of the genre come and go, and are soon forgotten
except by their fans.

These same heroes appear in the great Cockney comedies,
Kipps and *The History of Mr. Polly,* without the ceremonial
vestments of magic elixirs, time machines and space ships.
They have the absurdity of simple men, but far more absurd
is the senseless world mankind has built around them, its
hideous cities, its destructive human relationships, its ugly
clothes, its brutal sports, and its frustration of love. How
many of Wells' heroes, even in the post-war novels of his
decadence, opt out—better camp out in the wilds of Lab-
rador with the woman you love than pull the strings of political power in London, even for the best of putative ends.

Yet what happens? These heroic marriages always fail.
The so-called thesis novels, *Tono-Bungay, The New Machi-
avelli, Anne Veronica,* even *The Research Magnificent,* are
no more about the patent medicine racket, Suffragism, British
politics, than Henry James' *The Golden Bowl* is about a piece
of bric-a-brac. They are about the same thing that most of
D. H. Lawrence's best novels are about—the failure of the
last sacrament left to secular man, true marriage, in an all-
corrupting social environment. This is not underlined in any
propagandistic way. It is simply presented as the abiding
tragedy of twentieth-century man and woman, just as it is in
Lawrence's double novel, *The Rainbow* and *Women in Love,*
or as it is in Ford's *Parade's End,* or in most of Hardy. Who
would be so optimistic today, as the century draws to its
close, as to deny that, if love between a man and a woman is
the last channel to the assumption of unlimited responsibility
and realization, the Community of Love, it too has been

choked up and is almost closed. This is what the novels of
Henry James are about too, the corruption of the organs of
reciprocity. And it was Henry James who very early hailed
H. G. Wells as the finest stylist and the most sympathetic
analyst of human motives of the then younger generation.
There are two ways of approaching style—*"Sculpte, lime,
cisèle,"* like Flaubert or James, or forget about it and say
what has to be said, like Dreiser or Wells. All four are great
stylists, though Dreiser is a very odd one. Wells was a far
more conscious artist than Dreiser, and many of his remarks
about the unimportance of style are annoyed responses to the
Art for Art's Sake decadents. Whether in the last gloom-
drenched pages of *The Time Machine* or in the chapters in
Tono-Bungay—Wells' major *Bildungsroman*—which describe
the growing into manhood of a lovelost young man in smoky,
gaslit London, few people in this century have written better.

As for the utopias and other social criticism and the history, they are all haunted, too. Something has gone wrong.
How can it be repaired before it is too late? Toward the end
of his life Wells came to say in conversation that maybe the
opposite has happened to the benign catastrophe he describes
in *In the Days of the Comet,* where the earth passes through
the tail of Halley's Comet, an unanalyzable change takes place
in the atmosphere, everybody passes out and wakes up rational and good. Maybe somewhere around 6000 B.C. the
earth passed through a malignant cloud of interstellar dust—
hence the long epic of folly and failure we call civilization.
Before the gigantic flowers blossomed over Hiroshima and
Nagasaki, Wells was talking about mankind at the end of its
tether. Well?

Ford Madox Ford's
Parade's End

The great bulk of the world's prose fiction, contemporary and past, does not wear well. Almost all of it is soon forgotten, and of those books which survive the wear of time, only a few withstand the effects of time on the reader himself. Out of all the novels ever written there is only about a ten-foot shelf of books which can be read again and again in later life with thorough approval and with that necessary identification that Coleridge long ago called suspension of disbelief. It is not ideas or ideologies or dogmas that become unacceptable. Any cultivated person should be able to accept temporarily the cosmology and religion of Dante or Homer. The emotional attitudes and the responses to people and to the crises of life in most fiction come to seem childish as we ourselves experience the real thing. Books written far away and long ago in quite different cultures with different goods and goals in life, about people utterly unlike ourselves, may yet remain utterly convincing—*The Tale of Genji, The Satyricon, Les Liaisons dangereuses, Burnt Njal,* remain true to our understanding of the ways of man to man the more experienced we grow. Of only a few novels in the twentieth century is this true. Ford Madox Ford's *Parade's End* is one of those books.

This is not a rash statement. Most important contemporary critics who have read it agree that it is the most mystifyingly under-appreciated novel of modern times. Issued as four novels of a tetralogy from 1924 to 1928, it enjoyed a moderate success with the public and even was issued by one of the two largest book clubs. Since then, in recent editions in America, its success has been tepid. Its virtues, which are those of a relentless maturity, may have limited its audience. Certainly the modernism of its style is no longer a factor. Its style is conventional indeed in comparison with many recent successful novels, and the less sophisticated public of forty years ago found it acceptable enough.

Many critics down the years have pointed out that almost all anti-war novels and movies are in fact pro-war. Blood and mud and terror and rape and an all-pervading anxiety are precisely what is attractive about war—in the safety of fiction— to those who, in our over-protected lives, are suffering from *tedium vitae* and human self-alienation. In *Parade's End* Ford makes war nasty, even to the most perverse and idle. There is not a great deal of mud, blood, tears and death, but what there is is awful, and not just awful but hideously silly. No book has ever revealed more starkly the senselessness of the disasters of war, nor shown up, with sharper x-ray vision, under the torn flesh of war, the hidden, all-corrupting sickness of the vindictive world of peace-behind-the-lines. It is not the corporate evil, the profits of munitions makers, the struggles of statesmen, the ambitions of imperialists that Ford reveals at the root of war, but the petty, human, interpersonal evil of modern life, what once was called wickedness. Grasping leads to hallucination and hallucination leads to death, hate kills and compassion redeems—this is the thesis of so many great novels. In a sense, *Parade's End* is the *Tale of Genji* transposed to a totally different system of coordinates, but the human equation comes out the same in the end, the pattern of the curve of life against the curve of death.

As the books appeared, they were known as "the Tietjens series" after Ford's hero, and imperceptive critics made much of Tietjens' remark that he was "the last Tory." This label has injured both the understanding and the sale of the novel. Tietjens is a troubled, compassionate, gently sardonic man, and that phrase is the most wry of all his comments on his personality. If he is a Tory, it is not in the sense of Winston

Churchill or Harold Macmillan, but of Jeremy Taylor or William Law. He is humanist man, confronted after two thousand five hundred years with the beginning of the end of humanist civilization in the first major explosion, the First World War, of mass civilization, inchoate and irresponsible, ridden with the frustration and vindictiveness that come with depersonalization and the loss of all real life goals. He is a Tory in the sense that he is a Christian gentleman, a Thomas More in a world where almost everyone is a Henry VIII or Anne Boleyn. He seems perhaps unduly put upon and crucified, Christlike because those around him are continuously crying out, "Barabbas! Barabbas!" in a terrifying din. But he isn't crucified at last, he survives, and his compassion heals as many as it can touch.

Hate kills. In the midst of war the living deaths of the novel emanate from the hatred of Tietjens' wife, adulterous, guilt-crazed, unrelievedly hostile. She is the daughter of Ibsen's Nora or Hedda, who has got her way, which turned out to be no way at all. She is not as thrilling as Strindberg's deranged women, but she is more convincing because she is infinitely pitiable. We accept her with Tietjens' compassion. In a sense she is the heroine of the book, as the wretched Lear is the hero of his play.

Graham Greene once said of *Parade's End* that it was the only adult novel dealing with the sexual life that has been written in English. This is a startling superlative, but it may well be true. Certainly the book has a scope and depth, a power and complexity quite unlike anything in modern fiction, and still more unusual, it is about mature people in grown-up situations, written by a thoroughly adult man.

Like his contemporaries, D. H. Lawrence and H. G. Wells, Ford's best novels are all concerned with the struggle to achieve, and ultimately the tragic failure of what before them had been called the sacrament of marriage. Before *Parade's End* Ford's *The Good Soldier* was probably the best of all the novels on this subject which so tortured the Edwardians, in literature and in life. Besides being a much larger-minded work, *Parade's End* is certainly the best "anti-war" novel provoked by the First World War in any language. The reason is that the two tragedies are presented as one double aspect, microcosm and macrocosm, of a world ill. Ford builds his cast of English people at war like Dante built his tiers of eschatology, and reveals the war as a gigantic, proliferating hell of the love lost—known to itself as Western European Culture.

Ford liked to point out that Dostoyevsky was guilty of the worst possible taste in making his characters discuss the profundity of the very novel in which they were taking part. Ford's Ivan Karamazov and Alyosha would have talked only about the quality of the cherry jam and thereby have revealed gulfs known only to the discrete. The complex web of shifting time, the multiple aspects of each person, the interweaving and transmutation of motives, all these appear in the novels Ford wrote with Joseph Conrad, but here, where he is on his own, Ford's talent for once seems to have been fully liberated, to go to its utmost limits.

The result is a little as though *Burnt Njal* had been re-written by the author of *Les Liaisons dangereuses*. There is the same deadly impetus, the inertia of doom, riding on hate, that drives through the greatest of the sagas. There is the same tireless weaving and re-weaving of the tiniest threads of the consequences of grasping and malevolence, the chittering of the looms of corruption, that sickens the heart in *Les Liaisons dangereuses*. The reader of either novel, or the saga, emerges wrung dry. The difference in Ford's book is compassion. The poetry is in the pity, as Wilfred Owen said of the same war.

Japan

Japan and the Second
Greater East Asia Co-Prosperity Sphere

In the past year Japan has been continuously in the press—
the daily newspapers, the newsweeklies, the weeklies of editorial comment and analysis like *The Nation* and *The New
Republic,* and most especially the financial papers. I doubt if
a week goes by without an ominous story in *The Wall Street
Journal* or *The Journal of Commerce.* In addition, for the
past two years there has been a steadily growing number of
books on Japan, on the character of the people, the economic
explosion, "the growing influence of the Japanese military,"
and of course the economic threat of Japan to American business, both internally and externally. Most recently people have
begun to write about the catastrophic effects of industrial expansion, urbanization and a steadily rising working class
income in the country itself. The Greater East Asia Co-
Prosperity Sphere lost in the war has been won by peace—and
by default. Suddenly Japan has become the third great power,
a whole Third World in itself.

Accompanying economic expansion there has been an ever
increasing cultural influence abroad. Today it can safely be
said that classic Japanese poetry has a greater influence on
young American poets than does English or French, and incomparably greater influence than American poetry of before the
First World War, with the possible exception of Whitman.
Japanese painters are amongst the most successful in the
world. During the American-initiated abstract expressionist
movement the Japanese quickly demonstrated that they were
better at the style than their Western colleagues, and furthermore, that they were doing what came naturally, that the

whole esthetic of the movement, so novel to the West, was deeply rooted in Japanese tradition. The two most important postwar American painters, both independent of abstract expressionism, Mark Tobey and Morris Graves, studied in Japan and deliberately modelled themselves on classic Japanese painting. Significantly, they have survived all the "movements" of the past thirty years and are today amongst the most sought-after, and incidentally most expensive, painters in the world. If you knew nothing about them, you would find it hard to believe that they were not both Japanese, probably Zen monks.

Zen Buddhism began to influence American intellectuals on a large scale immediately after the Second War, and long before that the works of D. T. Suzuki had begun to influence a small elite. Today Zen can accurately be called the American form of existentialism, far more influential than French or German existentialists like Sartre and Jaspers. Now, although Zen is simply the Japanese pronunciation of Chinese *Ch'an* and Indian *Dhyana* Buddhism, it is really a specific and peculiarly Japanese development, bearing little relationship to the other sects of Mahayana Buddhism. Even before the Communist regime, *Ch'an* was almost dead in China, and nobody has ever been able to demonstrate the existence of *Dhyana* Buddhism in India. This autonomous development is significant.

Ever since Perry's gunboats forced open the sea gates of Japan in 1854, people, both Japanese and Western, have been talking about the Westernization of the country. Today, nearly 125 years later, we, both Japanese and Westerners, are beginning to wake up to the fact that the country has not been Westernized at all, it was simply modernized. With incredible rapidity Japan overtook in three generations the developed capitalist nations, and is now assuming a leading position in the world-wide technological civilization which is often called post-capitalist or post-modern. To this world civilization it is making its own, very specific, cultural contribution. Before discussing some of the aspects of this new factor in a world cultural synthesis, it would be good to go back and take up some of the allegations of the popular journalists of a new Yellow Peril craze which has manifestly grown before our eyes and which is a far more ominous factor than the sale of ramen noodles and rubber sandals in Durban, Rio and Boston.

There is no evidence whatsoever for the growth of the influence of the military on the general Japanese population. Quite the contrary. It is the government of the United States which has accelerated its pressure on the civilian government of Japan to increase its armed forces and its offensive armaments. Every such move by the American government has been passionately resisted by the Japanese people, including the five great trusts which dominate the Japanese economy. Japanese businessmen are only too well aware that they owe their ever expanding economy to the fact that seventy per cent of their taxes do not go for wars, past, present and future. It is self-evident that in the United States we have a war economy. Only the most vulgar politicians or editorial writers in learned journals like *Barron's Weekly* dispute it any more, and it is becoming equally evident that a war economy does not work and it is almost impossible to get out of, to kick the habit. Japan, West Germany, Sweden owe their present prosperity to a peace economy, something you don't have to get out of.

It is interesting to notice that without exception the authors of the current rash of Yellow Peril books are men who are known to have been employees of the American military and intelligence establishments and probably still are. This is a factor not to be ignored in the agitation and propaganda against "The Ugly Jap" in Southeast Asia and the Indian Ocean littoral. Riots against Japanese businesses suddenly erupted all over the place in November 1972. All over what place? Exclusively in American satrapies like Thailand, where nothing happens without the approval of the C. I. A. The riots consisted of a handful of kids and vagrants carrying placards.

Who paid them to demonstrate? For there was absolutely no popular movement of any sort which they represented.

The Greater East Asia (and Indian Ocean) Co-Prosperity Sphere has grown up by default of the Americans and in many instances in places where American power is absolute. The trouble with American business is that it is simply not interested in peaceful economic expansion in Southeast Asia. How many billions of dollars went into the Cam Ranh Bay military facilities? At the same moment, ordinary, peaceful business enterprise with and for the Vietnamese became dominated by Japanese business. The Americans were there in possession, but they were so busy making another kind of money that they didn't even notice.

The same holds true for the actual merchandise itself. You cannot run manufacturing plants, least of all those turning out technologically highly sophisticated commodities with super profits guaranteed by the taxpayers—even when by ordinary business standards you are bankrupt—and turn out good merchandise that can compete with ordinary business enterprise. The deterioration of quality is strictly proportionate to government subsidy of inefficiency and dishonesty. It doesn't take too long for the crooked economy of the Merchants of Death to invade the manufacture and merchandising of normal, peaceful industry and commerce. This is so obvious that it should not be beyond the grasp of a speaker and his audience at a neighborhood Kiwanis Club luncheon. The consumers' goods manufactured by a great American conglomerate born of the war economy cannot compete in Durban, Perth or Jakarta—or Saigon—with those manufactured by Mitsubishi, who cannot turn to the taxpayers to underwrite inefficiency and bad manners. It should never be forgotten that Japanese economic power has crowded American business in precisely those areas where the American empire's political and military power was uncontested.

Before the Second War, Japanese merchandise competed

with American, German, English because it was cheaper, and it was cheaper because the Japanese working class lived in a paternalistic, low-paying, oriental economy which had little to do with the capitalism described by Western economists, whether Marxist or anti-Marxist. What did it matter to the ordinary purchaser if the cement in the lenses of his Japanese camera yellowed after twenty years and that in the German it did not? Today the Japanese lens cement doesn't either. The Japanese "extended family" structure still survives in large part, but the wages, the standard of living, and much of the value structure and life aims of the Japanese working class have changed profoundly. They have not become Westernized. They are each and all factors in a peculiarly Japanese Neo-capitalism.

There are many great industrialists in Japan who, along with the scholars and publicists who they pay to write for them, genuinely believe that this new capitalism of Japan will be the country's major contribution to world civilization, and will influence the self-styled Free World and People's Democracies alike. They do not think of themselves in the spurious terms of American business propaganda of the Coolidge era, as you might guess, but quite to the contrary, identify themselves with the neo-Marxists of the West German Frankfurt Group and the Yugoslav Zagreb Group, with their theories of worker participation, but in a post-capitalist rather than a post-Communist utopia. Not only this, but they believe that their Neo-capitalism is the solution for the undeveloped countries over which their commercial influence is so manifestly spreading. They may be right. It is apparent now that an economy still functioning on nineteenth-century commercial and industrial principles cannot pull an under-developed nation out of a so-called oriental economy. India is today an overall dead loss and has existed since the Second War in a kind of receivership, and it is in spots far more developed than say, the new African nations or even Indonesia or Thailand.

There is certainly profound social conflict in Japan and

widespread alienation, but it differs from that in the West in that it has not yet destroyed the quality of work and therefore the quality of the commodity, nor has it destroyed initiative. As for the latter—they are still building mock-ups of the Wankel car in Detroit, but in Detroit itself you can buy a nice, new Japanese Wankel, right down the street from the Chevrolet and Ford agencies. Detroit and Flint claim that they cannot possibly meet the government pollution control standards on cars before five years and then only by drastically raising the price, but this coming Fall you'll be able to buy Japanese cars that already meet them. Why? American manufacturing and research and development have been preoccupied with the commodities of the war economy.

This "Japanese miracle" has not taken place without severe social strain. The economy is certainly what vulgar economists call "overheated." There are several different kinds of inflation. Japan suffers mostly from price inflation—there is more money than people know what to do with, even though a large percentage of it goes into savings and popular investment, and so back into the circulation of capital and the ever increasing expansion of the capital structure. There is still too much left over. So a Japanese nightclub or discotheque can cost twice as much as the most expensive in Paris. It would be hard to spend less than 200 dollars per person for an evening of geisha entertainment. The Japanese inn, devoted to the assignations of the rich and their mistresses, is more expensive than the most expensive hotel in New York. These things are trivial and perform the necessary function of sopping up money which is really only social loose change, but they are only a startling symptom of the disproportionate inflation of prices all along the line. The wage scale continuously presses against the price level. Today it is difficult for a skilled worker in the Tokyo area to support a family of four on seven thousand dollars a year at the standard of living he has grown to expect.

Western tourists in Japan never realize that there are several parallel economies in the country. Four to seven per cent of the budget of major industries goes to promotion and promotional entertainment (imagine what this would mean if it was the practice of General Motors). So there exists an expense-account economy—nightclubs, hotels, Love-Inns, geishas, courtesans—where the prices are like something in science fiction. Below this is the world of international and upper class internal tourism, now the most expensive in the world. Next is the level at which well-paid professional and skilled workers live, where wages are lower than they are in the United States, Canada or West Germany, and where prices for most things are about 15 per cent higher, and where housing, as in most rapidly developing countries, is expensive, inadequate and in short supply. Below that is the level of the ordinary Japanese worker, who is having a hard time making ends meet, but who is living in a style he never enjoyed before, and below that in the back country, and in the slums of the cities, there still survive the remnants of a pre-capitalist "oriental" economy, not quite as bad as the worst in the United States, but considerably worse than anything in Northern Europe. If the population were not so extremely mobile, and the overall economy so elastic, these levels could easily freeze into caste. As it is, the friction along their interfaces creates very considerable heat, but still, Japan's social relationships resemble far more those in 1850 San Francisco than they do those in medieval India. The social consequences of this gold or oil boom state of affairs in some ways are not unlike those of the San Francisco Gold Rush.

A community in the grip of a gold or oil boom has a compulsive and hysterical character—"Get it and get out!" The frantic activity does not lead to permanent satisfaction within the community itself. The relations between people are fugitive—one night stands. The value system itself lies outside the community. The tremendous gains in just plain naked wealth are not negotiable for permanent satisfaction. The community exists by exploiting natural resources which are consumed from the ground and vanish elsewhere. Japan imports almost all its raw materials—except one—its human beings with their "work ethic," group loyalty, and high skills. This raw material it is mining, not cropping, today.

A healthy human society completely recycles itself. It is a crop, not a mine. It lives on and with its environment; the boom town destroys it. Today the towns along Highway 49, the Mother Lode, have been cleaned up for the tourists. Thirty years ago they were rubbish piles, and the streams and forests around them had been ruined by ruthless butchery and finished off by gold dredges which turned hundreds of square miles into heaps of cobbles.

Japan is beginning to look like this, and for the same reasons, a get-it-and-get-out social morality which is spreading amongst a population which only recently had been the most fundamentally conservationist in the world. In the days before Perry, when Japan was closed to the world, it was very much a recycling space ship with a resulting ethic that pervaded all walks of life.

Read the great Japanese novels of the Middle Ages, from *The Tale of Genji* on, with the point of view of an economist. The life described has been called incredibly luxurious, but take note—what does the luxury consist of? Works of art and highly skilled craftsmanship. The materials involved are inexpensive, with the sole exception of beautiful fabrics, often imported from China or Korea in exchange for the gold of which Japan in those days produced a surplus. Japanese women didn't even wear intrinsically expensive jewelry until modern times. Cost was determined by skilled labor and hence wealth continuously circulated within the economy. Actual living conditions differed very little from those of the Polynesians in the South Sea islands whom Europe would have considered savages. Even a generation ago people still said that Japan competed unfairly with American labor because the

Japanese had a lower standard of living. By any sensible system of values, they had a higher one. They enjoyed a breadth and depth of permanent satisfactions without destroying their sources.

All this is no longer true. The conurbation that stretches from north of Tokyo to Hiroshima with little interruption is turning into an immense litter of jerry-built housing and flimsy industry. The air is thick with smog. But more important than this, as a symptom of what is happening, the Japanese have become unconscionable litterbugs. Take a walk through the mountains along a trail from temple to temple, past waterfalls and through forests. Everywhere there's garbage. Critics have said that this is due to the lack of an overall social responsibility in the Japanese, whose responsibilities were always to the family and to the clan. This is not true. A generation ago the Japanese, above all other people, were conscientiously respectful of the public good. They still are, off in the hinterland.

The social-spiritual resources for a reversal of the present trend in Japan are still there. The graciousness shown in interpersonal relations and in the choice of the pleasures of life that were so admired by Lafcadio Hearn and that he prophesied long ago would be subject to a terrible onslaught from a competitive, industrial system still survive, even in Tokyo, even in television programs.

The Japanese have often been criticized for their proneness to mass fads, crazes and collective hysterias. Usually this is a fault. But as the environment they have been creating around themselves has become unlivable, they have suddenly discovered ecology. In Japan ecology is already not a movement confined to freaks, hippies and New Left intellectuals. In fact the only intellectuals interested in the subject until just recently were disciples of the American poet, Gary Snyder. It is the government, the giant trusts, the royal family, the newspapers, the establishment that have become concerned about what is happening. As the American money which has poured into

Japan for expenses of the Korean and Viet Nam wars trickles out, a lot of the boom is going to die down in the Japanese economy. If the United States goes into an economic crisis, as it promises to do, this will have still more drastic effects on Japan. Even Nixon's trade and currency war is going to slow things down. We can look forward to a period of retrenchment and reorganization, and one of the forms that that reorganization is likely to take is the reclamation of the environment and the redefinition of the goals of the society. It is quite possible that Japanese business as a whole will adopt a Galbraithian economic program. It may well have no other way out except economic collapse. If it does so it will unquestionably overtake the United States—for Richard Nixon and his robber baron Janissaries are certainly not going to do so.

The World of the Shining Prince

The world's great fictions are remarkably limited in number. In fact, there seems to be but one sharply focused expression of each highly organized culture. Homer, the Scandinavian *Burnt Njal,* the Chinese *The Dream of the Red Chamber,* the Indian *Mahabharata,* the Spanish *Don Quixote,* and probably if we had the complete work, instead of the small fragment that we do, the Roman *Satyricon.* In spite of the illimitable output of fiction in the modern world, it is doubtful if we have a comparable work. Possibly this is due to the fact that Western culture, after the thirteenth century, has been too poorly focused and too disorderly. Certainly, we have never produced as great a novel as the Japanese *Tale of Genji.*

When Japanese culture was still in its infancy and the benefits of civilization were enjoyed by only a few thousand people at the most, set apart in the midst of a vast mass which was in fact at a lower level of civilization than the contemporary Polynesians, Lady Murasaki wrote what may well be the world's greatest novel. That is, it is a non-epic, non-dramatic fiction concerned with the shifting values and motives of what nowadays we call "interpersonal relations"—I suppose that could do as one definition of the word novel.

For a generation it has been a steady seller in Arthur Waley's beautiful translation. Parenthetically, this translation is itself the most illuminating of all documents on the Japanese text. It, rather than the original, has been translated into many languages, including the modern Japanese, and the extraordinary subtlety, exquisite refinement of sensibility, and psychological, moral and religious profundity are brought out by Waley to a degree that could easily be missed by even the most scholarly and sympathetic reader of the medieval Japanese text.

The literature on *Genji* in modern Japanese is immense. It is fantastically contradictory. In certain circles it is considered a sort of feminist tract and a denunciation of male promiscuity. Marxist critics have claimed it as a satire on the evils of the upper classes, a quaint notion comparable to George Lukac's whimsy that *King Lear* is a proletarian play. On the other hand, mystical Buddhists have seen in Prince Genji a bodhisattva, and modern commentators have compared Lady Murasaki to Marcel Proust.

Ivan Morris' *The World of the Shining Prince* takes sides in all these controversies only against the most fantastic interpreters. He has written a sort of social, historical Baedeker to the novel. He provides all the relevant information about life at the Heian court and amongst the common people of early medieval Japan. Beyond that he does not go. Lifelong Genjists like myself might wish for more and for an adventure into subtle and imaginative interpretation. We ferreted all these things out for ourselves long ago. But the book has been read by many, many thousands of people and nobody who ever read it ever forgot it or failed to be deeply moved, and only a handful of them even know how to find the relevant background information. It is for them that this book is written and it does a superlative job of meeting their needs.

I should not want to give the impression that it is either a dry or fatuous "Daily Life in Old Time Japan." It is an imaginative reconstruction of a tiny over-civilized world which flourished when Europe was sunk in barbarism. Nothing quite like the Heian court has ever existed; although certain parallels might be found in Persia or India, nowhere has civilization ever been entirely confined to so tiny a caste or, possibly for that reason, so intensely cultivated. Ivan Morris' picture is clear and accurate.

Nor is Ivan Morris insensitive to the ever receding subtleties encapsuled one in another, like Chinese boxes, that distinguish this novel from all others. It is possible that some of the more refined interpretations of these subtleties would only confuse the Western reader and so he leaves them aside. However, he makes it very clear that the greatest writing and the most profound drama occurs in the latter half of the novel after Prince Genji himself is dead, and he is well aware that the plot is basically the story of the working out, the reduction, and the final redemption of an evil karma, the consequence of jealousy, anger and irresponsibility.

I feel that Morris' guide to *Genji* is about as complicated as most people are prepared to take and I doubt if a short essay is the place to go into these complications. However, there's nothing like trying.

It is my personal belief that *The Tale of Genji* is a cryptic, artistic statement of Buddhist erotic mysticism. A bodhisattva, in case you don't know, is one who, at the brink of absorption into Nirvana, turns away with the vow that he shall not enter final peace until he can bring all other beings with him. He does this, says the most advanced Buddhist thought, "indifferently" because he knows that there is neither being nor not-being, neither peace nor illusion, neither saved nor saviors, neither truth nor consequence. This is the reason for that benign, world-weary expression on the faces in Far Eastern religious art.

Lady Murasaki presents Genji as a bodhisattva. "Hikaru," "The Shining One," is a bodhisattva epithet, and she gives him the distinguishing natural perfume of such a savior, but she presents him not only as an indifferent bodhisattva, but as an unconscious one, a religious notion of startlingly original profundity.

From a momentary spasm of the most extreme jealous anger on the part of one of his mistresses, Lady Rokujo, a being, an incarnation of evil karma, "takes foot," as the Japanese say, and struggles throughout the book with the grace that emanates from Genji gratuitously.

In succeeding generations, the karma, the consequences of a lifetime that belonged to him and to his beloved friend, Tojo no Chugo, crosses and re-crosses in their descendants and comes finally to a resolution when a young girl, beloved of both descendants, struggles with the demon and destroys it forever in a series of acts as gratuitous, as indifferent and unconscious as the original evil or the original grace. Needless to say, a complex of moral notions of this sort involves a kind of religious thinking which not only the Western world but even modern Japan might find outlandish. As I say, Ivan Morris avoids such speculations, but nowhere does he rule them out, and his book lays firm foundations on which the many thousands of English-speaking people who love the *Tale of Genji* may rear whatever airy superstructures suit their taste. The *Tale of Genji* is the incomparably great novel it is because it admits an indefinite number of such superstructures.

The only place I disagree with Ivan Morris is where he calls the *hannya* (the devil who speaks through the mediums who are called in when the girls it is killing are dying) the ghost of Lady Rokujo. It is not the ghost, although it speaks in her name. It is the embodiment of a single instant of wrath which grows by feeding on the souls it destroys. Lady Rokujo herself, in fact, goes off and becomes a priestess of Ise and dies in what we would call a state of grace. This idea is not Buddhist, but is derived from the Chinese philosopher Wang Ch'ung (A.D. 30?–90?) and from Shintoist animism.

The substantiating quotation:

Every long-cherished thought; every word, every impassioned piece of music; every violent emotion, love or hate; all that can be exteriorized by the living and can survive death; can subsist, can act, not always, but for a time, until satiated. Thence the power of magicians and witches, men and women trained to concentrate an intense passion in the formulas they utter. Then the special power, for good or for bad, of words uttered by little children, who always put all their strength into what they say. Then the cries one sometimes hears at night; exteriorized lamentations of the oppressed. Thence all apparitions which men call *kuei*. These are the subsisting loves or the persisting hates, which tend to satiate themselves. It was not the soul of Tu-po which killed the emperor Hsuan of the third dynasty; it was the subsisting hate of that unfortunate man, put to death contrary to all justice, which gratified itself, when the vital spirit of Tu-po had already been dissipated long beforehand. The blue dog which bit the side of the Empress Lu of the first Han dynasty, a bite from which she died, was not the soul of her victim Prince Ju-i, but the subsisting curse of that poor child, who gratified itself, and became extinct in its gratification, long after its death. In the music which still resounds among the reeds of the river P'u, there survives, not the soul of the musician Yen, but his perverse intention.

—Wang Ch'ung

Nō Plays

Donald Keene and his students have almost doubled the number of Nō plays available in English. With the works available in German and French, especially those of Noël Peri in French, Ezra Pound and Arthur Waley in English, this means that the Western world can now study a representative collection, seen from a variety of points of view, of one of the three most remarkable dramatic traditions that man has ever evolved.

There was nothing like Japanese Nō drama in the West until Thomas Sturge Moore and William Butler Yeats imitated the first Pound-Fenellosa translations. *Iphigenia at Aulis* and *Salome* bear a faint resemblance to Nō, but there is a fundamental difference. They are plays of action and of the developing interaction of persons, and they culminate in dramatic climax. The typical Nō play contains no action at all but rather the recollection of action, and although it commonly culminates in a dance, the dance is not a climax but the manifestation of the crystallization of the realization that has grown and pervaded the play. Many Nō plays concern revenants—ghosts who are bound by passion to re-enact the critical moment of bygone lives—critical not in a dramatic sense, but in the sense of decisive karma. At the end the prayers of a pilgrim priest, who has encountered a long-dead hero and heroine in a windy nightfall on a lonely moor, release them from the endless re-enactment of dead fate and consequence. They are unbound, and reciprocally, realization of the meaning of being itself pervades and saturates the minds of the audience, and precipitates a crystal called release. In other words the Nō drama is more like solemn high mass than it is like a Western play—although a process like this goes on, behind the scenes so to speak, in a very few great Western dramas, notably Shakespeare's *Tempest*. In the Nō drama this mode of esthetic realization is stripped to its essentials and reduced to an art form which is at the same time a Buddhist ritual.

It is quite impossible to convey, least of all by the printed text, the extraordinary novelty of a Nō play to an audience which has never seen one. The words are chanted in a slow, choking moan, in an accent incomprehensible to a modern Japanese who has not been taught it. The dances are considerably slower than any ritual motions anywhere in the West. The acting consists of highly stylized, symbolic gestures, unbelievably slow, whose significance is not apparent to the untutored. The costumes of stiff, elaborate brocade bear little relation to anything worn in the real world and the principal actors are masked. The stage is always the same—a small platform, like a boxing ring, with a resounding floor, approached from the dressing room by a bridge on which are three dwarf trees. The "backdrop" is a screen painted with a highly stylized pine. The chorus and orchestra sit on the stage and the chorus not only "choruses" but often takes over the actor's lines, especially while he dances. Finally, all roles are played by men.

All of this sounds so exotic that it would seem completely unexportable. Quite the contrary. The Japanese Nō drama represents an art form so highly purified that its impact is irresistible to any person who lays himself open to it. From William Butler Yeats to Bertolt Brecht to Paul Goodman to the Living Theater, Eisenstein, Maiakovsky or Genet, ever since the first translations, Japanese Nō has profoundly affected the best European theater. In addition there is probably no better closet drama except for a few plays of Sophocles and Aeschylus. The greatest Nō plays, especially those of Zeami, read in the study, are the finest dramatic instruments of meditation, objects of contemplation, in all literature, and when read, they certainly take less getting used to than seen performed.

Donald Keene gives a new version of one of the greatest Nō plays—*Nishikigi,* Pound's best translation—which Keene dismisses as too inaccurate. The difference is illuminating. Accurate the new version may be, but Pound's is great poetry, in spite of its pseudo-Irish accent, and the new version is not. Furthermore, knowing really almost nothing about Japanese culture, Pound did capture the *yūgen,* the mystery and revelation of Nō, to a degree no one has done since. That is not to quarrel with this new collection. It is really wonderful, and constitutes an addition to the non-Western supplement to the Hutchins-Adler 100 Best Books, a list so lacking in the deepest spiritual insights of non-acquisitive cultural traditions. Perhaps we can learn most about Buddhism by studying the beautiful objects it has produced, the frescoes of Ajanta and Horyuji, statues of Buddhas and bodhisattvas, poems of Ono no Komachi and Bashō, novels like *The Tale of Genji,* and perhaps its finest esthetic distillate of all, the greatest Nō plays.

It is not often in our omnivorously eclectic society that we can thank someone for giving us knowledge of hitherto unknown major accomplishments of the human spirit, and that of course is exactly what Donald Keene does. It is a little as though someone had turned up a thousand lines lost from Homer or Isaiah.

The Influence of Classical Japanese Poetry
on Modern American Poetry

There is a perceptive book on this subject, *The Japanese Tradition in British and American Literature,* by Earl Miner. It is close to definitive but it culminates with the work of Ezra Pound and William Butler Yeats and has little to say about developments since. In the last twenty-five years the influence of Japanese poetry has become far more pervasive than it has ever been. The postwar development has been quite different, a difference of distance. Japan was once for the West a far away world of lotus dreams, a paradise of decadent sensualists. Whatever it is now, it is certainly that no longer.

The first influence of Japan on Western culture came through the reports of the Jesuit mission in the sixteenth century, with their similar but more extensive reports and translations from China. For the *philosophes* of the eighteenth century, Far Eastern civilization was a model of rational order. As is well-known, specifically Japanese influence began with the wood block prints discovered used as packing and wrapping paper for Dutch imports of porcelain, tea, silk, and other commodities, and the influence of their asymmetric, dynamic balance on the then modern painters was revolutionary.

At the turn of the century art nouveau, directly imitative of Japanese art, coincided with a fad for things Japanese, from cheap porcelain in the ten cent stores to sword furniture and *netsuke* lovingly displayed in the homes of the rich. Then too the first great collections of important Japanese paintings were formed in the West, and the first imitations and translations of Japanese poetry were published.

It is amusing to think that in America the founder of the

"discipline" with which we are concerned here was Sadakichi Hartmann, a bohemian of bohemians if ever there was one. In many ways Hartmann was a wise and witty man. As a poet he was dreadful, and he began a long tradition of vulgarization and sentimentalization of Japanese classical poetry in translation. The translations and imitations of Yone Noguchi and Lafacio Hearn, and of E. Powys Mathers, from the French, were considerably better, yet no better than the best sentimental verse of the first years of the twentieth century. They established Japan in the literary imagination as a reverse image of America, a society whose system of values had been moved through the fourth dimension so that left was right and up was down. Japan became a dream world in the metaphorical sense—a world of exquisite sensibility, elaborate courtesy, self-sacrificing love, and utterly anti-materialist religion, but a dream world in the literal sense, too, a nightside life where the inadequacies and frustrations of the American way of life were overcome, the repressions were liberated and the distortions were healed. This isn't Japan any more than materialist, money-crazy America is America, but like all stereotypes some of the truth can be fitted into it. There are forms and expressions of the Japanese sensibility purified beyond anything in the West, where something quite unlike the spirit of Western civilization is to be found—for instance, Ashikaga ink paintings, the Nō drama and a great deal of the best classical Japanese poetry.

Modern Western civilization produces in most of its more sensitive spokesmen a profound alienation. Classical Japanese culture provides for some Americans one satisfying answer to that alienation. In Modern Japan the classic past can never become such a compensatory dream world for any but a few romantic, archaizing intellectuals any more than stories of George Washington, Thomas Jefferson and Abraham Lincoln can satisfy alienated American intellectuals. After all it's one's own world one is alienated from. Unless this is understood it is impossible to understand the peculiarly selective nature of the influence of Japanese poetry on American. "The Japanese do everything just the opposite to how we do," said the GI's of the Occupation. That is the point. Classic Japanese culture provided those nutriments for which the West was starved, or at least Western intellectuals persuaded themselves it did. A hundred Americans have read Arthur Waley's translation of *The Tale of Genji* for one who has read Kawabata Yoshinari's novels. A very few poets may have read translations of Yosano Akiko, but after her, contemporary Japanese poetry is almost totally unknown. Translations exist, but their sales have been infinitesmal.

The Nō drama had a revolutionizing influence on both Ezra Pound and William Butler Yeats. There is a fairly large literature of Western plays more or less in the form of Nō. Kabuki has influenced contemporary playwrights, sometimes via Bertolt Brecht, but I seem to be one of the few Westerners who ever goes to the Shimpa theater. The excellent modern Japanese theater is unknown in the West with almost the sole exception of a dramatic adaptation of Kobayashi Takiji's *Cannery Boat* in the early Thirties.

The myth of Japan provides a dream world in which the suppressed half of Western civilization can find imaginary fulfillment, but also, by a remarkable example of historical cultural convergence, the forms of Japanese poetry, of the Nō drama, and even of the Japanese language itself happen to parallel the development of poetry in the West from Baudelaire to Rimbaud, to Mallarmé, to Apollinaire, to the Surrealists. Ezra Pound was very aware of this, and beginning with his first little imagist epigram:

IN A STATION OF THE METRO
The apparition of these faces in the crowd;
Petals on a wet, black bough.

he called it "superposition." This example does resemble the structure of many classic *waka,* but is nothing strange to Western literature. It is scarcely a metaphor, rather a simile with the connective "like" suppressed. As Pound developed, the language of poetry became for him a vast field of metaphors in which relations could be established at the option of the poet to produce genuinely novel meanings, so that superposition becomes originative of new meanings as in the famous poem of Hitamaro's, *Ashibiki no*:

> The pheasant of the mountain,
> Tiring to the feet,
> Spreads his tail feathers.
> Through the long, long night
> I sleep alone.

whose complex of meanings so many translators have dismissed as purely formal and irrational. (Assuming of course that that is the meaning of the poem, which, as is well known, is disputable.) Before Pound little poems of Mallarmé like *Petit air* had already reached the same point—radical dissociation and recombination as in a cubist painting. As Pound moved on into his long, final work, *The Cantos,* this method which he was to call "ideographic" became his almost exclusive style.

In spite of inaccuracies, Pound's translations of three of the greatest Nō plays have never been equalled either as poetry or as conveying the dramatic essence of Nō. As he, and following him, William Butler Yeats realized, the Nō drama does not move through a deductive logical process to climax and resolution following the recipes of Aristotle's *Poetics.* The Surrealist leader André Breton once pointed out that the development of modern poetry in the West could be interpreted as a revolt against Aristotelian logic and Greek grammar.

Nō drama creates an atmosphere, but one defined in sharp, definite, imagistic terms, an atmosphere of unresolved tensions or longings or irresolutions, and this dramatic situ-

ation is resolved by an esthetic realization which evolves from
the dramatic situation as its own archetype. The dance and
the songs accompanying the dance have been compared to a
crystal of sugar dropping into a supersaturated solution—the
dissolved sugar crystallizes around the introduced crystal until
the solution is no longer saturated. What eventuates is not resolved climax but realized significance. Yeats's *Plays for
Dancers* do accomplish in their own terms the objectives of the
Nō drama with, by and large, its methods. There are long
tracts of Ezra Pound's *Cantos* that are not successful, but the
great passages owe their success to the same method, the
esthetic of Nō and the technique of radical superposition derived from Chinese and Japanese poetry.

Critics with some knowledge of the Chinese written language have made fun of Pound's essay on the Chinese written
character and of his advocacy of the ideographic method as a
new syntax of the sensibility for Western poetry. He got his
ideas of course from the Japanese informants of Ernest Fenel-
losa and although now the dissecting or parsing of Chinese
characters has gone out of fashion, it was once an intellectual
indoor sport amongst the more cultivated literati of the Far
East.

If Japanese, or for that matter, Chinese poetry is translated
into Western syntax and all the spark gaps of meaning are
filled up, what results is a series of logically expressed epigrams, usually sentimental, with a vulgar little moral interpretation attached, or at the best a metaphorical epigram of a
moment of sensibility like Pound's *Metro,* which most resembles, not classical Japanese *tanka* or even the best *haiku,* but
the more sentimental work of the late Yeddo period. It is this
compulsion to fill up the gaps and interpret the poem for Western readers which vitiates the work of so many translators,
both Western and Japanese. They too often believe that Westerners could not possibly understand a Japanese poem in all
its simplicity. Bashō's *Frog* is self-evident in any language, and

yet hundreds of words have been wasted extending and explicating it. As Western logical processes became popular with Japanese translators, and of course with Japanese poets writing in the modern style, Western poets were moving in the opposite direction.

Frances Densmore, one of the first American ethnomusicologists, published many volumes of Indian song—music, text and translation. The songs of some tribes consist of a large number of "abstract" vocables and a few meaningful syllables. In her translations Miss Densmore discarded all but the "real words" and so produced little poems which bear a remarkable resemblance to Japanese poetry:

> As my eyes
> Search the prairie,
> I see the summer in the spring.

> In the heavens
> A noise,
> Like the rustling of the trees.

> * * *

> The bush
> Is sitting
> Under a tree
> And singing.

> The deer
> Looks at a flower.

It is quite possible that Miss Densmore modelled these translations on Japanese haiku. They had a profound influence on the American poet Yvor Winters (and, by the way, on myself) who produced about 1924 a book of one line poems similar to haiku.

> HUNTER
> Run in the magpie's shadow

> SLEEP
> O living pine, be still.

In the Thirties and Forties American poetry in the international modern idiom lived on more or less underground. Imitation of English poetry of the Baroque era was the reigning fashion. The influence of Japanese poetry is apparent in those young poets like Louis Zukofsky, George Oppen and Carl Rakosi who were followers of Pound and of William Carlos Williams, who was a master of the epigram of the sensibility, of poems which resemble the late post-classical *haiku* and *senryū*.

The first really satisfactory translations from the Japanese appeared in Arthur Waley's *Japanese Poetry, The Uta,* a book which unfortunately was never very easy to obtain, which had an excellent introduction, an elementary grammar and vocabulary and the Japanese text *en face.*

During the Occupation, as has happened so often in history, captivity took captivity captive. Thousands of young Americans learned a little Japanese and came to appreciate the virtues of the Japanese way of life. A smaller number gained an adequate knowledge of the language, and a still smaller number, but still a large one, was converted, not to contemporary Japanese life and thought, but to the traditional religion and culture. For over a generation the work of D. T. Suzuki had been slowly making its way amongst Westerners interested in Buddhism. It is true that Zen as interpreted by Suzuki is a special religion and philosophy which differs in some ways from any common form of the religion in Japan. It has been called "Zen for Westerners." Perhaps so. Certainly it was eminently successful and became the popular American form of Existentialism, much more influential than the work of Jean Paul Sartre or Karl Jaspers, possibly because it was more meaningful and gave more profound answers. As a new generation matured after the war, Pound and Williams became old masters of the new American poets and their poetic practice and esthetics along with those of French poets like Mallarmé, Apollinaire and Reverdy and the classical Japanese and Chinese as expounded by Suzuki all converged to produce poets like Robert Creeley, whose best short poems are like those of Japanese poets who have wedded a thoroughly modern sensibility to the classical forms. The last twenty years have seen a growing flood of such poetry.

There is too much of it to discuss in detail. Western civilization is experiencing that secession of the elites and schism in the soul described by Arnold Toynbee. The poetic expression of the counter-culture, which has turned away from the values of the dominant society, has sought and perhaps found new life meanings in the Far East. What was once a social phenomenon confined to a small number of highly sophisticated intellectuals is now a mass movement.

Outstanding among the leaders of this movement are a number of poets who have lived for extended periods in Japan, who speak Japanese, are well read in classic Japanese and Chinese literature, who are usually Buddhists, either Zen or Shingon, and who have meditated long on the words of the Avatamsaka and Lankavatara Sutras. Gary Snyder, Philip Whalen and Cid Corman are outstanding. In the Far East such ideas are usually connected with reactionary politics, but these Western writers are about as radical politically as they could well be, and their criticisms of their own society are fundamental. Long before ecology became a world-wide fad, Snyder and Whalen, still in college, were talking about an ecological esthetic, a blending of American Indian and Far Eastern philosophies of cooperation with, rather than conquest of, nature. The *Tao Te Ching*, the writings of the Zen masters, the meditations of American Indian medicine men, provided them with the foundations for a life philosophy at avowed cross purposes with that of the dominant society. If the counterculture has an ideologist, it is Gary Snyder. In the last fifteen years this life philosophy has proliferated into all levels of American society accompanied with a poetry indebted to classic Japanese examples—from collections of *haiku*, both translated and American, for young children learning to read, to little poems scattered here and there through the works of most younger poets—small crystals of meditation, of the poignancy of nature, or of wit, to *haiku* contests sponsored by small-town women's clubs. American *haiku* and *tanka* show every variety of knowledge or ignorance of their Japanese exemplars or the classic Japanese sensibility, from true, original zen koans or profoundly Buddhist poems comparable to Lady Izumi's, to embarassingly sentimental nonsense.

Of the more significant young poets who have come up since 1955, a climacteric year in American poetry, at least twenty-five have written several, sometimes many, poems in Japanese style, and in longer poems the influence is more subtly pervasive. It can be safely said that classic Japanese and Chinese poetry are today as influential on American poetry as English or French of any period, and close to determinative for those born since 1940. I have tried to explain why this is so. Classic Far Eastern poetry speaks for all those elements of a complete culture, or factors of the human mind, of man at his most fullfilled, which are suppressed or distorted by Western civilization. This projection of a hunger in the West explains the weak interest in contemporary Japanese poetry, itself the expression, locally modified, of what, for better or worse, has become a world civilization. The contemporary Japanese poets best known in the West are Kitasono Katue, a translator and once somewhat of a follower of Ezra Pound, now one of the very finest concrete poets in the world, and the small group of friends of Gary Snyder who call themselves *harijans,* and who for a while lived in a commune on a remote volcanic island in the Ryukyus.

Six Japanese Novelists:

Hiroshi Noma, Osamu Dazai, Yasunari Kawabata,
Yukio Mishima, Shohei Ooka, Junichiro Tanizaki

Most of the novels, in all languages, dealing with the Second
World War have followed in the footsteps of Ford Madox
Ford and e. e. cummings rather than Barbusse, Rolland or
Hemingway. They have dealt, not with the horror and pathos
of war as catastrophe and death, but with its assault on the
personality, and owe their drama to the varying degrees of
resistance or collapse of their characters before this onslaught.
In other words, war, army life has been seen as one aspect of
le monde concentrationnaire, only an extreme development of
the human self-alienation characteristic of modern society generally. Contemporary military novels could be arranged in a
series shading imperceptibly into those dealing with prisons
and concentration camps in one direction, and totalitarianized
civilian life in the other.

Hiroshi Noma, one of Japan's leading realist writers, in
Zone of Emptiness focuses his attention almost exclusively on
this problem. Like *The Enormous Room* it has no battle
scenes. It is a story of life in an army prison and in barracks
in Japan, of the immense zone of emptiness, the gulf of alienation which grows and envelops a young Japanese soldier. Although we think, and no doubt justly, of the Japanese war
machine as a far more obliterative mechanism than the American, it is surprising that, at the end, one feels that more has
survived of Private Kitani, than, for instance, survived of
Norman Mailer's characters. Perhaps it is because Private
Kitani is a simpler person, and was already conditioned to

expect even worse than he got. The book might be said to have a specific message: no matter how pervasive the pressures and terrors of a totalitarian army, no matter how hopeless the doom of the personality, no matter how vast the zone of emptiness in which they are lost, men do survive as men, as long as they are alive—at least some do. Hiroshi Noma writes a clear, rapid, narrative style, with considerable sense of the dramatic, objective delineation of evolving character. This is not one of the greatest war novels ever written, but it is a moving story, and a curious picture of the naiveté and random discipline of what we thought of as an irresistible military machine.

Anyone who read Osamu Dazai's "Villon's Wife" in *New Directions 15* is not likely to forget it soon. Few stories give a more poignant picture of the sordid demoralization of those intellectuals of the modern world who have taken the world ill into their hearts and bowels without being able to digest it. Like most of Dazai's writing, it has an ominous, autobiographical ring. And well it might. After a life of maximum disorder, he committed suicide in 1948. *The Setting Sun* is again the story of the world ill, the collapse of values, loss of inner direction and outer valid interpersonal relations, the loss of the ability to love, which is as common in mid-twentieth-century Japan as it is in Paris or New York. This time the central figure is a woman of ruined aristocratic family of the type made familiar to Western readers in the novels of Kikuo Yamato. Her life is not just meaningless. She is immobilized in a stasis of moral decay. Nothing is possible. There is only slowly growing death, slowly mounting horror, the will-less entrapment and hysteria we first came to know in Chekhov's plays. In desperation she "abandons herself," as they say, to a depraved and wrecked writer, called Uehara here, but the same character that appeared in "Villon's Wife," Dazai himself. They spend only one pitiable, dishevelled night together, the eve of the day her brother, himself destroyed with drugs and despair, commits suicide. Out of that night comes a child, and the hope that, in this "first engagement," as she calls it, the smothering evil has been pushed back a little, and that later, with the help of the child "a second and a third engagement will be possible." "Somewhere, somehow, some kind of revolution must be taking place." In some way this act of sentimental, hysterical defiance, and its resulting creation, must be part of it. I don't know if this is strictly true, but it is a conclusion which touches our mercy, in spite of its sentimentality. With the exasperating eclecticism so typical of the intellectuals of contemporary non-Western cultures, Dazai echoes not only Céline, but Artzybashev. Today we have outgrown Artzybashev; we know he is sentimental. Perhaps Céline is too. A brief walk around Belleville or the Faubourg Saint-Antoine after the Second War would have convinced anyone that, bad as may be the world that met his eyes, *Death on the Installment Plan* and *Journey to the End of Night* are profoundly sentimental books. Perhaps what we are witnessing all over the world is simply the inability of a commercial, acquisitive culture to provide satisfactory goals, and not really a journey beyond the end of night at all—however awful may be the tortures of the sensibilities our civilization destroys.

Americanism, Catholicism, Marxism, Existentialism—any general cultural manifestation, take what you will, usually presents a "hard" and a "soft" aspect. This is true, certainly, of Japanese civilization. Against *The Tale of Genji* there is the *Forty-seven Ronin*. Against the Saikaku of *Tales of a Voluptuous Woman* there is the Saikaku of *Loves of the Samurai*, possibly the most sadistic fiction in all literature. In fact, it might be said that Japanese culture exhibits this dichotomy to an unusual degree. It is usually the hard expression

which lasts longest and is taken most seriously in the West—
"hard" and "Classic," e.g., long-lasting and exemplary, are
practically synonymous. In Japan, no. As Osamu Dazai represented hard Japanese fiction, so Yasunari Kawabata is an outstanding representative of soft. I do not think there is much
doubt as to the intrinsic merits of Dazai. His comparative
merits over against Kawabata are another matter. Both are
equally sentimental. Just because it is shocking is no sign
that emotional over-emphasis has ceased to be the definition
of sentimentality. Poe's childish horrors no longer scare us, and
we giggle instead of shiver. So too, Dazai's world is not "the
real Japan" and Kawabata's "an anachronistic fake." Both
treat of a world of dissolving and unsatisfying values, both
reflect the reality of mid-twentieth-century Japan in transition
to the unknowable future. Dazai evokes Céline; Kawabata
evokes *The Tale of Genji*. We feel that Dazai is more up-to-
date, but he isn't really, by very many years, because Kawabata's Genji is Genji seen through the eyes of Mallarmé and
his disciples. *The Izu Dancer, Snow Country,* and *Thousand
Cranes* are a sort of ultimate provincial expression of French
Symbolism brought to late, forced flower in a country which is
nothing if not overly generous with evocative and provocative
symbols. Also, it is a specific aspect of Japanese classical culture that almost exclusively interests Kawabata. Most of the
complex symbology and "hidden meanings" in Lady Murasaki's great novel are over the heads of Western readers. The
episode which everybody likes best, and can best understand,
is the chapter "Yugao," the story of the murder of a new,
beautiful and mysterious mistress of Genji's by the demon
which "took foot"—"became incarnate" from a moment of
jealous rage on the part of his royal mistress, Lady Rokujo.
Not, bear in mind, her ghost, or even the ghost of *her* hate or
jealousy—the moment of hate detached itself from time and
from its originator and became a ghostly person who strikes
down the beautiful and beloved for three generations. "Yugao"

is merely the most obvious episode in a long, subtle war of good and evil. Western readers do not need to be ashamed of their ethnocentrism. Most of the subtleties of *The Tale of Genji* are over the heads of the modern, non-specialist Japanese, too. It is precisely this episode which Kawabata, deliberately or not, "modernizes" in *Thousand Cranes*. Also, his modernization is no more and no less satisfactory than Sartre's or Cocteau's—or Ernest Haycox's—updating of Aeschylus. Like them, Kawabata settles for a lesser thing in every way—smaller, less noble, less complex, less profound—in a word (borrowed from Aristotle on tragedy), meaner.

Thousand Cranes is the story of a young, modernized Japanese, presumably a business man, unable to cope with the karma, the unsolved dilemmas and unassimilated and undisposable residues of his father's emotional relationships with two former mistresses. The older, blighted and de-sexed by a bygone moment of scorn—and marked with a hideous birthmark on her breast, like a demon beauty in a Kabuki play—destroys the other, gentle, loving, self-sacrificing mistress, the second woman's daughter who loves the son with a kind of hypnotic, all-consuming guilt (the daughter is, as it were, the medium through whom this spirit of destructive hate operates), as well as destroying possibly the girl "Thousand Cranes," whom she had tried to affiance to the protagonist, and finally the son himself. Just like in Osamu Dazai, everybody commits suicide, but here the action centers around the tea ceremony, and takes place amongst the palaces and temples of Kamakura, whereas in Dazai it centers around dirty little bar rooms and verminous one night hotels in the slums of Tokyo. It is largely a question of decor. For the important thing about *Thousand Cranes* is its difference from its classical model. In Kawabata's novel the bad woman is bad and the good woman is good and the girl is guilty and hot and the youth is weak—and Kamakura and the tea cottage and gardens and the castles and temples are souvenirs of a noble past—of classical Japan.

But Murasaki wasn't a classic. She was just a Japanese court lady writing a novel about her friends and enemies. And Lady Rokujo wasn't bad; in fact, she has a kind of glory otherwise reserved for Genji himself; she hardly figures in the novel, but she seems to be anything but ill-tempered and unforgiving. Yugao is not "good" nor is Genji "unfaithful," although the modern Japanese movie of the novel portrays him that way. All these people are just people, not mean, but rather noble as Aristotle liked them to be, caught in life with its endlessly unravelling consequences. So it would seem that Kawabata's *Thousand Cranes* raises the old question, "What makes great art great?" For it is after all, only a very touching, very engagingly written modern sentimentality. On the other hand, now, after she had been dead so many years, Lady Murasaki is a classic and will go on, providing models for other popular novelists, in that otherwise unknowable future.

If Mallarmé had ever written a novel, it might well have resembled Kawabata's *Snow Country*. It is all very *fainéant* and aimless and precious. Shimamura is a young business man. He had been an authority on Japanese drama, the Nō and Kabuki, but it came to bore him, so he took up Western ballet. He writes articles on the ballet. He is a leading authority. But he has never seen a ballet and has no desire to see one. On the way to a weekend at a mountain village, one of those Japanese resorts with a hot spring and ski slope, he sees a girl on the train. He does not look at her, but watches her face, brightly reflected over the moving, snow-bound night landscape outside the window. This is the central symbol of the book, changes are rung on its elements, night, snow, bright light, a fleeting face, and the plot such as it is revolves around them.

Shimamura has a desultory affair with a geisha, a companion of Yoko, the first girl. At long intervals he returns to the village, drawn, not by love, but by his inability to love. He never becomes intimate with Yoko and his intimacy with the geisha Komako, who loves him deeply, is empty of meaning. At last, several melancholy winters later, he decides to break off the affair and not return. On his last night Yoko is injured in a fire, from which she is rescued by Komako. Shimamura is overcome with vertigo, possibly he faints, in the night, in the dark crowd, before the blazing building, in the cold, under the Milky Way. All of the symbols converge to a climax that is melodramtic but—empty of meaning; at least Shimamura is incapable of using its meaning. In the morning he will go and not come back.

Since about 1920 it has been impossible to write a novel like this in a Western language and make it stick. If one were published it would seem as silly as those lamentable Midwestern free verse haiku once so popular with sensitive housewives. But *Snow Country* comes from a country where haiku were invented and are still written, though possibly not as well as once they were, and so it does really have the poignancy it strives for, and a terrible sense of the waste of love and of all bright, fleeting things that flicker out against the dark background of the winter world. It is sentimental even to say that—but the Japanese are possibly the only people who have made sentimentality bearable. In fact, they have made an art of it.

Yukio Mishima's *The Sound of Waves* has been compared to *Daphnis and Chloe*. It does resemble a Greek peasant or fisher's idyll—but then, as has been pointed out so often, the typical Western thriller meets all of Aristotle's tragic desiderata —as Euripides, for instance, does not. It is a question of what you want in an archetypical sort of story—the farewell of Launcelot and Guinevere can be made pretty trivial and still stick close to the plot. It is not just style—or at least it is style as the reverberation of hidden depth.

Yukio Mishima is an inordinately busy writer. Born in 1925, he has published eight novels, four Kabuki plays, a

travel book, fifty short stories, ten one-act plays, and several
volumes of essays. Well, there's just one *Daphnis and Chloe*
and not very many *Idylls* of Theocritus. I am afraid to disagree with the considered judgment of my peers. Yukio
Mishima was "the guest of the State Department and the
Partisan Review," which should really pin down the opposition at both ends, but *The Sound of Waves* reads like a piece
of routine commercial fiction to me. It does have the sound of
waves of a small Japanese fishing village, a sense of the life of
the men who fish and the women who (as in Utamaro's famous
prints) dive for abalones, and a sympathy for very young and
simple love—all very admirable qualities which go to produce
an entertaining story—on a level, I should say, slightly below
much American magazine fiction.

Mishima's *Five Modern Nō Plays* is more corn, but not of
the same kind. It is 1921 Little Theatre corn of the "Hist!
Dimitri! The saws are in the kasha!" "Ah! Feodora Feo-
dorovna, what of your tuberculosis?" variety. It carries me
back to my childhood on the stage of the Dill Pickle Club,
but it may not have that effect on other people with a different
past. I sometimes wonder if rewriting the great classic tragedies
is ever a good idea in any language. Perhaps it really is ir-
reverent. It is hard to get the modern adulteration out of your
mind the next time you see the classic, and this is certainly
a disservice. Rarely does the rewriting open up new perspec-
tives. The French do it best of all. Yukio Mishima does it
badly. He is far indeed from Cocteau or Sartre. *"They face
each other in silence. Weird music."* Un hunh. My understanding of the terrible, embodied hate that has taken foot and
walked away from Genji's mistress and is destroying his wife
and will destroy everything he loves for generations is not in
the least deepened and enriched by this sort of thing.

Shohei Ooka's *Fires on the Plain* is a shocker about a soldier
lost on Leyte after the Japanese collapse. He shoots a defense-

less woman. He becomes deranged with starvation. His companions trick him into cannibalism. He is captured and sent back to Japan where he ends his days in an insane asylum. Shohei Ooka (pronounced *oh, oh,* not as in "snooks") is a competent writer. He knows how to get the effects he wants, convincingly and with economy. He is never cheap the way Yukio Mishima is always cheap. Still, the book, for me at least, seems to miss its final intention completely. There is a social meaning in the portrayal of a man at the ultimate extremity of inhumanity. Is there a tragic meaning? Like Aristotle long ago, I think not. Furthermore, as many have pointed out before me, horror stories about war defeat their purpose if that purpose is to make war undesirable. The great evil of modern life is *tedium vitae, accidie,* the awful boredom that comes with self-alienation and lack of life aim. It is precisely the horror of war that makes it attractive—at least to the imagination of the passive reader. Ford Madox Ford's Teitjens series, e. e. cummings' *The Enormous Room* are the great books they are precisely because they show that underneath the blood, sweat and tears, war is simply the humdrum evil of precisely the same old civilian peacetime world enormously hypertrophied. The real cannibals are in swivel chairs, boudoirs and cocktail bars, just like always. So the war horror novel is dishonest almost in strict proportion to its horror. *Fires on the Plain* is one of thousands, written all over the world, a slightly better example of a bad type.

Junichero Tanizaki's *The Makioka Sisters* is one of the most ambitious of Japanese twentieth-century novels. Whether it is better than Kawabata's *Snow Country* is a matter of taste. It is not an exercise of the sensibility, but a family epic of a type going back to Chinese novels like the *Chin P'ing Mei* (*Golden Lotus*) or *Hsi Men and His Six Wives*. Originally I suppose there was a moral to this type of tale—"When the future is in the hands of women, the house will fall." The plot is still the same, but the Makioka sisters are viewed with considerably more sympathy. The blurb speaks of "a great family," "upper class life." But that is just the point—these are daughters, not of the upper class, but of the ambitious and pretentious higher ranks of the employee class.

Father Makioka was on his way up; the daughters were raised to be fine ladies, but he is dead and the whole novel is concerned with the struggle to hold the pathetic position already gained, of course by distinguished marriages. But the social pressure is always downwards. The girls have nothing to back them up as brides, and have to make do with what they can get. In each case the defeat is sordid, disastrous, or just dull. None moves on to become the gracious wife of a mercantile aristocrat.

The Makioka Sisters is certainly an eminently Far Eastern story, but it could also be by Balzac or Thackeray. It resembles Thomas Mann's *Buddenbrooks*. In addition, although Tanizaki may not be a better writer than Balzac, he has things the French writer lacks—the close narrative plotting, almost as dense as Dick Tracy or a soap opera, derived from the great Chinese novels, and of course the poignant imagism of a writer saturated in Japanese poetry. Perhaps the best characterization would be to call *The Makioka Sisters* the seamy side of Jane Austen. The story opens with the Makioka family administering vitamin B injections to each other. The last sentence of the novel drives this characterization home with a vengeance. Yukiko is the central figure, the problem sister of four problem sisters. "Yukiko's diarrhea persisted through the twenty-sixth, and was a problem on the train to Tokyo!"

Japanese Poetry Now

In the past twenty-five years there have been a number of collections of translations of contemporary Japanese poetry published in the United States. There are so many poets in Japan and the scene changes so rapidly that Thomas Fitzsimmons' collection is by far the most contemporary. He has also managed to make his choices exceptionally convincing as poetry in the American language. Japanese poetry in classic forms has been widely translated into all the European languages and has in many instances exerted a strong influence on Western poets. Only a few modern poets who write in the classic forms have ever become at all widely known amongst readers of poetry in the West. Poetry in modern forms has met with even less appreciation.

Today we live in what, in spite of ideological differences and historical evolution, is one world-wide modern culture to which each nation or culture area gives its own special character. Modern Japanese poetry is not "Westernized" any more than is the Japanese novel or cinema. It is, in a general sense, an expression of the post-modern sensibility of human beings who find themselves in a mass civilization, dominated by an ever accelerating technological revolution, yet it is at the same time specifically Japanese, as Japanese as the novels of Tanizaki or the films of Kurosawa. On the other hand it is far removed from the poetry of the great classic anthologies, of the tenth to the seventeenth centuries, the *haiku* of the succeeding period, or the poetry of the *Nō* drama.

Superficially it would seem easier to find echoes of the older Japanese poetry in Western poets than in Japanese poets writing in modern forms—as do all the poets in this collection.

However the ancient tradition is still very much alive and far
more *haiku* in seventeen syllables and *tanka* in thirty-one
syllables are written than poems in modern forms. There are
even contemporary *Nō* plays. By and large verse in the ancient
style is a mass sport rather than an art. Thousands of *haiku*
are written every month, and every important event calls forth
additional thousands. Hardly ever is one of these little verses
anything more than an exercise in sentimentality. Still, there
are poets who do write important poetry in the old forms, more
often *tanka* than *haiku*. Until recently such poetry was usually
more profound than that in the new forms, which are less than
a hundred years old and only now have become vehicles for
complete poetic expression.

For over a thousand years Japanese poetry changed—at
least to Western eyes—very little indeed. The earliest collection of history and myth, the *Kojiki*, contains extensive passages in verse, both narrative and lyric. With extremely few
exceptions these are all in patterns of five and seven syllable
lines, and there is a tendency for the lyrics to move toward
the strictly limited forms of the later poetry.

The first great Imperial anthology, the *Manyoshu*, was
gathered in the eighth century, probably a generation after
the *Kojiki*. It contains a number of "long poems"—*naga uta,*
elegies, narratives, folktales, but none of them are long by
Western standards, seldom more than a few hundred words.
Commonly they end in little codas which are usually thirty-one
syllable *tanka,* which sum up the long poem and exist as poems
in their own right. There are a few irregular poems, a few
sedoka, thirty-eight syllables, arranged 5–7–7, 5–7–7, a few
dodoitsu in twenty-six syllables, which would become the
common folksong form, but the vast majority of the over
four thousand poems in the *Manyoshu* are tanka in thirty-one
syllables. After the Manyoshu the *naga uta* died out, or at
least ceased to be considered literature, or to be included in
the successive imperial anthologies, but survived in a some-

what different form, still five or seven syllables, in the folk songs of itinerant story tellers and entertainers.

The poets of succeeding ages have returned again and again to the *Manyoshu* as the embodiment of the purest Japanese sensibility, comparatively uninfluenced by Chinese culture or by Buddhism, both of which in fact were penetrating the country by the time the collection was made. However it is true that the poems in the *Manyoshu* are characterized by a fundamental classicism, simple, sensuous, passionate—"wholeness, harmony and radiance"—and the collection has played the role of a basic exemplar during all but the most effete periods of Japanese poetry, something like the Chinese collections, the *Shih Ching*—the Book of Songs—folksongs, purportedly collected by Confucius, and *Three Hundred Poems of the T'ang Dynasty,* have played in China. Movements of poetic rejuvenation and purification have returned to the *Manyoshu* for support. Its influence is by no means dead. Just as the poetry of Chairman Mao echoes the *Three Hundred Poems of T'ang,* so contemporary poets like Hitoshi Anzai, along with influences from French and English, owe much to the direct language of presentational immediacy of the *Manyoshu,* although this is not apparent in translation.

The long period when the imperial capital was at Kyoto and the emperors had not become purely ceremonial figures saw the publication of a succession of imperial anthologies beginning with the *Kokinshu.* This is the period Westerners know in its flowering time through Arthur Waley's translation of *The Tale of Genji* by Lady Murasaki—widely considered the greatest novel ever written. It contains almost eight hundred poems, some of very great beauty. *The Tale of Ise,* which purports to be a factual account of the love life of the great poet Narihira, is actually fiction written around a collection of his poems. The great poetic diaries of the time, mostly by women, have a similar structure. The modern novels of Kawabata and others have an analogous pattern, but the poems have disappeared, and have been absorbed into the narrative. The Heian (Kyoto) period was one of exquisite sensibility, luxury wedded to simplicity, and an all-pervasive sense of the Buddhist pathos of life and an ever increasing refinement of poetry. Qualities like these are obviously susceptible of decadence, and so it happened. Under the Ashikaga and Tokagawa Shogunates, when the Emperor became a purely cult figure, and the actual capital moved to Kamakura, there was a revival, but when the court moved to Edo (Tokyo) and the commercial middle class came to dominate Japanese society, the thirty-one syllable *tanka* sank into formalism and triviality, and was replaced by the seventeen syllable *haiku*.

The *haiku* evolved out of the highly artificial *renga*, the linked verses popular in seventeenth-century poetry parties where each person contributed half a *tanka* and the verses went on, each stanza by stanza, linking one into another. Since these verses were uttered on the spot, they had to follow strict rules of subject and style. The result was seldom profound. Although there are a few deeply moving *renga*, they usually represent poetry reduced to a fashionable amusement, and a trivialization of poetic inspiration. A few Japanese critics consider these faults to be characteristic of the entire enormous mass of *haiku*, numbering many millions, which have been written since, and even reject the great practitioners of the form, Bashō, Buson, Issa, as trivial and sentimental. This judgment is comparable to that Japanese taste which rejects the *ukioye* wood block school—Hokusai, Hiroshige, Kiyonaga, Utamaro—as sentimental and decorative, and prefers the hieratic painting of the Heian period and the great Ashikaga ink painters. There is something to be said for this point of view. The fact remains that for over two hundred years most Japanese poetic inspiration found expression in *haiku*. When Westerners think of Japanese poetry they almost always mean *haiku* and imitations of the form are today popular in all the major Western languages.

The opening of Japan by Perry's gunboats in 1854 coincided with the decadence of the simple mercantile culture of the Edo period, the revival of early classic Japanese literature, and a movement to overthrow the Shogunate and reinstate the Emperor as the actual ruler of Japan, which culminated in the Meiji restoration, the assumption of power by the Emperor in Tokyo and the liquidation of the Shogunate. The Meiji revolution was prevented from being an archaizing mummification of Japanese culture, like similar movements in ancient Egypt, by the fact that it coincided with the opening of the country and the, at first, overwhelming impact of Western industrial civilization. The effects on poetry were drastic, although they took some time to get under way.

A few Japanese who were in contact with the Dutch trading post at Nagasaki were aware of the vast difference between Western and Japanese poetry. The Japanese for centuries had been writing fairly long poems in Chinese, but the esthetics of this poetry differed from that of the West even more than the form. In 1882 there was published *A Collection of New Style Poems,* mostly verse translations of European poems, for instance, Gray's "Elegy," but also containing poems by Japanese in imitation of European models. These were long by Japanese standards and rhetorical rather than imagistic. The collection was accompanied by critical statements which were really manifestoes, attacks on the "little vibrations of thirty-one syllables."

For the next twenty years there was a craze for European romanticism, and little magazines were filled with imitations of Byron and Shelley. Most of this stuff was of scant value and is mercifully forgotten. The movement produced one outstanding poet, Tōsōn Shimazaki, who is still read today, and who is considered the founder of modern Japanese poetry. Much of Tōsōn's work was in free verse. It was becoming apparent that the imitation of the prosody and rhyme of European verse usually produced nothing but jingles in the

Japanese language. At the beginning Tōsōn does not seem to have known very much about contemporary French poetry, but even his earliest work sounds more like Verlaine than it does like Shelley. This was a fortunate coincidence because from 1900 on, especially after the publication by Bin Ueda of translations from French Parnassian and Symbolist poetry, this influence became predominant. Echoes of Baudelaire, Verlaine, Paul Fort, Émile Verhaeren, and, after the First World War, Arthur Rimbaud, Alfred Jarry, and Tristan Corbière, can still be found in Japanese poetry of the mid-twentieth century. French poetry even influenced the poets who wrote in the classic forms but in modern language and of modern life. This is certainly true of the two greatest *tanka* poets of the beginning of the century—Takuboku Ishikawa and Akiko Yosano—and of the *haiku* poet Shiki Masaoka.

As in Europe, where the Symbolists and Decadents produced an almost immediate reaction, there soon grew up a movement of what nowadays is called Socialist Realism, of poetry also not just in ordinary written Japanese, but in the colloquial language. This transition was made easy by the example of Verhaeren, who in the taste of the time was the leading post-Symbolist and certainly a poet with a social conscience. The Russo-Japanese War was opposed by many on essentially pacifist grounds, including both Akiko Yosano and Takuboku Ishikawa, and much more by younger people who were discovering Walt Whitman, Edward Carpenter, Richard Dehmel and the revolutionary poetry of Europe. Reaction to the First World War and the Russian Revolution raised poetry of this kind to a dominant position, especially after Mayakovsky and the French modernists were translated into Japanese. It should be borne in mind that most young people who wanted to become writers, especially poets, learned French in high school and if they could, took a trip to Paris, just as would-be engineers and businessmen studied German or English. Unlike American intellectuals, Japanese are not monolingual, and

French poetry throughout its great days in the early twentieth century has been more accessible to Japanese poets than to American or English poets.

All the movements and cults of French verse found imitators in Japan almost as soon as they were launched. During the period between the wars, largely under the leadership of Sakutarō Hagiwara, whose esthetic theories sound like Mallarmé or Paul Valéry with their emphasis on "abstract" musical qualities, but whose practice was more like certain American free verse poets, and Junzaburō Nishiwaki, an objectivist and surrealist, Daigaku Horiguchi, Hakushū Kitahara, Yaso Saijō, Haruo Satō, one very definite thing was accomplished with Japanese poetry. In spite of the fact that these people led different movements, had different reading publics, and attacked each other critically, they established a free verse prosody for Japanese which does not simply echo Walt Whitman, William Carlos Williams or Paul Éluard but is peculiar to the language and would seem to be, if one grants the exhaustion of the five and seven syllable patterns of the old *naga uta,* the most natural way to write moderately long poems in Japanese.

As the military despotism grew within Japan and the country became ever more deeply involved in the Chinese war and then in the Second World War, Japanese poets fell silent, or (very few of the better ones) wrote patriotic verse glorifying the great military adventure. Unlike France with its many poets in the underground and its publications like *Poésie* or *Editions de minuit,* effective resistance was impossible in Japan. The choice was either silence or prison, and most likely, death. Most of the Communist writers were exterminated. Takiji Kobayashi, the world famous author of the best proletarian novel, *The Cannery Boat,* was tortured for days in prison until he died.

A little like Spain as Franco's dictatorship relaxed its totalitarian thought control, Japanese poetry started off after the war where it had stopped in the late Thirties. Also of course

the catastrophic defeat, the wholesale destruction of the country, the two atom bombs, and the systematic humiliations of
the Occupation produced a state of shock in Japanese poets
—along with everybody else. If any one emotion is characteristic of the postwar years it is a kind of desperate sarcasm.
This is true of all except the purest "modernists," but even
Katue Kitasono, the one Japanese poet well known to other
modernist poets in the West, and the translator of many of
them, changed the name of his prewar magazine *VOU* to
Cendres during the years of ruin, but significantly changed it
back once Japan had recovered. (*VOU* is not a Japanese word.
Kitasono says it means "vow.")

The "cubist" poetry of Pierre Reverdy, Dadaism, Surrealism,
all were absorbed and transmuted into Japanese forms. There
are still Japanese surrealists writing and, as in the West, a
number of young "Neo-Dadaist" poets. Katue Kitasono has, in
his latter years, become one of the most impressive concrete
poets, and his constructions, like "WHITE" are in all the standard Western anthologies of the movement.

The New Left in all its manifold complexity of sects and
grouplets was at least as active in Japan as in the United States,
France, or West Germany. The conflicts and demonstrations of
the Sixties resulted in a great outpouring of revolutionary verse.
Much of this was topical and overtly propagandistic. Moving at
the time, it served its purpose and is forgotten. Where it probed
more deeply, to levels of the revolution of the human sensibility, it survives as part of the general movement of contemporary Japanese poetry.

Postwar Japanese poetry was very specifically that of a
postwar generation. An extraordinary number of important
young poets were born between 1919 and 1925, the generation
that actually fought in the war. Commonly their work at first
most resembled that of the early W. H. Auden, the poet of an
imaginary ruined England slipping into a new Dark Age—
except that their ruined Japan was by no means imaginary.

Their pylons really were toppled and their trains didn't run. "Get there if you can and see the land you once were proud to own"—ruled by a foreign, military bureaucracy whom cultivated Japanese consider representatives of barbarism, and over it all the umbrellas of Nagasaki and Hiroshima. This was a case in which it was more blessed to receive than give. Japan and her poets and other "symbolic critics of value" recovered far more quickly than the United States from the terrible moral wound of the atom bomb. In fact, America never recovered at all. But Japanese poets only recovered by accepting total alienation as the primary assumption for any and all creative expression. A generation after the war, with Japan the third richest country in the world, this is still true.

There is very little important poetry anywhere in the world in the latter years of the twentieth century which accepts the values of the dominant society. In Japan there is none. There are no Yves Bonnefoys, nothing like England's "The Movement," nothing like the United States' government-supported Establishment. There is not even a Left Establishment—no Günter Grasses, no Robert Lowells touring with political candidates. Contemporary Japanese poetry may be technically influenced by the best of such people, but it takes off taking for granted Allen Ginsberg or Paul Celan.

This does not mean that all important poetry written by poets born since 1925 is technically "modernistic" or ideologically revolutionary. Some of it is archaistic, rejecting contemporary values for those of the Japanese past. There are still significant poets writing *tanka,* but more important, there are many whose work shows deep-seated influences of the classic past, particularly of the most classic—the "pure" poetry of the *Manyoshu*—although these influences may be perceptible only to very cultivated Japanese or a few Western Japanologists. For the subject matter of these poets is certainly not bush warblers (*uguisu*) singing amidst the drifting cherry blossom petals, or cuckoos crying under the setting moon. Most recent poetry is overtly, obviously, related to a world-wide counter culture whose spokesmen are poets like Ginsberg, Leonard Cohen, Bob Dylan.

Just as Osamu Dazai was the novelist of alienation who really meant business, more even than Céline, Miller or Kerouac, so Kazuko Shiraishi is certainly the outstanding poetic voice of her generation of disengagement in Japan. And there is certainly no woman poet of this kind anywhere near as good elsewhere in the world. Joyce Mansour in France is far inferior and Lenore Kandel in the United States equals her only in one or two poems. Like Osamu Dazai, her work has a fierceness and an exaltation that makes most of her Western colleagues in disaffiliation seem positively mellow. In the final analysis of course, what makes her preeminent is sheer poetic ability. If you hear her read aloud, with or without jazz accompaniment, you know that, even if you don't speak a word of Japanese, Shiraishi is the last and the youngest and one of the best of the generation of the Beats in America, the Angry Young Men in England, Vosnevschensky in the USSR.

Just as the Beats were succeeded in the United States by the Flower Children, so in Japan, the most significant movement amongst the younger generation has moved beyond alienation to a mystical life acceptance, a more fundamentally subversive, more revolutionary attitude by far. The group who call themselves *harijans,* centered around the magazine *Psyche* and communes in Tokyo, Kyoto and a small island in the Ryukyus (the latter about to be totally destroyed and "developed" by a resort hotel chain), owe much to the inspiration and guidance of the American poet Gary Snyder. Their rejection of modern industrial competitive society goes down to the very sources of what is now a world civilization. Mystics, revolutionaries, communalists, committed to an ecological esthetic and life practice, they have managed to unite the most ancient and enduring traditions of the Far East with the movement of creative withdrawal of the West. They are also of course a natural and to-be-expected reaction to contemporary Japan, caught in an explosive mining-boom-town economy and a destruction of the environment unparalleled even in America or the USSR.

Japanese poetry in modern forms has been criticized as lacking in profundity. It is true that *tanka* poets like Akiko Yosano and Takuboku Ishikawa at the beginning of the century were capable of richness and depth, and a profundity of implication beyond anything of Tōsōn Shimizaki or even Daigaku Horiguchi with his echoes of Baudelaire. Akiko's famous poem,

Press my breasts,	*Chibusa asae*
Part the veil of mystery,	*Shimpi no tobari*
A flower blooms there,	*Soto kerinu*
Crimson and fragrant	*Kokonaru hana no*
	Kuremai no koki

echoes the most cryptic verse of the *Tao Te Ching*:

> The valley's soul is deathless.
> It is called the Dark Woman.
> The Dark Woman is the gate
> To the root of heaven and earth.
> If you draw her out like floss
> She is inexhaustible.
> She is only to be possessed without effort

and all the erotic mysticism of neo-Taoism, Shinto, and Shingon (tantric) Buddhism that has come after it. After her day the doors seemed to close on the classic Japanese tradition. Shiki Masaoka could connect with the Zen Buddhism of the *haiku* poet Bashō and the great Ashikaga ink painters, but with the beginning of the "China Incident," Zen, so popular in the West, became identified in the minds of young Japanese with the high command of the Imperial Navy and the most dedicated officers of the Thought Control Police, and after the war it remained identified with the eccentric Chicago millionairess Ruth Sasaki, and the family of Kyoto's leading investment bankers, and unfortunately for him at first, Gary Snyder, all of them Zen monks.

Snyder could find in Zen a subversion of all the values of the dominant society, but unlike Akiko, Shiraishi could not connect with the Shingon erotic mysticism of that most profound of all the world's novels, the *Tale of Genji*. It was a closed book to her, at least for purposes of creative subversion, as the myths of Washington chopping down the cherry tree and Abe Lincoln splitting rails were to Snyder.

Classic Japanese culture has had a profound influence on the counter culture of the West. It had little on similar people in Japan until the appearance of the *harijan* poets and others amongst the youngest poets. More than anything else, this is what is most important about the youngest people now writing. In the Occupation hundreds of the more literate GI's brought home a system of values unassimilable by a commercial predatory system. The West reworked and reinterpreted the East and returned it to Japan, which had certainly become a part of world civilization, commercial, competitive, predatory, but where at last the oldest traditions of Japanese culture are coming to play a new role.

Religion

Lamennais

For a modern liberal Catholic, particularly for an American, cleric or lay, the alignment of forces in the Church in Europe in the first years of Restoration after the fall of Napoleon is almost incomprehensible. This is specially true since the Johannine revolution, as theological, ecclesiastical, and political radicalism have finally converged. Yet it is essential to understand the religious situation in France—where the action was—as Restoration, counterrevolution, and the Holy Alliance shut down over Europe—because it was then that the major tendencies for reform came into being. Otherwise what is happening today would seem quite falsely to be a total overturn, the work of forces born since Vatican II.

The problem is one of sorting—at their birth the forces of change in the Church were not only contradictory then, and amongst themselves, but some of them have since completely changed their meaning. Plus has changed to minus, radicalism to reaction, and vice versa. After all, well-organized groups within the Church holding beliefs which were bundles of contradictions still existed commonly only a short time ago. The most politically radical American Catholic group were not only Maximalists, believers in rigid and naive interpretations of the Tridentine creed and the decisions of Vatican I, but given to the veneration of dubious relics and questionable miracles, and amongst their more far out members, something very like grossly superstitious practices—all this coupled with a social vision of an anarchist utopia where all men were brothers under a theocracy of the confessional, under a Pope infallible in faith, morals and everything else, *ex cathedra* or not. In contrast the average theologian interpreting St. Thomas to mean the opposite of what he said, or the Biblical scholar who accepted the Higher Criticism of his liberal Protestant brethren, were very likely to be political conservatives and with no pressing sense of social responsibility—for the simple reason that, triply cloistered within the ghetto of Catholic life, within the cloister of the Catholic academy, and within the sanctuary of the clerical and usually the religious life, they were unaware of anything that went on in society beyond the pale.

In France, with the Bourbon Restoration the Church was brought face to face with all the problems that had been kept more or less smothered since the beginning of the Counter-Reformation. During the height of the Revolution she had been compromised or demoralized or driven underground. Large numbers of clergy and religious had been executed or had left the Church. Outside of a few religious orders which taught a thoroughly mechanized Thomism, the Church had no philosophy. A well-educated, devout layman in America today is far more familiar with the *Summa Theologica* than was the average French archbishop in 1820. A popular philosophy was an amorphous Cartesianism, lightly sautéed in holy water.

The Vatican had spent the years of the Napoleonic Empire in Babylonian Captivity. In the eyes of the restorers of Europe, Castlereagh and Metternich and Alexander II, the Papacy was compromised. It may have well been Metternich who first said, "How many divisions has the Pope?" After all, it was the Czar, whom no one would accuse of being a Papist, who invented the notion of the Holy Alliance, and who supported the territorial claims of Rome against Metternich's ambitions for Austrian control of all of North Italy.

All during the eighteenth century the ancient nobility and beauty of ritual and liturgy had been subject to the attrition of vulgarization, reactionary modernization and secularization. The non-juring clergy who had refused allegiance to either Revolution or Napoleon were back in power and were intransigently legitimist. They had forgotten nothing and learned nothing. Christianity to them meant obedience to the house of Bourbon. Those who had collaborated were on the defensive, not just for their positions in the hierarchy, but for their right to the sacraments. On both sides, legitimism to the contrary notwithstanding, a tidal wave of wholesale bourgeoisification was sweeping the Church. Except for a few eccentrics, even the strictest religious orders were out to meet the *nouveaux riches* of the *nouveau siècle* more than halfway. Very simply, the Church was being vulgarized in every aspect. It was in these years that stopwatch masses and plaster statues with glass eyes, the computerized confessional and the anti-mind pedagogy began.

More important than all this tawdriness in exterior things was an ever-growing spiritual vulgarity. Mysticism was the dirtiest word in the pastoral vocabulary and over-indulgence in prayer far worse than the sin of impure touch. As for contemplation, the average priest, if asked to define it, would say it was something actresses did with mirrors. In society generally, complete skepticism was almost universal. The ruling class of the Restoration were punctilious in their attendance at Mass as a political demonstration. Voltairean skepticism had given way to pious fear, not of God, but of the people. Superficially regarded, the Church seemed to be only a flimsy mask of piety for the restored *ancien régime,* which was in fact neither old nor capable of ruling without the support of Russian bayonets. The French Church looked as though it would not survive the only too obviously doomed dynasty of the Bourbons. Instead it experienced the most vital revival since the Council of Trent.

The first influential spokesman for this revival was Chateaubriand, founder of Catholic estheticism, out of which has come everything from the pre-Raphaelites to the churchiness of people like Oscar Wilde and Rémy de Gourmont, but also all those movements of de-vulgarization, usually the revival of a purged medievalism, the rebirth of pure Gregorian chant, the reform of vestments, and the appreciation of medieval Latin poetry, the great dignity and beauty of the liturgy amongst certain religious orders and Anglo-Catholics.

Joseph de Maistre was the founder of irreconcilable, intransigent Maximalism, but in support of secular autocracy. The Holy Father was not just holy, but *Trisagios,* and the throne was only doubly holy.

Out of Lamennais came almost everything else. In addition, in one way or another, and at one time or another, he was also a spokesman for, or an influence on, all the other movements and forces of that *aggiornamento.* This was not due to opportunism or intellectual instability, quite the opposite. Behind the contradictory and antagonistic positions assumed by Lamennais in the course of his life, stood the massive consistency of the man himself. Lamennais as a person changed hardly at all. He remained a very specific kind of spiritual personality. He has been called a prophet in the literal sense and that he was, not just one of the major or minor prophets accepted into the canon of Scripture but brother to all the anonymous *nabis* who appear now and again in the Biblical narrative, holy men out of the hills and deserts whose function is to correct the relations of high priest, king, and chosen people to that all-enveloping transcendence and ever-elevating immanence which was the meaning of the term "chosen" in "Chosen People." Since from the very beginning his role as prophet was frustrated, he repeated, as ontogeny repeats philogeny, the spiritual history of Israel. He moved from prophecy to apocalypse.

If apocalyptic can be defined as disappointed prophecy, there is a spiritual quality which unites the two and that is an ecstatic mysticism which is at the same time the most intense ethical activism. This is a kind of prayer and a life so lived is a life of prayer, just as much as that of any Trappist or Carthusian. Here is the real and abiding heritage of Lamennais. With a few exceptions indeed his has been the personality or spiritual sensibility shared by all those who have come after him to take up the struggle to recall the Church to the apostolic life. Not in the Catholic Church only—the Quaker, George Fox, or the Methodist, John Wesley, or the Socialist Anglo-Catholics in their slum parishes who went to jail for putting candles on the altar, and Albert Schweitzer, who probably did more than any other one man to popularize the apocalyptic ethic—all are brethren of Lamennais. Today, it is apparent to all but those who have eyes and see not and ears and hear not, neither walk they with their feet, that apocalypse at last has come and that even with fools' luck if man goes on another million years, we are at this moment living morally in the Last Days. It is Lamennais' personality, not the details of his changing theology and philosophy, that embodies the archetype of these men of renewal. His doctrines changed, his life did not, and so it is his life and the literary, one might say, poetic, expression of that life consistency which is important. Nobody is quite sure how many people wrote the book called *Isaiah*. It shifts from prophecy to apocalyptic back and forth with the changing relations of Israel and the Persian Empire, but it is one poem, one kind of prayer. As Isaiah to the Persian Empire, so was Lamennais to the world of France of the first half of the nineteenth century.

Felicité Robert de la Mennais was born in 1782 into a family of wholesale merchants and ship owners at Saint Mâlo in Brittany. His father had been ennobled by Louis XVI, but he managed to survive, and even for a while grow rich, by a careful adjustment of his activities and opinions to the Revolution and to Napoleon. In his latter years the business declined, but until he was himself middle-aged, Lamennais never had any economic problems. His uncle, M. des Saudrais, was a man of considerable learning with a large library. He assumed the responsibility for the boy's education after the death of his mother when he was five, and seems to have solved the problem by turning him loose in the library, letting him read whatever he liked and sometimes discussing it with him. Later Lamennais helped his uncle in his own literary career.

1787 to 1797 were the years of ferment and passionate discussion, of idealistic reformation, of Terror—which the family narrowly escaped, and finally of get-rich-quick vulgarity and compromise. The young Lamennais spent them reading, teaching himself languages. Like many home-taught or autodidacts he was immensely erudite and thoughtful. He seems to have formed early—perhaps that's the wrong term—perhaps he was physiologically so constituted—as to be given to an habitual state of passionate meditation. Slowly through the years of adolescence, both he and his brother Jean turned back toward the Church. It was a strange church they turned to as they neared their majority—compromised, persecuted, manipulated and very nearly emptied of content, if the true content of the Church is life modeled on the historic Jesus. Both brothers returned to the Church, not as submissive converts, much less as frightened bourgeois conformists, but as passionate reformers. It was pretty close to impossible for a religious man to return to the Church for any other reason in those days.

Their first two books were joint productions, *Réflexions sur l'état de l'église en France pendant le xviiie siècle, et sur la situation actuelle* and *Tradition de l'église sur l'institution des évêques* (*Reflections on the Situation of the Church in France During the Eighteenth Century and on the Contemporary Situation,* and *Church Tradition on the Istitution of Bishops*). Napoleon's police suppressed *Réflexions*. That action is a good measure of the subjection of the Church. It was not so much the position of the brothers on the question of the relations of Church and State, empire and papacy, Pope and Church that Napoleon considered dangerous, it was the intensely religious revivalism that pervaded every page. All that *Réflexions* really advocates is what today we would call Home Missions, ordinary discipline of a large, authoritarian, corporative body, decency and order in worship, adequate training of the clergy, education and conscientious pastoral care of the laity, responsibility on the part of the episcopacy and a commitment to a

Christian life for all professing Christians. Such notions as these Napoleon had the good sense to understand were totally subversive of the values of his empire. Bonapartism may be an arguable political ideology, but it is not one of the Theological Virtues.

Between *Réflexions* and *Tradition de l'église,* Felicité Lamennais translated from Latin *The Spiritual Guide of Louis de Blois.* It was the first indication of his extraordinary genius for the exquisite transported rhetoric—in the best sense of the word—which was to assure him a place as one of the greatest writers of the Romantic era and the first of many other works of devotion and meditation that are seldom included even in bibliographies, much less in the various editions of his collected works, and are today amongst the rarest books of the period. The famous ones are *Les paroles d'un croyant, De l'esclavage moderne, Le livre du peuple, Une voix de prison, Du passé et de l'avenir du peuple,* the pieces which make up the Classiques Garnier volume and are known to all educated French people. They are really works of devotion, prophetic and apocalyptic ecstasy, which only seems to become ever more and more *laique* as Lamennais moves away from the established Church. The evolution of his ideas can be described as facts in the intellectual history of himself, and of the early nineteenth century of which he was an incarnation, but the real Lamennais is to be found only by reading his devotional works—prose poems calling mankind to total moral revolution, eschatological prayers.

Before we can understand the development of Lamennais' ideas, from Napoleon's Concordat with the Pope in 1801 in his first books, to his *Des progrès de la révolution et de la guerre contre l'église* in 1829 and the second revolution and the bourgeois monarchy in 1830, it is necessary to understand the special situation of popular Catholic apologetics in which he began his career.

Immediately after the Concordat, Chateaubriand, probably

the most fashionable writer of the period and a master of sentimental rhetoric, published *Le génie du christianisme*. Catholicism suddenly became fashionable with the excessively sentimental *nouveaux riches* of the new empire. Greek and Roman costumes and furniture might still be chic amongst Bonapartists but the old neo-classicism of the French Revolution was being corrupted by the sentimental medievalism of the young Romantic movement.

Thousands—no, millions—of pages have been wasted on definitions of Romanticism. Whatever else it was, it was literature for women—idle, luxurious and usually young. The audience for literature had shifted its balance—the husbands were too busy making money to read Chateaubriand or Benjamin Constant. Chateaubriand sold the Church to this new class on miracle, mystery, authority and millinery, those virtues Ivan Karamazov would consider its principal vices. Chateaubriand did not make Catholicism convincing; he made it fascinating, something like sin. The tradition he established has lasted until our own day, although its last notable exponents were the English Decadents and Joris Carl Huysmans, who returned to the Church because he found High Mass more thrilling than Black Mass. It is not just Chateaubriand's prose, Béchamel sauce full of false rubies, that is contemptible, it is the argument that one should re-enter the Vatican because it resembles "The Fall of the House of Usher." Napoleon's new aristocracy did not find Chateaubriand contemptible. They thought him simply divine.

Joseph de Maistre was a horse of another color. He was the archetype of the steely, razor sharp, relentless Maximalist. There was nothing new about Ultramontanism, nothing new about a rigidly uncompromising interpretation of the most disputed doctrines and passages of Scripture. What was new about the new Ultramontanism was its quality and meaning, its justification and purpose. De Maistre's *Du Pape* had very little indeed to do with Christianity and nothing to do with Jesus of

Nazareth. He believes in authority, not because he believes, as did St. Thomas, that the order of the universe and the order of the mind are reflected one in another and are, because of the nature of reason, hierarchic in structure, but because he does not. He believes in the infallibility of the Pope because he believes in the fallibility of everything else. He believes in Papal infallibility because he believes in absolute authority. He believes in absolute authority because he believes in absolute power. He believes in absolute power because without it there rages a chaos of disorder and delusion called the Revolution, or, more simply, the people, who at any moment, if control were to weaken and become less than absolute, would rise up like a storm of lava and melt away all the newly minted gold in the pockets of the new self-styled aristocracy. This is a kind of reverse Jacobinism. As Marx did Hegel, so de Maistre stood Robespierre on his head. This was not literature for idle young brides living *la vie luxeuse,* but for their husbands. It shows in the prose. De Maistre writes like the snapping of a chain of steel traps. When reading Chateaubriand one is often tempted to giggle. Nobody ever giggled over *Du Pape* except perhaps the Holy Father himself, very nervously, in his Babylonian captivity to the Emperor of the French.

In practical politics de Maistre, who spent most of his life in the diplomatic service of the House of Savoy, was a moderate legitimist, but his moderation was not due to any disbelief in the divine right of kings. He simply believed that the secular power of any throne was infinitely inferior—of a different order of being—to the spiritual and temporal power of the Vicar of Christ. Also since he was aware that no state could exercise unlimited power, unchallenged, he trusted no state, however totalitarian. It was this profound suspicion of the effectiveness of secular power sowed by *Du Pape* which germinated the radical and eventually even revolutionary Ultramontanism of succeeding generations. It was de Maistre who began a process which would end in the anarchist communalism ruled solely by the

hierarchy of spiritual authority that is still in our day even a
quasi-respectable Catholic theory of the state.

Any variety of Ultramontanism was subversive of Gallicanism, the Church-State relationship which was peculiar to
France and was the heritage of the Constantinian Church, of
the days when the Christian Church moved into the deserted
legal structure of Roman paganism. The "Gallican privileges"
place the French church under the control of the state almost
to the degree of the Russian. Like the Russian, the French
state-sponsored and paid hierarchy and educational structure
were enthusiastic supporters of the authority that supported
them. The Revolution and Napoleon had impoverished the
Papacy and abolished the Papal States. The Vatican was certainly not in the position to pay anybody's wages in Paris. Once
the restored Bourbon monarchy, the Russian Czar and the
Austrian Emperor had guaranteed again the integrity of the
Papal States, the Vatican was not in a position to challenge the
Gallicanism of the French throne and episcopacy. Furthermore
it was uneasy with any extreme Ultramontanism. If the authority of the Papacy was as absolute as that of the Deity Incarnate,
the temporal authority over an impoverished and rebellious
central Italy was not really very important.

Behind all these controversies about the relation of Church,
State and individual lay a metaphysical crisis. Where was the
principle of order in the universe and in man to find its foundations? De Maistre's most trenchant logic is to be found in his
devastating attack on Locke, but it was an attack, like Hume's
or Kant's, which imperceptibly destroyed the attacker along
with his enemy. The problem would eventually be solved not
by logic but by an ever spreading revolution of the sensibility.
Lamennais was one of the first, most potent, and most vocal
exponents of that sensibility. It is what makes his life massively
consistent in spite of all his changes and self-contradictions, as
an expression of that sensibility, he was soon to discover his
own peculiar "principle of order," his other major life consistency of thought.

To return to his life. In 1809 Lamennais was tonsured and from then on lived mostly at his family's country home, La Chesnaie, where he gradually developed around himself a semi-monastic community, an Oratory remarkable for its utter freedom from episcopal or other ecclesiastical control. During the Hundred Days he fled to England fearing persecution for a pamphlet he had written on Church control of the university and for anti-Bonaparte passages in *Tradition.* He made a few friends but mostly he hated the English, English culture, and the Anglican Church, a passion which was another of his life consistencies. However revolutionary he became, he never became an internationalist, least of all *vis-à-vis* England.

In London he placed himself under the spiritual direction of the famous Abbé Carron, who persuaded him to enter the priesthood. Through the Abbé he also met a young man, Henry Moorman, modest in circumstances and demeanor, whom he converted from Low Church Anglicanism. The letters which are a record of this friendship Lamennais later published as *Lettres sur le protestantisme.* The book is seldom discussed by biographers of Lamennais, although recent and fashionable psychoanalytic ones have made everything of it. Henry Moorman was a lonely, chronically ill boy with a stepfather and no sense of home, one of the first of the many lovelost people who would be drawn to Lamennais. One does not have to be a psychoanalyst to see that this is the decisive love relationship of Lamennais' life, himself a person who never was securely confident of the love of others. The boy ran away from home, came to La Chesnaie, but returned home on the advice of Abbé Carron, without seeing Lamennais. His mother and stepfather finally accepted his conversion. As he was planning to return and become one of the brotherhood at La Chesnaie, he died. Lamennais was to fall in love later in a rather desultory fashion with a couple of women, but Henry Moorman remained to him as did Beatrice to Dante.

What characterizes *Lettres sur le protestantisme* is their passion. There is nothing sexual about them. They are love letters, the record of a courtship of which conversion to Roman Catholicism, rather than sex, was envisioned as the culmination. Today we realize there is nothing wrong with all of this. A generation ago vulgar Freudian critics made much of this aspect of Lamennais' career. Monckton-Milnes, possibly the most notorious *milord deviant* of his time, visited La Chesnaie and wrote about it, and one of his most eccentric lovers, Charles Justin McCarthy, the nephew of the Rector of the English College at Rome, Dr. Wiseman, later Cardinal Archbishop of England, was probably Lamennais' most troublesome spiritual protégé. Quite possibly it was his knowledge as confessor and counselor to such people that threw his very prose into paroxysms of rage when describing the besetting sin of the English—their hypocrisy, their universal conspiracy against the facts of life. McCarthy was a character out of Baron Corvo or Ronald Firbank. He actually seems to have had some kind of brain disease. McCarthy remained a passionate defender of Lamennais through all his later troubles with the Vatican, although eventually his help came to consist largely of dishing the dirt about inner Vatican politics to the innocent and easily disturbed Lamennais. McCarthy eventually straightened out, or turned straight, and went off to become governor of Ceylon. McCarthy is important because it is through him that Lamennais' influence penetrated to the glittering, perverse, and exceedingly churchy young men who became so common in late nineteenth-century fashionable intellectual circles. Lamennais' purity of heart could not be better shown than by the spiritual beauty of his innocent letters to such incense soaked denizens of churchy high society.

Chateaubriand, de Maistre, Lamennais to the contrary notwithstanding, the real secret of the society of the Bourbon restoration is that nobody believed anything, except Charles X himself, who was deficient mentally. Lamennais attacked, not skepticism, but spiritual indifference, head on, with one of the major works of his career, *Essai sur l'indifférence en ma-*

tière de religion. It is one of the great books of apologetics in the history of the Church. Like most polemicists, Lamennais operated from the premises of his opponents. He established once and for all what even to this day is probably the occult philosophy of most French Catholics, Catholic skepticism. It is implicit in Pascal, at least vestigial in both Bossuet and Fenelon, and it is the whole hidden meaning of de Maistre, but in Lamennais' *Essai* it is forthrightly stated. The book is not just an attack on rationalism, but upon the validity of individual reason. The first volume is an even more devastating, because more emotional, demolition of the rationalists of the Enlightenment than de Maistre's. The difference is that Lamennais not only believed, but he was a man consumed by faith as a virtue, passion, and habitude, physiological in intensity. Faith to Lamennais, as it had been to St. Paul, or would be to George Tyrrell, was not an act of acquiescence in creed or catechism or *Summa Theologica*, it was not even a "way of life" but life itself, a life of prayer. Lamennais does not look like a contemplative because he jumps around so much, but it is ecstasy, not argument, that demolishes Diderot and Voltaire in the *Essai*.

When Lamennais tried to find a cornerstone for this faith, an ultimate principle of authority, he developed a notion which is probably the most naive in the entire history of the epistemology of religion, the *sensus communis* which he translated as *consentement commun*. The Latin might mean anything, from common sense to the *Zeitgeist* and the French is vague enough. What Lamennais meant by it was something like the general reason, even sometimes, the group mind, even sometimes something like Jung's collective unconscious. Sometimes he talks as though he was using that favorite apothegm of High Church Anglican theologians, the Canon of Vincent of Leirins, the *consensus orbis terrarum*, "that which has been held by all men at all times everywhere in the church." Sometimes, and as his life went on, increasingly, he is sort of an epistemological Averroist and "common sense" becomes a universal intellectual soul, and since *le peuple,* the working class, are more universal than anybody else, they become, for the last half of his career, the source of authority.

It is only too obvious that there are no principles which can be stated as such—logically verbalized—which have been held by all men everywhere. If so, there would be no need for speech or logic. Society would simply run by mute consent. It is even more obvious that there is not an iota of the Christian creed which has been held by all men everywhere at all times and that the Vincentine Canon is a purely circular definition. As for any more philosophical definition of the term, it would be very nice if it were true, but it all too obviously is not. And furthermore there is embedded in it a kind of epistemological construction of the Socratic fallacy. Men knowing the good rationally do not necessarily choose it, and good men may well be more irrational than not. But it is true that Lamennais carried over into the nineteenth century what can only be called the revolutionary Averroism of the Left of the Revolution, the mystical notion of The People as the ultimate source of value and validation. We should not forget that Marx and Engels and Bakunin read everything they could get of Lamennais—enthusiastically—no matter how much they might disagree with him, and in the Revolution of 1848 he was incomparably more influential than all three of them put together.

The *sensus communis* was certainly an incongruous cornerstone to choose as a support for the Petrine Throne. Lamennais always talks as if he knew practically nothing of any part of the world except Western Europe, and little of that except France. The notion that the peculiarly French structure of Catholicism, whether Gallican or Ultramontane, could be developed from any *consentement commun* could arise only in a mind of an innocent and holy chauvinist. Perhaps this Frenchiness is the reason, along with the magnificent rhetoric, and the discrediting of Voltaire, that led to Lamennais' marching with one step, the *Essai,* into the very center of French intellectual life. He became what he would call "world" famous overnight.

As the volumes of the *Essai* went on Lamennais moved from a concept of the relationship between regal and papal authority not greatly different from de Maistre's to an ever increasing Ultramontanism. The reason lay not just in Lamennais himself, or in the development of his ideas, but in the relations of church and state in France. It was becoming obvious that Gallicanism did not represent "freedom from Rome" as an Anglican would put it, but domination by a monarchy which, behind all its medieval trappings (Charles had insisted on being annointed at Rheims just like Jeanne d'Arc's Charles) was fundamentally secular and bourgeois and busy sprinkling Marx's primitive accumulation of capitalism with holy water licensed by the state. It was always necessary to bear in mind that Lamennais flourished in the period described in Engel's *Condition of the Working Class in England* and the horrifying chapters in Marx on primitive accumulation. If that was the condition of the working class in England, their condition in France was worse.

Meanwhile Lamennais had become one of the most famous men in Europe, the darling of Pope Leo the XII, and immensely fashionable in circles he never visited and which, of course, did not read him. It is still disputed whether toward the end of his reign the Pope made him a Cardinal *in petto*.

Through it all Lamennais continued on his way, the leader of a brotherhood remarkably like the Catholic pietist ones which flourished in the Rhineland before the Reformation. So it is not surprising that as an antidote to apologetics and controversy he translated and annotated Thomas à Kempis' *Imitation of Christ,* still the best translation in French. It is hard to see how he found time to write such many-volumed works. His correspondence was immense and he was available as a spiritual counselor and confessor to all who came to La Chesnaie. Lamennais survives in the written word, and so is thought of as an apologist, a kind of nineteenth century Origen, but he was actually far more a pastor. His power was based on prayer and the pastoral sacraments of the altar and confessional. All of his apologetics preach faith, not as belief or, like Pascal, submission to the articles of a creed, but as life.

In 1825 and 1826 he published *De la religion considérée dans ses rapports avec l'ordre politique et civil,* another definite step on the road which now we can see was already marked out for him. Lamennais no longer trusts the state and has come to think of society in fundamentally apocalyptic terms. The only practical conclusion to be drawn from the book would be a complete papal theocracy in which the secular power would just be a government department with a cabinet post, the exact reverse of the Church in relation to the French Monarchy. But now there is a third power. Lamennais has seen the dark satanic mills, and he does not as yet know where to place them in what is becoming more and more the vision of a cosmic struggle. The people appear as an apocalyptic beast. Lamennais recognizes in them a supernatural dynamism. He cannot make up his mind whether they are one of the animals that draw the chariot in Ezekiel or one of the Great Beasts of Chaos in *Revelation.*

In the next book, *Des progrès de la révolution et de la guerre contre l'église* (1829), every secular power has been weighed and found wanting. Lamennais has become a complete apocalypticist. The communal society headed by the representative of the Messiah and governed by the sacraments is the Kingdom. "He who is near to me is near the Fire. He who is far from me is far from the Kingdom." Although Lamennais would be lost in the eschatological Higher Criticism that would come at the end of the century and was never interested in such matters anyway, it is here that he belongs. From now on, far more than Albert Schweitzer, his is an ethic of the end of the world. But the vision of Apocalypse is one form of contemplation, one of the highest forms of prayer.

With the fall of legitimacy and the establishment of the bourgeois monarchy of 1830, Lamennais' vision was able to take concrete form as a revolutionary program and take flesh in a group of disciples who would become the most brilliant Catholic spokesmen of the first half of the century, notably Montalembert, Lacordiare, and Maurice de Guerin. Guerin can be read about in Matthew Arnold's famous essay. Arnold unknowingly communicates the special temper fostered by the oratory of La Chesnaie which Newman characterized as "unwholesome." In 1830 they founded the daily paper, "L'Avenir," dedicated to *Dieu et liberté*. Within two years "L'Avenir" became the most influential thing of its kind in the world. Its subscription was mostly amongst seminarians, young clergy and radical Catholic aristocrats of the kind who would later become a force in the Church (like Lord Acton or Baron von Hügel in another generation), but for every subscriber there was a multitude of readers and discussants. The paper was pushed by its opposition in the French hierarchy, the Roman Curia, and the ranks of the reactionary laity, bourgeois or aristocratic, further and further toward what today we would call the left, but what was in fact a concept of society identical with that of the Apostles awaiting the Coming. There is an uncanny resemblance to the narrative of *Acts* in the story of *"L'Avenir,"* and the memoirs and letters of its little apostolate. They attacked the secular power in the name of the Pope and in defense of the people. But the Pope was completely dependent upon the dying Holy Alliance, and, if the secular power were challenged, totally, fundamentally, intransigently, the power of the Papacy would be subverted along with it. The power of the Papacy was not the power of Peter and Paul wandering Romewards along the shores of the Eastern Mediterranean, ragged and barefoot, preaching the Coming of the Kingdom. Leo was dead and Gregory XVI was terrified of the revolutionary Ultramontanism of *"L'Avenir."* He did not even dare attack Lamennais directly, but in the encyclical

Mirari vos condemned him anonymously. The result was the most apocalyptic prayer in French, *Paroles d'un croyant*, 1834, comparable to Blake's Prophetic Books or Christopher Smart or in some ways to Lautreament's *Les Chants de Maldoror*. At the end, not unlike the Gospels and Epistles, *Paroles* preaches rendering unto Caesar, or Caesar's heir as Pontifex Maximus, the things that are Rome's, and unto God the things that are God's, and lays great emphasis on the societal duties of an evangelical community. In substance the book is a long, apocalyptic prose poem. It is the work of a nineteenth-century Zealot. It reads as though it had been found in a jar in a cave in the desert. Perhaps Lamennais says, "Those who live by the sword shall die by the sword," a statement of course as equivocal as "Render unto Caesar. . . ." But he only preaches abstention from the sword of iron because he believes that there is available to each man of the people a sword of the spirit infinitely more effective.

The book went off like a nuclear explosion in the intellectual community of Europe. Although Lamennais, with the holy foolishness that comes from a diet of honey and locusts, was unaware of it, the Vatican had sealed his fate. The situation had become intolerable, and he and his comrades decided to go to Rome and submit the future of *"L'Avenir"* and themselves to the Pope. The Pope responded with unqualified condemnation. Montalembert and Lacordiare submitted, and what is most shocking, broke personally with Lamennais, their spiritual father. Lamennais went over to the Revolution.

His revolution, like his Ultramontanism, was his own, and quite unlike anybody else's. Most writers on Lamennais are interested in him almost exclusively as a Catholic apologist who came to a tragic end. They write from within the Church, Roman or Anglican. Most of them dismiss the entire latter part, and in fact, most influential part, of his life, as lived out in poverty and obscurity. This is nonsense. He always lived in poverty. He gave up his beloved La Chesnaie and lived in poor rooms in the working class quarters of Paris, but it never would have occurred to him to do anything else. True, he managed his money affairs badly, but he didn't believe in money at all. As soon as he was condemned by the Vatican, he entered as an equal into the ranks of the leaders of the French intellectual Left. Many of his most powerful writings come from these latter days—*Le Livre du peuple, Une voix de prison, Du passé et da l'avenir du peuple, De l'esclavage moderne* are the works by which most Frenchmen know him, and that make him a "classic." The earlier are lost to the *laique* world in the ghetto of the history of theological controversy. He never loses the apocalyptic vision. His style remains that of a visionary on Patmos. Probably the people for whom and to whom he spoke scarcely understood him, but they loved him and his presence was always greeted with enthusiasm. After all, it is very flattering to an auditorium full of strikers in Lyon to tell them they are a cosmogonic force.

For the rest of his life Lamennais was tirelessly active in the support of every revolutionary cause in Europe, or at least, in Catholic Europe. He never got over his antagonism to, and ignorance of, Protestant Europe. Like most Frenchmen he was completely ethnocentric. He talks a great deal about the world and all mankind, when what he really means is France and Frenchmen. His prose poems in defense of the Polish Revolution, motivated by unconscious French geopolitics—as Marx always was by German—were what first frightened the Pope. From then on his name appears on what today we would call all the "radical front groups" and committees for defense and relief of the oppressed and persecuted, but he was also extremely active personally.

By 1840 in *Le Pays et le gouvernement* he had come to advocate defensive violence in the Revolution. The authorities put him in prison for a year of fantastically fecund production. There he wrote many of his best works—including another apocalypse which was probably the direct inspiration for Nietzsche's *Thus Spake Zarathustra,* however differing in intent. *Amschapands et Darvands* derives its imagery from the *Zend Avesta,* a deliberate choice. Like most prophets who have seen the community of love stillborn, or even murdered in its cradle by its parents, Lamennais had come to look upon the cosmos as the theater of a struggle between the Good and an almost, but not quite, equally omnipotent evil. As Chesterton once remarked, it is much easier to believe in a personal devil than it is to believe in a personal God.

In prison he also worked on his *Esquisse d'une philosophie.* This immense and unfinished work surpasses Trotsky's theory of the Permanent Revolution because it places the revolution at the center of ontology. The Good, the True, and the Beautiful are the revolutionary powers of God, something like the Trinity—something like the *Sephiroth* of the *Kabbalah.* No one but scholars reads all of *Esquisse* (an ironic title if ever there was one) today—but the chapters on art and the beautiful are still read as the strongest statement of the esthetics and the theory of the relations of art and society usually identified with Tolstoy. I have never read anything about the influence of Lamennais on Tolstoy but it is impossible that he should not have read him and the resemblances are obvious. The difference is that Lamennais, trained in the Church, is more of a systematic metaphysician and so grounds his theory of art, as what a skeptic would dismiss as revolutionary propaganda, in the very nature of being itself. Art is the derived secondary formal manifestation of the Beautiful which is the primary form of the True. As such it is only a stage toward the realization of Truth. The final activity of man in relation to God is science, the understanding by the intellect of God as the True, the infinite being who is the Intellect of intellects.

Reading such mentalism in the midst of the poisoned tares sown by Science unrestrained, this vision of being probably strikes most of us today as rather awful, a bit like Aristotle filtered through Arabic and thence through the mind of a skeptiç scholastic. Although Lamennais was a man of great love, the God who is Love plays only a minor role in his final philosophic synthesis. He must have realized this because as he grew old and death became for him an ever present reality, he thought of life after death as the end of Time when even the noblest fetters would fall away and the soul of man would expand like an infinite blossom under the sun of an infinite love.

On the trip to Rome Lamennais stopped off in Germany and met Döllinger, Möhler and Schelling and von Baader, and corresponded with Schelling for quite a while afterwards. Certainly they influenced each other. Von Baader, who owed so much to Boehme, may well have not introduced him to, but involved him with the thought of Lamennais. For Lamennais is certainly a kind of Gallic Boehme, as he is also a Gallic Blake.

Every other aspect of Lamennais' multifarity has been written about, but I know of no paper called "Felicité Lamennais, Boehmenist," yet the resemblances are worthy of further study. Boehme lays quite outside almost all later Catholic thought, so it is easy to forget how influential his ideas were in those days. Louis St. Martin, *"le philosophe inconnu,"* had died in 1803, but Martinism was still extremely fashionable. St. Martin was the leading mystical writer of the Revolutionary period, and translated almost all of Jakob Boehme during the very years of the overturn of all things by fire. To him the Revolution and Terror were a kind of sacramental showing forth of the Last Judgment. He was an apocalypticist if ever there was one. Furthermore, he believed in the withering away of the Church into a communal theocracy not unlike the Jesuit communes in Paraguay. The guiding principle of human association, action, and faith would be precisely Lamennais' *sensus communis*. The great difference is that he interpreted this basic, initial motion of being and knowing as an overflowing of the infinite, uncontainable, Divine Love. It is quite impossible that Lamennais could not have read him from the very beginning of his self-education in his uncle's library. In the latter days of his life he was to come to a not dissimilar belief. St. Martin, one of the saints of religious Freemasonry like Jacques de Molay, died uncensured by Rome, in the grace of the last sacraments.

Franz von Baader, one of the strongest of all apologists for Catholicism, combined Jakob Boehme, St. Martin, and anticipations of Kierkegaard, along with late medieval Rhenish mysticism, Ruysbroek, Meister Eckhart, and even St. Mechtild of Magdeburg and St. Hildegard of Bingen, into a unique synthesis. He too believed in a millenarian communal theocracy, ruled by grace flowing from the sacraments. Like Lamennais, and unlike St. Martin, he placed the main emphasis on God as Truth and the divine human relation as one of knowing—but only prior to the Fall. For fallen man, God appears as overflowing love, and the life of faith a life immersed in that love, as fish in water. There was a strong Lutheran tinge to von Baader's moral philosophy which relates him to Kierkegaard. By the Fall, man has totally alienated himself from God—total insignificance, total contingency, over against totally omnipotent absolute Being. But across that unbridgeable gulf flows God himself as love, immanent and incarnate. Man's salvation lies not in faith as belief, and not at all in works, but in faith as absorption in the divine life. Once again we come back to the ancient sequence: knowledge is being (not the other way around), being is illumination, illumination is love. Von Baader was a contributor to *"L'Avenir,"* a frequent correspondent of Lamennais', and wrote a pamphlet passionately defending him in his hours of tribulation after the journey to Rome. Eventually forbidden to teach philosophy himself, he was the only friend who stayed in the Church to remain loyal to Lamennais.

In the Revolution of 1848 Lamennais got more votes than anybody else, including Victor Hugo, and was elected freeholder to the Committee for a New Constitution. He submitted

Projet de constitution de la republique francaise (1848) but a little group of radical politicians whose responsibility was the result of bargaining, compromise or pressure, were not prepared to build Jerusalem in France's green and pleasant land. In the elections for the new assembly Lamennais increased his vote by 9,000, from 104,000 to 113,000. When Louis Bonaparte seized power in 1851, he retired and spent his last three years translating *The Divine Comedy*. Again, one of the best translations in French. Lamennais' translations, incidentally, which include the Gospels, are full of notes and exegesis by himself and make fascinating reading.

At the beginning of 1854 while finishing the *Divine Comedy,* the same book Blake was illustrating on his death bed, Lamennais died, after a very short illness. He refused all ministrations of the clergy and any hint of reconciliation with the Church. He said, "I wish to be buried in the middle of the poor and like the poor, with nothing to mark my grave, not even the simplest stone. Carry my body straight to the cemetery and do not bring it to any church."

His friends decided on a day for his funeral. The government, afraid of a demonstration, insisted that it be performed before dawn and forbade any demonstration procession to follow the coffin, and refused entrance to the cemetery to all but a handful of his friends. Before dawn on the morning of March 1st, the tiny procession began its march to the cemetery through a dense fog. The band of faithful disciples, as they started up the boulevards through the poorest workers' quarters of Paris, were joined at the Place de la Bastille by a crowd of maskers returning through the fog-bound streets from all-night Mardi Gras revels. Their shouts attracted the attention of the first workers on their way to work.

From person to person, and door to door, and window to window, the word spread through the streets of the poor, through Saint Antoine and Belleville and the Marais to Clignancourt—"Lamennais is being carried to his grave!" Soon the funeral cortège that had started out so tiny and even so, guarded by the police, was an immense throng that had to battle its way to the new-made grave. He was buried without oratory and someone said, "That is all. Go home," and there remained only a heap of new earth marked with a cleft stick, in it a piece of paper—"Felicité Robert de la Mennais."

There are many thousands gone—clerics and laymen—from devotion to the living, historic Jesus, step by imperceptible step, *pedetemtin,* into defense of an ecclesiastical power structure. Most French apologists were apologists for the Church, not the apostolic life modeled on Christ. It is a peculiarity of French Catholic apologetic that it is singularly un-Christian, or shall we say, very Catholic, but very un-Jesuslike. The story of Lamennais is the reverse of the usual. He started out as one of the most powerful apologists for power, but he based that power on a principle, his *sensus communis,* which could only make sense if it was translated, "The Communion of the Saints" and if that in turn was translated "The Communion of the Nazarene Personality in All Men." This is certainly the Living Body, the Hidden Church, the body and blood of the creative principle of the universe. So it is only too obvious that, like many other thousands gone, before and after Lamennais, the Church as a power structure left him, he did not leave the Body of Christ. To the end his writings are a form of prayer and he died with Dante's immense mystical vision of the conflict of power and illumination in his hands—just like Blake before him. In his day two roads diverged in a yellow wood, whose leaves were the gold of the cash nexus. One led from the Beatitudes to the Vatican Council; the other to Marx's apocalyptic poem inserted in *The Communist Manifesto.* Somewhere at that point of divergence there is a transcendent signpost erected by Lamennais and only now is its direction becoming fully legible. It points to an *ekklesia katholikos* in the most ancient sense of those old Greek words.

The Evolution of Anglo-Catholicism

I. FROM THE REFORMATION TO THE OXFORD MOVEMENT

Si jamais les chrétiens se rapprochent, comme tout les y invite,
il semble que la motion *doit partir de l'église d'Angleterre* . . .
elle peut être considerée comme un de ces intermèdes, capables
de rapprocher des éléments inassociables de leur nature.
> —Joseph de Maistre, *Considérations sur la France.*

It is easy to form a distorted impression of the growth of the Anglo-Catholic Movement in the Church of England and those churches in communion with it. The dramatic story is that of the Oxford Movement. The dramatic character is Newman. The dramatic moment is his conversion to Roman Catholicism. Evangelicals, Low and Broad Churchmen, and Roman Catholics, have always seen the movement as a Romanizing one, reflecting in its theology and ritual orthodox Roman Catholicism, and have defined its objectives as implying "submission to Rome" as a necessary consequence. Nothing could be less true. Even to this day, many Anglo-Catholic clergy have never been inside a Roman Catholic Church or read a "Romanist" theological work written after the Council of Trent.

The growth and development of modern Anglicanism stems from seeds dormant in the Anglican church from its beginning. Newman's theory of development of doctrine may or may not apply to the evolution of post-Tridentine dogma, but it certainly applies to the Church he left. On the other hand, the influence of the Oxford Movement, and the ritualist revival which succeeded it, has had a profound influence on Roman

Catholicism and Lutheranism all through the latter part of the nineteenth century and the early part of the twentieth.

Today the devotional and liturgical life of both Protestantism and Catholicism have been assimilated to a world-wide movement of purification and restoration which unquestionably first began with the Oxford reform. This influence of course did not only operate externally. Again and again Catholicizing priests, and sometimes whole religious orders, "swam the Tiber" from Canterbury to Rome, having lost hope of defending the Catholic heritage of the Church of England against militant Protestants, politically-appointed bishops and a secular Parliament. Once they got there however, many of their old practices and beliefs slowly re-asserted themselves and acted to purge the Roman Catholic Church in England of many of the distortions and abuses and superstitions which had crept into the practices of the Church in the long dormant period of the eighteenth and nineteenth centuries.

Looking back over the controversies that drove many an embattled and despairing priest to renounce the Anglican Communion and deny the validity of his own priesthood, and even question that of his baptism, it is tragic and ironic to realize that many, perhaps most, of these were over points of practice and doctrine then considered hopelessly Protestant or even sacrilegious which are now common in the Roman Catholic Church since Vatican II—the vernacular liturgy, open communion, communion in both kinds, birth control, divorce, married clergy, the redefinition of scriptural, traditional and magisterial authority, of baptismal regeneration, and justification. Once the now apparently inevitable permission for a married clergy is granted, many Anglican and even some Lutheran churches and priests and ministers will be considerably more "High Church" than their Roman Catholic fellows.

The importance of Anglican Catholicism is precisely that it worked out, for over a century in a far from authoritarian environment, most of the implications of a free Catholicism and demonstrated that even in so touchy a subject as the Higher Criticism of scripture, liberty was the mother, not the daughter, of order; that at the end of the process of freedom for development within a Catholic context, hardly defined except as a way of life based on a way of prayer, true Catholic orthodoxy would not be weakened but immeasurably strengthened. It is for this reason that the developments in Anglicanism since the beginning of the Oxford Movement are of such crucial importance and are so illuminating of the problems now confronting the Universal Church.

In all this history the coming and going of John Henry Cardinal Newman is only a minor episode. It would be tempting to be defiant and try to write the story of the Oxford Movement without mentioning him. That would be a foolish thing to do. Distortions of history cannot be corrected by equal and opposite distortions. It should be borne in mind in studying the Oxford Movement that Newman is a separate problem, just as it should be apparent on inspection that he represents a divergent tendency. He "went to Rome." The other leaders did not. Certainly it was after his conversion that he became that special theological and even philosophical influence that is his unique contribution.

Historians of the Movement commonly represent it as saving the English Church from an abysm of sloth, indifference, simony, slovenliness, and secularization, into which it had sunk in the eighteenth century. This is only partially true, and it was nothing peculiar to the Church of England, but characteristic of religion in eighteenth-century Western civilization taken as a whole. The eighteenth century was not only the heyday of a secularizing rationalism, but it was the heyday of Erastianism as well. The State was supreme in secular affairs in Sweden as well as in Bavaria; in Prussia as in Spain; obviously, as we all know, in France and England, but also, as we forget, in Rome.

In the Papal States the State as such was as "value neuter"

as anywhere else. It was just far less efficient than most, and was responsible for the Balkanization of central and southern Italy. Had the Borgias established the Papacy as an hereditary monarchy, things might have been different, but since the secular power of the Papacy was actually powerlessness, the Papal States were the victims of the maneuvering of great powers whose interest it was to keep the heart of Italy barbarous and weak. We forget that only a few generations ago the city of Rome was a wilderness of half-buried classical ruins, ill-kempt churches, ruinous Renaissance palaces, cow pastures and slums. The Light never went out in the Church, true. But it never went out in Canterbury either, although in both cases its rays shone far more from the Inner Light than from the radiance of the cathedra.

We forget too, that William of Orange was an aggressive Presbyterian and Calvinist publicly, and devoid of religion privately, and that from the death of Queen Anne the throne of England has been occupied, until recent years, by rulers who were not really members of the Church of England at all, as it had been defined by the Elizabethan Establishment, or by the great theologians of the Elizabethan, Jacobean and Caroline days. For two hundred years the entire tendency of the secular authority, whether throne or Parliament, was against the Anglican heritage. This did not mean that the heritage was forgotten, or that the Christian life died out, or went underground in the eighteenth century.

Samuel Johnson is a perfect example of a devout but worldly Anglican layman of those times. His religious opinions and prejudices can be found in Boswell, distorted by Boswell's worldly and secular bias—as is the whole Boswell-Johnson—but his religious life is revealed in the rare entries in his diary, always at least at Easter, the anniversary of his wife's death, and usually his own birthday and New Year's Day and in his prayers and few personal poems. True, he only went to communion on Easter. That's all anybody else did, anywhere, except for a few specially devout persons and members of religious orders. Coleridge is another example at the end of the century. As a theologian and philosopher he may be very confused, but the tremendous importance of religion in his life could not have existed in a completely irreligious milieu, nor even grown out of it by reaction.

Religious life in the Church of England was pretty well confined to the Nonjurors, the Evangelicals, the old High Church party and the pietists who were influenced by French Quietism, German piety, and the writings of William Law. Again the eighteenth century was the flowering time of Quaker piety, when Quakerism turned from an apocalyptic Pentecostal sect into a society of lay monastics. The printed literature of spiritual diaries kept by Friends in the eighteenth century is immense, and reveals the continued existence in England on a very wide scale of that lay monasticism that is the characteristic form of the English religious life. Of course the Society of Friends were a people apart, an alternative society; nevertheless, they existed within the dominant culture, would have been something very different without it, and radiated an influence all about them.

This kind of devoted, "concerned" Friends call it, life appears in the first English religious writing. It can be found in Bede as well as Walter Hilton, *The Cloud of Unknowing*, Julian of Norwich, Richard Rolle, Marjorie Kempe and all the other great English mystics of the end of the Middle Ages. It can be found in the devotional literature of the English families who remained true to the old religion, and where, in an underground church, the religious life was necessarily the family life. It can be found in the poetry of Herbert, Henry Vaughan, and even Herrick, and it is perfectly expressed in Walton's *Lives* of Donne, Herbert, Sanderson, Hooker, Wotten. All of them were distinguished by a domestic monasticism, a cheerful piety and a gentleness of disposition. At least three of them—Donne, Wotten and Herbert—were fishermen, wanderers by quiet streams and flowered meadows, contemplating the mysteries of life in moving water. *The Compleat Angler* itself is a book about the contemplative life, under the symbolism of fishing. This is not a witticism.

To understand the profound changes which took place in the Church of England through the nineteenth and early twentieth centuries it is necessary to establish the sympathy of a special mood, and that mood can be found in Roper's *Life of St. Thomas More* and in *The Compleat Angler* as well. England's special contribution to monasticism was the Order of St. Gilbert of Sempringham. The Gilbertine villages or city communities were organized with a convent of nuns at one end and of monks, both contemplative and active, at the other, and in between the homes of lay monastics whose religious life was the fulfilment of family life. I myself have always hoped to see, amongst the many other revivals of a purified medieval monasticism within the Anglican Church, a revival of the Gilbertines. Perhaps as we enter the Apocalypse that will be the final resolution of *aggiornamento*.

Contrary to popular belief, Henry VIII was not interested in founding a "Church of England." Nor was he interested in reforming the Church. He was interested in robbing it. The looting of the monasteries was occasioned by the impending bankruptcy of a vastly over-extended international policy. The coming and going of Henry's wives reflected political forces, and policies national and international, not unlike the coming and going of prime ministers in later days. As Henry's chancellors and queens succeeded each other, the doctrinal position of the Church under its royal head swung like a pendulum. As long as Henry was alive it did not swing very far. The succession of official formularies from the parliamentary declarations of 1529 to 1536 summed up in the Ten Articles, *The Institution of a Christian Man* (The Bishops' Book), the Act of Six Articles, 1539, *The Necessary Doctrine and Erudition of a Christian Man* (The King's Book, 1543), Archbishop Cranmer's *Primer* issued in the last year of Henry's life, were all considerably more orthodox and more specifically Roman than much of the liturgics and theology popular since Vatican II—always saving the Royal Supremacy. It should be borne in mind that quarrels of king and throne were nothing new in the history of either the Western or Eastern Church. The extreme lengths to which Henry had pushed the Royal Supremacy fell far short of the claims of most Byzantine emperors. Had the personal revolt of Henry VIII not coincided with the Reformation on the continent and the attendant political struggles of the German states, France, the Holy Roman Empire and Spain, the schism of the English Church would have quietly healed over with changes in the occupants and policies of the throne. The Communion Service of the first Prayer Book of Edward VI was still unmistakably a Mass. Even the second Prayer Book was susceptible of a Catholic interpretation and would be reformed drastically in that sense by Elizabeth's bishops.

There was a great deal of iconoclasm and destruction throughout all these years, but it is extraordinary how much of the artistic heritage of the Middle Ages survived to be destroyed by the Protestant revolt in the next century. Nothing shows the comparative superficiality of the Henrician and Edwardian Reformation than the comparative ease with which Mary was able to restore the Roman obedience. The persecutions of Mary have made her name a household word. In fact the majority of the clergy and the vast majority of the populace quietly submitted. Serious revolt did not begin until the marriage to Philip of Spain.

In those years the Council of Trent was in session (1545–1563) and those doctrines that we think of as specifically Roman were then far more rigorously defined. The council did not attempt to ameliorate any of the differences with the reformers, but attacked them head on. Practices and doctrines that were peculiar to the contemporary Western Church were made binding for all times and places. Behind its counter-attack in the field, the Church became a fortress church. What this meant in actual fact was that what had hitherto been considered the Universal Church, the body of all Christian men, synonymous with society as a whole, in Western Europe at least, accepted a position as a subculture or a sect. As on the continent, many of the persecutions and burnings of the later days of Mary's reign were for doctrines and practices which had been matters of dispute amongst the fathers and doctors of the Church until the sixteenth century. Many of the abuses, for example, the sale of indulgences, had been attacked by the entire consensus of medieval Europe, from the great scholastics to Chaucer and Langland.

The intransigent policies of Cardinal Pole, Mary's archbishop and cousin, bear comparison with the Papal suppression of the Jesuit Mission in China two centuries later. There was a brief chance to make the Catholic Church truly catholic without sacrificing doctrine to the more intransigent Lutherans and Calvinists. Under the driving intolerance of Mary, Philip, and Cardinal Pole, and with occasional gentle, ineffectual demurrers from Rome, the universal church in England was turned into a sect and so remained. It is necessary to understand this to appreciate more the psychology than the doctrines of the Anglo-Catholic divines under Elizabeth, James and the two Charleses, who built up a philosophy of the English Church as a *via media,* a "bridge church" between Rome, Orthodoxy and Protestantism, a branch of the Church Universal —which, ironically sheltered under the royal supremacy, they hoped, would someday restore true universality to Christendom.

Throughout the sixteenth century all Western European churches were becoming national churches, whether Protestant or Papal in their allegiance. The Spanish Church was and remained until Vatican II essentially a national church, less markedly so than the English but more than the Gallican

French church, for the simple reason that over vast periods of time the Spanish throne alone or in combination with that of the Holy Roman Empire controlled the Papacy, not the other way around. Ironically only Calvin in Geneva kept alive the idea of a theoretically ruled divine society which had been at least the putative vision of Hildebrand.

Similar processes of course had gone on in the Eastern churches. Northern Orthodoxy was nationalist—Serbian, Russian, Bulgarian, etc.—while nationalist and ethnic tendencies in the South had produced schismatic churches—Monophysite, Monothelite, Nestorian—in Syria, Egypt and the Orient, all denying, incidentally, the Orthodox charges of heresy against themselves—denials that were later to be accepted by the Roman See in some instances, by Canterbury in others in admitting various Uniat Churches to communion.

Hooker, Laud, Hall, Andrewes, Cosin, Bramhall, Bull, Stillingfleet, Shillingworth, Pearson, Morton were amongst the most learned theologians of their day. Parallel with their theology was reborn in the English Church its characteristic piety —John Donne, Sir Thomas Browne, Herbert, Nicholas Ferrar, Jeremy Taylor, Thomas Traherne, Henry Vaughan, as well as Andrewes and Laud, were all devotional writers of a type more meaningful to us today than most of the contemporary Counter Reformation mystics on the continent. They are only the more articulate few out of many. It is the capacity of the English Church to produce so rich and deep and manifold a life of prayer which nineteenth- and twentieth-century Anglo-Catholics considered the principal sign of her catholicity, because it reflected the continuity of her sacramental life.

The theologians constructed an apologetic for a reformed Catholicism, protestant only against what they considered specific Roman abuses and claims. Baptismal regeneration, confirmation, the Real Presence as distinguished from transsubstantiation, the Eucharistic sacrifice, the reservation of the Eucharist, auricular confession, unction, invocation of the saints and the Blessed Virgin—all can be found in the Caroline divines.

This entire theological edifice was constructed not by appeal to recent Roman Catholic theology or the medieval doctors but was based solidly on Scripture, the apostolic Fathers, the patristic period, to and including St. Augustine, and the Councils of the undivided church. In every instance the emphasis is on the apostolic life. Christianity is envisaged as the pattern of life shown forth by those persons who had been in intimate contact with the incarnate Lord, who had walked and talked and eaten and drunk with the living Jesus. The Church is thought of as itself a sacrament, social, but embodied like the Eucharist, of the Christ-life.

The brief interlude of James II only consolidated the Anglo-Catholic tendency amongst bishops, priests and laity. Archbishop Sancroft and six bishops remonstrated against the liberties granted Dissenters and Roman Catholics, were brought to trial and acquitted. This crisis was used by essentially irreligious forces to overthrow James and deliver the crown to William of Orange, husband of James' sister. He was one of the wealthiest men in Europe, the leader of an essentially economic revolution. Once again, Sancroft and eight bishops refused the oaths to William and Mary. They considered that even though he was a Roman Catholic, their oaths to James were personal and so still binding. The archbishop, five bishops, four hundred clergy were deprived and were followed by a large but unknown number of laymen. From then on the throne was no longer in fact head of an Anglican church, but a Protestant, continental power over against it. Certain of the bishops consecrated others and the most irreconcilable of the Catholic party went into schism—the so-called Nonjurors—which lasted as an effective body all through the eighteenth century. Towards the end of the century there were some 50 congregations in London!

Most of the Episcopal Church of Scotland refused the oaths.

That Church as such became and has remained disestablished. (William established the Presbyterian Church in Scotland.) The Scottish Prayer Book and the English Nonjuring liturgy returned to the first Prayer Book of Edward the Sixth, with considerable improvements in the Catholic sense taken mostly from eastern liturgies. These included the epiclesis or invocation of the Holy Spirit upon the elements of bread and wine, lacking which the Roman rite is considered defective by the Orthodox. Incidentally, the Book of Common Prayer of the American Episcopal Church and American Orders are derived from the Scottish Church and the Nonjurors, not from the English Church.

The Nonjuror schism is extremely important in the background of the Oxford Movement. Bishop Ken and the great eighteenth-century mystic, William Law, profoundly influenced Pusey, Keble and Newman. The later generation of Young Turks around Newman—Ward, Oakley, Pattison, the Romanizers—were specifically in revolt against the old Anglo-Catholic tradition, quite as much as against the Evangelical and Broad parties.

As the years went by, and its distance from the Church widened, the little schism of the Nonjurors came, in the polemical writings of its apologists, to be more and more sacramentally oriented. The Apostolic Succession was looked on as a succession of the sacraments, the episcopacy an enduring channel of the divine life blood. It was the sacraments with their all-pervading gift of grace which bound the Church together with an authority far surpassing Pope or king. Isolated as they were from their parent body and totally unknown to the Church as a whole, the Nonjurors emphasized the purely transcendental and mystical universality or catholicity of the Church. It was for this reason that the Alexandrine and Cappadocian Fathers, but especially the Syrians, appealed so greatly to them. There had been plenty of exterior authority of all sorts in the Roman Empire in the East. The Church was still loosely knit, with long and easily broken lines of communication. The appeal against imperium to charisma was to limited supernatural communities, the congregations of faithful whose power preceded others' because it operated on a higher plane.

It would be difficult to overestimate the importance of William Law. The household of William Law was a direct descendant of Little Gidding, the household of Nicholas Ferrar, as both were of the household of St. Thomas More. The principal difference is the increasing strictness forced by the effort to distinguish a devotional community from a world in which prayer, meditation, contemplation and asceticism were at ever increasing discount.

William Law is only the most famous of the Nonjuring divines, due probably to the cogency of his literary style and the conscious attempt to avoid sectarianism in his writings. He was a late-arrived Nonjuror who refused the oaths to George I. In spite of the strictness of his own life, his controversial writings against deism, against the egoistic morality, Mandeville's *Fable of the Bees,* against Protestantism, against Roman Catholicism are for their time singularly liberal in tone and echo the judiciousness of Richard Hooker. It was on Law's controversial writings and some of the more orthodox ruminations of Samuel Taylor Coleridge that in the next century F. D. Maurice was able for his own purposes to erect a bridge back to the main Anglo-Catholic tradition of the seventeenth century.

It is Law's *A Serious Call to a Devout and Holy Life* by which he is known in the history of English literature and by which he profoundly affected the course of religious development in England. It was a seminal book for the Evangelical Movement, a turning point in the spiritual life of the Wesleys, but it also deeply influenced, in their notions of a dedicated life, people as unlike Samuel Johnson and Edward Gibbon. It is a devotional manual of the type popular in Catholic circles on the continent in the eighteenth century and amongst

the Quakers and other Pietists in England and the Germanic
countries. Today its asceticism seems impossibly strict for anyone living in the world unsupported by a monastic regimen.
Yet it is a direct descendant of the works of the medieval
English mystics who were anchorites, hermits or even housewives but almost never conventuals.

Law was more learned in the mystical tradition than most
English pietists, and so his book describes a more systematic
cultivation of the interior life than any other English work of
his time. Then, too, his influence was much greater because
more public, and not so closely confined to the audience of a
sect, due to the great literary merit of *A Serious Call*. It is
still read by thousands of people of different religions, or none.
In his fifties, after a life of occasional curacies and many years
in the home of Edward Gibbon's father, where he lived first as
a tutor, and then as a kind of chaplain and spiritual counselor
to uncounted people of all parties in the Church, or none, who
came to consult him, he retired to a cottage in the country at
Kings Cliffe, his birthplace, and established a kind of little
convent with two ladies, Mrs. Hutcheson and Hester Gibbon,
the aunt of the historian. Until his death twenty-one years
later, the three devoted themselves to a strict religious life of
prayer, contemplation, teaching in two schools for poor boys
and girls, and charity, the latter so undemanding as to seriously disturb the neighboring rector.

It is in this later period that Law wrote the bulk of his mystical works and published his beautiful edition of the works of
Jakob Boehme. With his hierarchic cosmogony and his dynamic vision of the supernatural world and the soul's place in
it, Boehme verges on Gnosticism. Although he takes over
much of Boehme's mythology, Law is in fact less gnostic than
the pseudo-Dionysus or Scotus Erigena. The total impression
given by his visionary writings is his close kinship with St.
Bonaventura and the long tradition of "By Light, Light"—going back to Philo, Christian Neoplatonism, and the Merkabah

mysticism of Judaism and its later descendants in the Kabbalah and Hasidim. What Law does is to adjust the ancient Gnostic emanationist melodrama to the interior life as a set of symbols of the progress of the soul, what in our day Martin Buber or even Carl Jung have done. This is not the highest level of mystical experience, but it is a most effective propadeutic, and when it is adjusted to Catholic Christianity and to life modeled on the historic Jesus, a most captivating one.

Law's influence on Evangelicalism and on the revival of Anglo-Catholicism would be hard to overemphasize. It is more than a taste in reading matter in the Fathers of the Church. It is even more than a witness to the special lay monasticism so specially English. It is above all else an apocalyptic vision of the Church as the body of Christ, the manifestation of the Creative Word, and itself a great Sacrament whose body and blood is concentrated and communicated at the altar. Law spoke from Patmos. To him the trinitarian process, the Incarnation and Atonement were of the substance of which the great cosmogonies of the pagan Orient had been but dim rememberings. Although no one would know of them for two hundred years, Law's direct visionary experience, rising from his meditation on Bochme and on the Fathers, was a kind of redemption of the Memphite Theology, the earliest tractate of Egyptian religion, and of the cosmological dramas of Mesopotamia and Syria. Viewed from the vantage point of William Law the endless polemic of Fraser's *The Golden Bough* falls quietly into place as prophecy not only of the Christian myth but of the Christian life.

It is relatively easy for us, sophisticated with all the writings of comparative religion of two centuries, to absorb Law's transmuted Boehmenism. What it gave to Pusey, Keble and Newman could have been little else than the mood, the tone arising from a kind of physiological conviction that they lived in the tissue of the Living Body.

Law's contribution to the more systematic apologetic of

later Anglo-Catholicism was of more considerable importance, although the influence was seminal rather than at large. He established the appeal to experience, what today we would call existentialism, as the effective answer to the rationalism of the Enlightenment, and from him stems all the anti-rationalistic polemic of Coleridge, Newman, Butler, down to the Modernists. As, in a sense a corollary of this appeal to experience, his doctrine of the Atonement follows naturally. He demolishes the forensic theory, that the sacrifice at the cross was a debt to be paid to the bookkeeping of heaven, with a direct appeal to the experience of at-one-ment, the divinization of human nature by its lifting up into the Incarnation. This appeal is as ancient as the early Fathers and is reiterated again and again in the semi-Platonic mysticism of English Franciscan philosophy and poetry—

> Honde by honde then schulle us take
> Ant joye & bliss schulle us make
> For the devil of Hell man hagt forsake
> And Christe our lauerd is makit our make.

This is a theological tradition which would come to flower in the combination of Bishop Charles Gore's theory of kenosis and the generally prevailing Anglican doctrine of the incarnation and atonement which begins to gather force with G. Mauberly, then L. S. Thornton, Coleridge, F. D. Maurice, Frank Weston, the Bishop of Zanzibar. In later years the mystical, semi-gnostic notion of the equivalence of macrocosm and microcosm would be forgotten, but in Law it is the essential explanation of the experienced fact—"The divine drama is in you." And last of all, Law re-established a specific kind of devotion still characteristic of Anglican piety. *A Serious Call* has often been compared to St. Francis de Sales' *Introduction to the Devout Life*. It is most interesting to read them together, supplemented with Law's final devotional works—*The Spirit of Prayer, The Way to Divine Knowledge* and *The Spirit of*

Love. They led one of his editors, the Quaker, S. Hobhouse, to claim him as a Quaker. It would be just as easy for someone saturated in St. Thomas More and the late medieval English mystics to claim him as a Roman Catholic, more traditional by far than the rococo devotional manuals of his time.

Much could be written about the saintly Nonjuring Bishop of Bath and Wells, Thomas Ken. His devotional writings would best be read in the idyllic setting of the cathedral he occupied for so short a time, along "Ken's Walk," by grassy battlements and greenish moats and swanny pools, with the splendid cathedral in the background. His hymns are the most deeply devotional of their kind, poetry of great simplicity and power, although the enormous bulk of verse, not hymns, which he left behind him in manuscript is seldom poetry at all. It is tragic that so gifted a *bone pastor* should only have held his see for three years, and significant that he is still the legend of the place. But the most significant thing about him is that he is the only man in the history of theology ever to write an explication of the cathechism, titled, and most deservedly, *The Practice of Divine Love.* Ken is a divine far better quoted than discussed.

When the love of God is produced in my heart, and is set on work, my last concern is to preserve and ensure and quicken it; It is preserved by Prayer, the pattern of which is the Lord's Prayer; It is ensured to us by the Sacraments, which are the Pledges of love; and more particularly it is quickened by the Holy Eucharist, which is the feast of Love; So that the plain order of the Cathechism teaches me the rise, the progress, and the perfection of Divine Love, which God of his great mercy give me grace to follow.

* *

O thou whom my Soul loveth, I would not desire heaven but because thou art there, for thou makest heaven wherever thou art.

I would not, O Jesu, desire life everlasting, but that I may there everlasting love thee.

O inexhaustible love, do thou eternally breathe love into me, that my love to thee may be eternally increasing and tending towards infinity, since a love less than infinite is not worthy of thee.

* *

Lord, what I need I labour in vain, to search out the manner of thy mysterious presence in the Sacrament, when my Love assures me thou art there? All the faithful who approach thee with prepared hearts, they will know thou art there, they feel the Virtue of Divine Love going out of thee, to heal their infirmities and to inflame their affections, for which all Love, all Glory be to thee.

O merciful Jesus, let that immortal food which in the Holy Eucharist thou vouchsafest me, instil into my weak and languishing Soul, new supplies of Grace, new life, new Love, new Vigour, and new Resolution, that I may never more faint, or droop or tire in my duty.

To God the Father, who first loved us, and made us accepted in the Beloved; to God the Son who loved us, and washed us from our Sins in his own Blood; to God the Holy Ghost, who sheds the Love of God abroad in our hearts, be all Love and all Glory for time, and for eternity. Amen.

—from *The Practice of Divine Love*

* *

Forty-five years old, just before the swift decline of his powers, Coleridge was to write in *Biographia Literaria:*

The feeling of gratitude, which I cherish towards these men [George Fox, Jacob Behmen, and William Law] has caused me to digress further than I had forseen or proposed; but to have passed them over in an historical sketch of my literary life and opinions, would have seemed to me like the denial of a debt, the concealment of a boon. For the writings of these mystics acted in no slight degree to prevent my mind from being imprisoned within the outline of any single dogmatic system. They contributed to keep alive the *heart* in the *head;* gave me an indistinct, yet stirring and working presentment, that all the products of the mere reflective faculty partook of DEATH, and were as the rattling twigs and sprays in winter, into which a sap was yet to be propelled from some root to which I had not penetrated, if they were to afford my soul either food or shelter.

Coleridge was certainly the most influential—what shall we call him—certainly not theologian, but rather, theological speculator—of the early years of the nineteenth century, but it is difficult to isolate any stable and consistent ideas, much less a system from his work. His literary remains are an immense mass of notes. Like "Kubla Khan," they begin in dream, emerge into reality, and are interrupted by the unwelcome appearance of persons from Porlock before they have become completely realized.

His opinions evolve steadily from deism or Unitarianism to an acceptance of what he claimed was Anglican orthodoxy, but all along the way and in the final summation he is never worried if he contradicts himself—like Whitman: "Do I contradict myself? Very well then, I contradict myself." But, like Whitman, there certainly can be no question but that Coleridge was a man with a system, but a physiological system, a temperament, a tone, a way of coping with life and its problems. And there is no question but that he is often very muddled reading. His opponents have called him "muddied," and have put down the confusion of his thought to the effects of a lifelong opium habit. The major Broad Church theologians of the nineteenth century looked back to him as an ancestor, practically a founder, and his influence on the greatest of them, F. D. Maurice, was very strong.

However, it is only an accident of history, of politics, the extreme Fundamentalism, in the modern sense of the word, of the Oxford Movement, that prevents him from being acknowledged equally as an ancestor of latter day Anglo-Catholicism. After the defection of Newman and "the Romanizers"—Ward, Oakley, Manning, and the rest—from the Oxford Movement, it was F. D. Maurice, the Coleridgean, and the Cambridge group under his influence, along with Pusey and Keble, who provided the synthesis, such as it was, that guided the intransigent so-called ritualists in their slum parishes in the last half of the century.

The point to point visibility in Coleridge's speculations may be low, but it is possible to triangulate the whole field of his thought from the few clear, outstanding summits achieved in his maturity.

What Coleridge accomplished was a qualitative change. His inchoate speculations are incomparably more profound than the rationalistic, scholastic, or sentimental theology of the eighteenth century. He was also infinitely better read in the philosophy and theology and literatures of several languages. He was a voice of the revolution in sensibility paralleled abroad by persons as widely separated as Baudelaire and Hegel—both of whom he resembles. Like Blake, Baudelaire, Hölderlin, Stendhal, Coleridge is talking about what we talk about, or at least did until it became apparent in the middle years of the twentieth century that Western civilization was not sick, but had ceased to be alive.

He brought Anglican theology up to date and out into a wider world. Few clergy indeed in his time were familiar with the German language, much less German philosophy and theology, and probably none with the significant literature of the continent. Few, strange as it may seem, read the Cambridge Platonists, Cudworth, Henry More, Whichcote, John Smith, and the rest, the most significant counter movement to English empiricism and rationalism. This possibly was due to the sheer badness of writing of both German and English idealists. The combination of their two turgidities goes far to account for the opacity and disorder of Coleridge's own prose. *Biographia Literaria, Aids to Reflection, The Friend, Confessions of an Enquiring Spirit,* and *On the Constitution of the Church and State* must be read in a context that includes Baudelaire's notebooks and even the decadent diary writers, Amiel, Bashkirtsiev and Barbellion.

Coleridge was penetrating the world of romantic alienation finally defined by Rimbaud and Proust. The argot of technical divinity conceals this from himself. Unfortunately he could no longer transmute the quest for illumination into poetry. The poems of his latter years only say badly what is already formless enough in his prose, but they lead straight to Baudelaire's *"La Cloche Felée,"* the first major poem of spiritual alienation.

Coleridge tirelessly and passionately attacked the eighteenth-century inventors of evidences and proofs for God or Scripture, always with the appeal to the unalloyed experience of faith, the confrontation of the contingent I Am with the absolute It Is. He was quite right to characterize this as purified Lutheranism.

He took over from the Cambridge Platonists and Kant the distinction between two kinds of knowing, which he called reason and understanding. Today we would probably reverse the meanings of these two words as Coleridge uses them. This is an unfortunate habit of Coleridge's; his distinction of act and potency suffers from the same fault. However his "reason" is not emotional intuition. He carefully distinguishes the whole man, acting in comprehension, from the anti-intellectualism of the bigot, the emotionalism of the enthusiast, or the rationalistic, religious apologetic of the orthodox—especially as the latter was represented in the external, mechanical rationalism of Paley, famous for his watch and watchmaker "proof," the argument from design. God, Coleridge pointed out, is not a watchmaker deduced from a watch found in the road, but an experience far more veridical than the watch itself, an experience which blasted away the sensate prudence of the British man in the street to whom Paley appealed. Until the banality of Paley had been banished from the theological universe of discourse, there could be no room for the supernaturalism of the Oxford Movement, not even for the conventional piety of Keble, much less for the sophisticated skepticism of Newman.

Coleridge dismissed the epistemological dilemma which still bedevils British empiricism by simply denying the initial assumption of Locke—*"Nihil est in intellectu sed quod fuerit in sensu"*—with the quip of Leibniz' *"Praeter ipsum intellectum"* The orthodox had been accepting the terms of the deists; Coleridge denied them altogether and moved the dispute to another court. This is his primary importance. English philosophy had continued to attack Hume's skepticism from positions Hume had demolished. Kant and Coleridge after him (and more confusedly the Cambridge Platonists) accepted Hume's attack on rationalism and empiricism, and began over again with Hume's skepticism as the foundation for a new definition of a different kind of "reason."

Justification, whether by faith or the sacraments, had not been a pressing issue for generations. After violent controversy, the Establishment had come to rest content in the contradictory XI and XXVII Articles of Religion, "Wherefore, that we are justified by Faith only, is a most wholesome Doctrine and very full of comfort." "Baptism is . . . a sign of Regeneration or New Birth. And the Baptism of young children is retained." The Protestants took one article, the High Church the other, and rested content.

In *Aids to Reflection* Coleridge put justification by faith in the center of his subjectively validated religion. God is known as the beginning of thought, by an integral response, not by ratiocination or the association of experiences. This response is a moral assent, the assumption of responsibility of the absolute by the contingent—Faith, which justifies and saves prior to any good works, or any works at all. The epistemological process is moral, and begins directly with God. This is philosophical Methodism, without the emotional crisis of Wesleyan "conversion," without the "enthusiasm" of the

Methodist and Evangelical revivals, and of course without "merit." So it is not surprising that Coleridge can find no place for the sacraments of Baptism and the Eucharist except in sentiment, as symbols of Church Order and tradition, and very little place for the Incarnation of the actual historic Jesus.

This judgment may be unfair to Coleridge. His great magnum opus was to include a large section on Baptism, the Eucharist and the historic Jesus, the notes for which were either never written or have not survived. All of his notes are now being published by the Bollingen Foundation, and Coleridge, already complicated enough, turns out to be even more complex and difficult. But his theological influence can only be discussed in terms of what was available then in his published writings. Still he says, "I hope to be saved, not by my faith in Christ, but by the faith of Christ in me."

Kant's "pure speculative reason" becomes Coleridge's "the Higher Reason," operative in the noumenal realm, its object the self. The subject becomes its own object. As Coleridge says in *The Friend,* "Thus God, the soul, eternal truth, etc., are the objects of reason: but they are themselves reason." The Theoretic Reason mediates noumenal (Higher Reason) and phenomenal knowledge (understanding) and validates the latter with the former. With this modified dualism Coleridge escapes from the rigorous monism of the seventeenth and eighteenth centuries, at least to his own satisfaction. Since the Higher Reason operates in the world of self, God, freedom, immortality, the realm of morals, it is the true instrument of the Will and the Will is cut off from the phenomenal world. So the Higher Reason becomes faith.

Initially this would establish a system of double truth, but powerful conceptual entities like these—Will and Higher Reason—tend to devour all around them. Coleridge drifts towards the will mysticism of the late nineteenth century. "As If" creates "Is." This is the metaphysic of radical pragmatism, and lies behind most theological speculation, except Neo-Thomism, from then on. The enemy will say, "The head has surrendered unconditionally to the heart." Coleridge shies away from the ultimate consequences embraced by some of his successors, in favor of the existential confrontation of total experience, but the practical consequence endures. The Higher Reason is an eye opening on the immediate vision of God of the mystics and that eye is opened by the will.

A hundred years would pass before it became common again to say, "Since the statements about the noumenal order have no phenomenological basis, they are pseudo-statements." Coleridge's descendants can only retort, "The same to you and many of them." In Coleridge are foreshadowed most of the post-Kantian disputes.

If faith is not objectively negotiable but dependent on each man alone, the direct communion of the faithful on earth is dissolved in transcendent individual communication coming only through God. The Incarnation, and still more, the sacraments become unreal, and there is only the conversation of omnipotence and contingency. This is the road out of Coleridge or Kant taken by Kierkegaard and the neo-Lutherans, Barth and his followers. Newman, action Catholicism, the neo-Catholics and the Catholic Modernists took another.

In practice Coleridge simply emotionalized the reason and gave it over to the rule of the will confronted with the life of faith. "TRY IT," says Coleridge. This is precisely the "grammar of assent." The will after all is stimulated by the phenomenological world. Does Coleridge choose one of these alternatives consistently? No. But no philosophical system can be closed in perfect consistency. Godel's Proof applies to metaphysics as well as mathematics. Coleridge clings to the Church.

Coleridge shifts his ground completely to say that proofs in the noumenal realm of the Higher Reason are only reflections of processes which hold for the understanding in the phenomenal realm and cannot be logically final—only convincing

—by a leap—of the will. The rationality of the universe, the order of nature, the law of contradiction, the unity of thought and being, are only plausible revelations, like the ontological proof of the existence of God, or the specific revelations of Scriptures and Church. This way lies a Humean, if not a simply skeptical, Catholicism. It is permissible to believe anything that works, can be plausibly proved, cannot be disproved, and satisfies the will via the emotions. All that is necessary is to purge Christianity of errors of fact and disprovable notions, and move religion bodily into the realm of its own transcendental consistency. Faith sees all being with the anagogic eye.

This is etherialization, the climax of the movement from tribal cult to world religion. It had already happened on a minor scale at the critical point when Christianity moved out into the wide world of Classical civilization. Origen and St. Clement, although always saving the literal meanings, did the same thing by treating Scripture as an inexhaustible system of metaphors. After Coleridge, the main task of theology becomes, in one guise or another, etherialization, or, as Marx and Engels would call it, the transformation of quantity into quality.

Since an etherialized system cannot violate the mundane understanding, it becomes easier to believe mysteries and impossibilities—that the infant Jesus came through the maidenhead of his mother like light through glass—than to believe in the troubled factual narrative of the latest Gospel synthesis. So Lord Acton could say, "I have never been troubled by an intellectual doubt," to the confusion of simple minds ever since. The only rule is *"Entia non sunt multiplicanda praeter necessitatum"*—a matter of taste—not certainly of the logic of the understanding, because nature too obviously multiplies entities beyond necessity.

Coleridge introduces into the indeterminacy he had created a determinant which is in fact esthetic and socially conditioned

—"the law of conscience which peremptorily commands belief." Following on this, the voice of God calling in the garden, and the Will responding, come all the religious emotions, the loneliness of the soul in the abyss of contingency and the welcome comfort of the accepted Fatherhood of God. "TRY IT," says Coleridge, "Christianity is not a theory or a speculation—not a philosophy of life, but a life, and a living process—TRY IT." "The facts of Christianity are not invented by imagination, but they are transmuted by it from a lower to a higher form."

Coleridge's speculations about the Trinitarian process follow naturally from his will philosophy, and lead to a triadic dynamism much like that attributed to the Hegelian dialectic. Like most theogonies, Coleridge's is really a disguised psychology, a projection of the processes of the self. This may be interesting reading, but its influence was minimal and much of it has not been published until today.

Many critics have made a great deal of Coleridge's theories of the relations of Church and State. They are unreal because they are posited on the assumption of a Christian society which had ceased to exist in his day, and has vanished in ours. He thought of the Church as two churches, an Establishment of the clerisy, the *responsibles,* the liberal professions and arts, and the administrators of policy, and this body intertwined between, and nourishing and being nourished by, the purely secular power and the Church of the spirit. This is Plato's *Republic* as worked out by Thomas Arnold and the nineteenth-century British Public School mystique. No doubt many members of the British Establishment still exist who think of society in these terms, but alas, it is, and probably always was, a hoax, the institutional form of the Social Lie. It assumes what does not exist, a Christian society. Via F. D. Maurice, William Morris, Ruskin, and the like, Coleridge might be called the originator of Christian Socialism, Guild Socialism, and other more benign theories of a sanctified, corporative state. This is a beautiful dream and something like it doubtless would have come to be, if the Catholic Church had won the world. Today, as the Church faces apocalypse and an underground life, it is an irrelevant pattern for the Christian community, although medievalists of the older generation may well think it by far the most Catholic of all Coleridge's ideas.

Coleridge taught apologetics how to talk to the alienated clerisy—the clerkly class dispossessed and prostituted by a predatory society. Newman summed up Coleridge's qualitative change of venue for all English theology after him:

And while history in prose and verse was thus made the instrument of Church feelings and opinions [by Scott], a philosophical basis for the same was under formation in England by a very original thinker [Coleridge], who, while he indulged a liberty of speculation which no Christian can tolerate, and advanced conclusions which were often heathen rather than Christian, yet after all instilled a higher philosophy into inquiring minds, than they had hitherto been accustomed to accept.

—*The Prospects of the Anglican Church*

The Evolution of Anglo-Catholicism

II. From the Oxford Movement to Lux Mundi

History seems to occur according to the theories of the philosophers of history who are contemporary with its facts. Certainly the early years of the nineteenth century were very Hegelian times. Again and again social forces and organized movements were pushed to critical points where they turned into their opposites, or where "quantity turned into quality." This was especially true of the Little Counter Reformation that accompanied the Holy Alliance's restoration after the fall of Napoleon. In the case of Lamennais the whole process was embodied in the life of one man, developed consistently and in a straight line. In England things moved slower. Development depended on the resolution of conflicting forces and the influence of antagonistic individuals. Furthermore, England, with Austria and Russia, was the source of reaction, not as France, or the Rhineland, or North Italy, the victim. But it was socially and economically a peculiar kind of reaction. England was the most industrially advanced state in Europe, and the ideologue, or at least rhetorician, of British reaction was completely a man of the Enlightenment—Edmund Burke. Whatever his political maneuvers, he was the voice of a secular society ruled by an oligarchy of aristocratic capitalists, who were great entrepreneurs of the oncoming industrial civilization because, as great landowners, they possessed almost unlimited resources for capital investment. The economics of the Manchester School, the belief that the sum total of private evils would result in the public good, was not only secular and immoral; in practice it shattered the structure inherited

233

from the old feudal society and created one of hopelessly antagonistic classes tending towards final, total atomization.

It is this irreparable schism in society that produced, by immediate reflex, the schism in the soul of what might be called the Romantic Left—Sade, Blake, Holderlin, Stendhal, Baudelaire, and not least, Lammenais. In England the secular society was larger than on the Continent, more democratized; its material benefits seeped lower down the hierarchy of castes and classes. Reflecting this consent of the majority was the almost complete secularization of religion. By far the most conspicuous things on the British landscape, urban or rural, were the steeples of churches, and dotted amongst them were almost as many chapels of the Dissenters. The architectural symbols of a homogeneous society have misled many even to this day. England had ceased to be a Christian state.

Coleridge had envisaged a reorganized England, once again socially dense, hierarchically structured, and governed by a supernaturally sanctioned clerisy, a system which curiously enough greatly resembled the Enlightenment's notion of the Confucian polity of the Chinese Empire with the addition of the mystery and ritual of a revamped medievalism. This idea, a kind of metaphysical Radical Toryism, was never to die out in England. Ruskin, the Pre-Raphaelites, William Morris, Belloc, Chesterton, Eric Gill, Herbert Read—it survives to this day and remains at the heart of the vision of most Anglo-Catholicism.

That is not the way the Oxford Movement, the mother of the Catholic revival, started out. It started as reaction pure and simple, but reaction committed to an unassimilable principle—the idea of a Christian society. The hysteria of the response of the Oxford Reformers to the first moves of the secular state strikes us today as comic, a tempest in a vicarage teapot, until we understand that behind bigotry and old-fogeyism, these men were the survivors of a cohesive society which they thought still existed around them. They were oblivious

to the fact that society was in the process of atomizing itself
and that the process was irreversible and would continue for
a century. In such a context any theory of, any movement
towards a coherent, cohesive social order was bound to be
revolutionary if pushed to conclusion. They did not know
this. They thought they were conservatives, counterrevolu-
tionaries, reactionaries.

In 1832 the Established Church in England, long incompatible with the secularizing society, had become in detail
intolerable. In 1833 there appeared anonymously the extraordinary *Black Book,* an exposé of abuses of the state church
almost incredible to us today. Many bishoprics, cathedral
chapters and certain great churches were immensely wealthy
and disposed of thousands of livings and benefices with income
sufficient to move their recipients immediately into the lower
echelon of the upper classes. The aristocracy, even the landed
gentry and many old feudal corporations disposed of other
livings—perhaps the majority—which ranged in income from
a modest competence to modest wealth. Evelyn Waugh once
pointed out that the standard of living of a successful Holly-
wood movie star or director did not differ greatly from that
of an early nineteenth-century country rector with a well-en-
dowed living—the differences were alcohol, sexual promiscuity
and a swimming pool. These livings were awarded, except in
rare instances, with little or no regard to learning or religion,
commonly to the younger sons of the aristocracy.

In most of the wealthiest benefices and in almost half of
all the others the vicar or the rector was not resident. The duties
of his pastoral care were discharged by curates, seldom more
learned or religious than their employers, who were paid a
poverty wage, a hundred pounds a year or less. Such a minister
was dependent upon his house, the produce of a few acres,
"stole fees," and the gifts of his congregation to keep his
usually large family above the level of destitution. The Russian
Church in 1830 might seem to us to be very exotic and very

barbarous. Economically the situation of the pastors was much the same, just a different flavor of ignorance, superstition, semi-literacy, Erastianism, and lack of sanitation. Perhaps the Russian clergy preserved more vestiges of piety.

The picture drawn in the *Black Book* has established itself in history, but it is overdrawn. Things were like that, but they weren't all like that. The Established Church had preserved the idea and the form of a supernaturally sanctioned clerkly class, a caste of *responsibles,* devoted to learning, prayer, and the cure of souls. Scattered all through the body of the English Church, like white blood cells in the bloodstream of a very sick man, were dedicated men who spent their lives living up to their priestly vocation, piously unaware that their colleagues looked on them as fools, or at the best, fossils.

It was not the theology of the Established Church or its pastoral relations, however defective or nonexistent in many instances these were, but its structure, which was intolerable to a society entering the era of free competition and capital accumulation. Nowhere was this more evident than in the Irish Anglican Church, where the old bishoprics were supported by the full power of the state and the enforced tribute of the entire population, Roman Catholic or Presbyterian. In the early summer of 1833 Parliament moved to suppress ten of the most redundant of the Irish Anglican bishoprics. And on July 14 John Keble of Oriel College preached a sermon on the national apostasy—the church in mortal danger. For the rest of his life John Henry Newman was to say that this sermon marked the beginning of the Oxford Movement. Reading it today it seems to us hysterical and hypocritical rant, yet John Keble was a gentle soul and far from being a hysteriac or a ranter. The secular state had moved to remedy a terrible injustice—at considerable profit to itself. The parliamentary agitation for reform of the Established Church was motivated by sentiments of profitable equity and respect for the religious liberties of Protestants, Roman Catholics, Jews and non-religious people, whose numbers already were approaching a majority even in England—if we include the bulk of the population who were really indifferent and who conformed to the Church only rarely for convenience. Parliament was beginning, in practice and with maximum pious hypocrisy, to recognize that Great Britain was not really a Christian nation, much less an episcopal one, and that the Church as the spiritual executive arm of the society had lost its monopoly of power. Keble ignored all this. He attacked Parliament, and the organs of the state, and behind them the consenting population, on moral grounds. There was no hint that the Establishment itself was, by its very nature, profoundly immoral. For Keble it was the other way around. The indifferentism and infidelity and even mockery with which the unsanctified viewed the Established Church was due to their own evil; in fact to their allegiance to a personal devil.

The Church is a supernatural institution whose officers are the direct descendants of the Apostles; their authority is guaranteed and made holy by sacrament, by the direct physical action of the Holy Spirit descending, by physical imposition of hands, from the flame of Pentecost. England is a Christian nation, absolutely bound in all matters spiritual, and in many temporal, to love, honor and obey the voice of the Third Person of the Trinity speaking through the Living Apostles— amongst whom of course are the Irish Bishops.

Hildebrand could not have been more forthright—as a matter of fact, he was less so, and he spoke from more substantial grounds. It is easy to see why Newman felt the national apostasy sermon launched the Oxford Movement. Behind the pious rhetoric it is all there. Society cannot escape its Christian nature, except into conscious sin. Spiritual authority is supernatural, hierarchic, and in its own realm, absolute. The Church is the guardian and purveyor of embodied grace, of the sacraments which place the Christian in direct communication with God. Outside this sanctified body there can be no salvation.

The function of the state in all its organs—the British state in 1833—is to enforce the communion of the citizens in this supernatural body. Anything outside it is simply sin. Authority is finally vested in the living representatives of the Apostles and that authority in any final confrontation overrides any other authority whatever.

Here are all the claims and contradictions of the Oxford Movement. Its primary fallacious assumption that nations in the nineteenth century were still Christian; its oblivious blindness to the world of ordinary affairs around it—Keble spoke with the unworldly isolation of a medieval anchorite—its glorification of what after all is only an administrative structure—episcopacy—to the point where not Baptism or the Lord's Supper but Holy Orders, the apostolic succession, becomes the principal sacrament, and last, but not least, what seems to us its unfortunate tone of hysterical self-righteousness.

It is easy for us to think of the Oxford Reformers as bad men. They were not. They were simply innocent, sealed away from the social and religious realities of the world around them by the peculiar monastic life of the Oxford colleges of their day. They were no more priggish or bigoted than the other Christians of their time. As their movement grew, they certainly demonstrated that truly religious values were still matters of life and death importance to vast numbers of Englishmen. The unreality of the world which they constructed for themselves was eventually to prove their salvation. Confronted with the facts of life, the Oxford Counter Reformation would turn into its opposite. Beginning as the most intense reaction, it would eventually become the most active and comprehensive and enduring movement of Catholic liberalism.

The story of the Movement has been told innumerable

times. It is a historical romance played out on a limited stage and full of the most intense drama. To judge from the immense number of successful books still being published, it fascinates thousands of people who have no interest whatever in religious questions. I have no desire to retell the story but it would be to the point to summarize the characters and careers of the leaders of the Oxford Movement and define the relation of each to the growth of a New Catholicism.

Even in the heyday of Newman's leadership, and certainly after he left, adherents of the Movement were known not as Newmanites but as Puseyites. Dr. Edward Bouverie Pusey, Regius Professor of Hebrew, was the only professional theologian of the group and one of the few who came to the movement from a High Church, rather than Evangelical, background. He was also the only one familiar with contemporary European theology. In fact he had deliberately gone to Germany to study "infidelity" at its sources for the purpose of combating it. He was also the only leader of the Movement whose family were wealthy aristocrats.

Pusey spent only four and twelve months studying in Germany altogether, but that was sufficient to make him far more of a scholar in Biblical criticism and patristics than anybody else in England. He gave bottom to the movement, for his contributions were nothing if not weighty. His first contribution to the famous "Tracts for the Times" was the thirty-fifth, on Baptism, a tract of over three hundred pages, inexpressibly dreary reading today. Pusey has been shut out from posterity by his prose style. Even his most controversial sermons are unbearably dull and his own translations of the Fathers of the Church make those passionate men so boring that today we can read them only by the most powerful exertion of the will, no mean accomplishment in the translation of Augustine, Clement, or Origen, masters of classical rhetoric. Nevertheless it was Pusey's concentration on Scripture, on the Fathers and on the Apostles that gave the Movement a content that could be passed on to the next generation of Anglican Catholic reformers.

He inaugurated comprehensive projects of translation of the Fathers and republication of the great English divines which would take final form in the many volumes of the *Library of the Fathers,* the *Ante-Nicene Christian Library,* the *Select Library of Nicene and Post-Nicene Fathers,* and the *Library of Anglo-Catholic Theology.* Although schoolboys in England were caned if they could not write bad Greek and Latin verses, there is little evidence that the English clergy read extensively in the Fathers and Doctors of the Church in the original tongues, but the huge sets inspired by Dr. Pusey can be found in most large second-hand bookshops in the English-speaking world to this day, and give evidence of once having been thoroughly read.

It is impossible to overestimate the importance of this availability of the past. Pusey's sermons may be uninspiring, even Newman's may sometimes depend on a bygone religious sensibility, and a bygone taste in style, but it is impossible to read the powerful minds that put together a Church, a communion, a polity and a philosophy that would survive both the collapse of the Western Roman Empire and the establishment of the Church by Constantine without being deeply moved. The Oxford Reformers themselves never spoke of themselves as Puseyites, or Newmanites, or Anglo-Catholics (least of all High Churchmen, which they most certainly were not) but as Apostolics, and their appeal was to the Apostolic life, and the life of the Church of the Fathers, when the Church was very far from being an establishment, but was a saving remnant in a dissolute and dissolving society—a position in fact almost exactly like that, did they but know it, of the Church of the faithful in the days of George IV and William IV and of the horrors of what Marx called the period of the primitive accumulation of capital.

Each of the Oxford Reformers was an ancestor of a type of clergyman that would endure in the Anglican Church until well into the twentieth century. Pusey was the only one from an aristocratic family or one that remained wealthy—Newman's father went bankrupt. This harsh, uningratiating man made the movement fashionable. Before his wife's death he was in the process of becoming a society clergyman of the common type. After her death he became convinced that God had punished him for loving her more than Himself. Pusey turned into a dishevelled fanatic, wore a hair shirt and subjected himself to penances that embarrassed the conventional and domestic Keble, who he insisted on making his confessor. This of course only made him more fashionable.

About the time of Newman's defection, the members of the movement re-established auricular confession as a general practice of their lay followers, and soon as a matter of obligation. They had almost from the beginning gone to confession to one another. Pusey became a fashionable confessor, although penitents had to seek him out in his isolated parish.

It is usually said that the obsession of the Oxford Reformers with the depravity of man was an inheritance of their evangelical youth, but only Newman was raised as a typical twice-born evangelical. Furthermore a glance at Roman Catholic, Lutheran, or High Church manuals of devotion of the late eighteenth and early nineteenth century reveals that conviction of utter sinfulness was no monopoly of the followers of the Wesleys and Whitefield. For that matter, it is the constant reference to the sinfulness of the congregation that distinguishes, over and above the comparative triviality of liturgics, the language of the Book of Common Prayer from that of the Roman or Orthodox Mass and breviary.

Pusey, Keble and Newman all wrote devotional works. They all, but Pusey's most of all, are top heavy with guilt. Prayer, meditation, and contemplation show little progression. Anyone who took them literally would find it almost impossible to get beyond the logjam of his own sin and into the un-ruffled waters of contemplation. Yet none of the leaders who, as far as the Ten Commandments were concerned, led prac-tically blameless lives, seem to have been aware of their own besetting faults, spiritual pride, social irresponsibility, and willful ignorance. This was precisely the kind of piety members of the English upper and middle classes found most congenial in the days of the dark, satanic mills.

Pusey more than anyone else was also responsible for a re-lentless emphasis on fundamentals of Catholic doctrine and practice. He was anything but a Ritualist. For most of his life he was content to celebrate the Eucharist in surplice and scarf, long after chasubles, candles and incense had become common in the city parishes of the Movement. Similarly he avoided the hundred flowers of post-Tridentine doctrine and devotion which became popular after the middle of the century. He was uninterested in the Sacred Heart or the Immaculate Con-ception. As Newman became hypnotically fixed on the author-ity of the Papacy, it is obvious that Pusey ceased to be able to understand him. Pusey was content with the Church of the Fathers and the early Councils that he had constructed around himself and surrounded by an impenetrable wall. Again this might be called pride and ignorance, but it was also rigorous insistence on fundamentals. The basic flaw in Pusey's system was the terrific tension set up in its narrow prayer life, at once intense and impoverished.

What did John Keble contribute, not to the movement but to the future of the Catholic revival? Really very little, except again, an enduring clerical type. He was unbelievably bigoted, but his bigotry had a certain comic charm. He would cut dead or overtly insult lifelong friends for petty differences of theol-ogy or even for churchly political divagations. He was unable to recognize the validity of any intellectual differences with himself. Those who did not agree with him were both sinful and stupid. Since his intellectual capacities were of the slightest, this confined his social contacts to a narrow world. Keble did not think of the materialists and utilitarians and positivists of his day as stupid and sinful. If he thought of them at all it was very rarely and with a shudder for the hopelessly damned. His condemnations were reserved for members of the Church who showed tendencies toward monothelitism and Oxonians who voted for Broad Churchmen for professorships.

Within his extremely limited world Keble was a sweet and good humored man, who loved everybody who agreed with him and minded him. Can we say he established the type of simple-minded Anglo-Catholic country clergyman? Perhaps the qualifications are unnecessary. Keble was just a typical clergyman of any socially acceptable denomination. Without this type the Church would not have endured past the first century. Ironically he was Professor of Poetry at Oxford, a position at least as respected as the laureateship. He seems to have had no feeling for poetry whatsoever, and his religious verses show no feeling for religion in the deepest sense either. Geoffrey Faber, whose *Oxford Apostles* is corrupted by too much amateur psychoanalysis, places his finger on a serious defect in all the leaders of the movement. They wrote terrible doggerel. Newman and Keble had reputations as poets, Newman even to this day in some circles. The others wrote occasional verse. Only John Mason Neale, of the more or less independent Cambridge Catholic revival, who translated an immense number of Greek and Latin hymns, had any real feeling for poetry whatever. The poetry of Anglo-Catholicism would not come until Christina Rossetti. It's not just that they wrote doggerel; if they appreciated poetry they did so for the wrong reasons, wrong even for eary Victorian times.

Richard Hurrell Froude was the older brother of the historian, J. A. Froude, who early left the movement for skepticism. Froude again established a type, the young Anglo-Catholic, interested above all else in outraging the Establishment, who, if a layman, rattles his rosary against the pew during Holy Communion in a Low Church, and who, if a clergyman, uses immense quantities of incense and preaches sermons on the miracle of Fatima and venerates both Pacelli and Charles Stuart, King and Martyr. When he came up to Oxford from Dartington in Devon, a passionate sportsman and rider to hounds, his beauty and vitality struck everyone with awe. Already he was well advanced with tuberculosis. It was probably Koch's bacillus rather than principle which accounted for the febrile, impassioned, deliberate defiance of his behavior and his writings. When after his death Newman published his manuscripts, the *Remains of Richard Hurrell Froude,* in two volumes, he caused a major crisis in the Church.

Froude was the only member of the group who from the beginning was Romeward set, in both theology and practice, and he was the only one who commonly went to Roman Catholic services, not only on the Continent but in England. Most of not just the Oxford Reformers, but members of the Catholic Revival until recent years, never attended Roman Catholic services. Many of them had, and have, never entered a Roman Catholic church. Froude was to have many descendants, most of whom would eventually leave the Anglican Church, from the group of young Turks around Newman to Father Ronald Knox. A characteristic common to all has been a compulsive obsession with inconsequentials, as can be discovered by reading Knox's *A Spiritual Aeneid.* Ronald Knox was not the first person of whom it was said around Oxford that he was two weeks ahead in the Breviary and two months behind in the Prayer Book, both of which he felt bound in supernatural obedience to read simultaneously.

Yet had it not been for the "Romanizing" tendencies set in train by Hurrell Froude, the Anglican Church today might still be a rather stark but holy spiritual environment. Froude was a High Tory of a purely mythological sort, as unlike Disraeli or the Chamberlains as it would be possible to imagine. He knew that England was bourgeois through and through, and he was out to *epaté* the bourgeois with all the ritual and romance and colorful superstition he could muster.

Froude was an actor on a far wider stage than the narrow parochial and academic one of Keble and Pusey, the stage of romantic revolt, alienation and rejection of all the values of the acquisitive society. In some ways he could be called the most influential of the first leaders of the movement—except that in fact his actual influence pretty much died with him, to revive as Ritualism after 1850. Its grave danger was its tendency, especially in controversy, to confuse the instruments of Catholic life with its meaning, to confuse ends and means. Far more than any of his colleagues, Froude was aware of the terrible social evils of his time. His answer was that of a romantic reactionary, but at least it was an answer. In the next generation it would turn into its opposite. By the middle of the next century priests would be saying Mass in the streets at sit-ins and demonstrations.

Newman has been called not only the greatest, but the only Catholic theologian of the nineteenth century. He has been called not a theologian at all. He has also been called one of the founders of anti-rationalism and anti-humanism, along with the Marquis de Sade, of a line that leads straight to Nechaev, Nietzsche and Lenin. Carlyle said he had the mind of a rabbit. Many who shared none of his beliefs read him for "the most beautiful English prose in two hundred years," others considered his style syrupy and evasive. What this all means is not that Newman was a neurotic bundle of contradictions, but that his was a most complex character; a personality more sensitive and sophisticated, and a mind broader and deeper, than his colleagues'.

Although he was the public spokesman—today we could call him the public relations man—of the movement and its political organizer, his development only paralleled the movement and eventually diverged sharply from it. Newman was engaged in creating a new orthodoxy. Keble and Pusey were quite confident they were in possession of one which only had to be uncovered. Newman was seeking a religion. The others never lost it. Although he wrote the majority of the "Tracts for the Times," preached and published his tremendously moving sermons, and wrote at least three theological works that are still of great importance during the years that he was considered the leader of the movement, his real and enduring influence was to come later. At the time he was simply over the heads of almost all his audience. Not least was this true of the little group of young men, children of Hurrell Froude, or for that matter, de Maistre, defiant, dramatic, *jeunesse dorée* of political reaction and romantic Catholicism, obviously Romeward bound. They entered the Roman Church with him and almost immediately became his enemies, for their Catholicism was essentially political and esthetic—not in combination but in compound, esthetic-politics or political esthetics. It is significant that once they cut loose from the middle class life of the Establishment, most of them moved far to the left of Newman.

Bourgeois-baiting was the last thing in the world Newman was interested in. Although he was the only middle class member of the original leadership he scarcely knew the middle class existed. The very special aristocratic mercantile family-centered life of the Newmans provides a strong support for the very shakily substantiated notion that his father was Jewish. Also that his father failed in business after Newman had enjoyed a childhood in surroundings of quite considerable and very gracious wealth is significant. The number of great *alienees* of whom this is true is astonishing. An established and thoroughly cultivated capitalist family which loses its wealth seems to explode and blow its children completely out of the social pyramid, where they become members of a new aristocracy of the intellect, a clerkly caste of *responsibles,* suspended outside the class structure.

In the harbor of Marseille, on his trip to Italy with Froude, Newman may have refused to even look at the detested tricolor flag on a nearby vessel of the French navy, but he was not a real Tory, even an archaizing Tory like Froude. He was an anomaly. It was only after the Established Church, thoroughly Catholicized by the inheritors of the Oxford Movement, became a refuge for anomalies, that Newman, so to speak invisibly, returned to it.

In the later nineteenth century there were probably more philosophical Newmanites in the French Church than in the English, either Roman or Anglican. The opening of early nineteenth-century Anglicanism to a large new spiritual world is Newman's primary contribution to the early years of the Catholic revival. Had it not been for him the Establishment could have assimilated the religion of Pusey and Keble. They never realized it, but when Newman left the Oxford Movement he made it unassimilable. At first it did not leave Toryism. Toryism left it. As the movement had begun in reaction to a maneuver of the state, so it came to an end, not with Newman's defection, but with a change in phase in the state. Toryism became Victorian Toryism. That was something that bore little resemblance to the high Toryism of the eighteenth century and the Regency, and none whatever to the idealized Stuart and Laudian Toryism of the old guard of the Oxford Movement.

As a young man the most dynamic leader of the next generation, Steward Headlam, listened to but one sermon of Pusey's and found him a crashing bore. Already things had changed so much that Headlam was unaware that he would never have existed as what he was, had it not been for Pusey. On this dichotomy and generation gap Newman, safe across the Tiber, was to have an indirect, underground influence. So it is most profitable, I think, to treat of Newman by himself, in the much wider, and at the same time, much more intensely personal, context which he created for himself, and which is his real contribution to "the development of doctrine."

Where had all the flowers gone? After Newman crossed the Tiber, religion, all the rage for fifteen years, suddenly became unfashionable at Oxford. All the bright young men who had become Roman Catholics were gone. They could not then be members of the Oxford Colleges, even had they wished, without provoking the wrath of the "magisterium." As any movement does when suffering a severe tactical defeat, the Catholic Revival consolidated its position, and operated on interior lines. It also shifted its base. The stark domestic monasticism which was Catholic practice as understood by Keble and Pusey survives even to this day, but it does not provide a way of life negotiable at large in the vast, secularized modern world.

What had the Oxford Movement gained? Whatever Parliament or Cabinet or throne might think, it had freed the Church from its Babylonian captivity as a department of State. It had returned to the Church its own authority, a collective rather than an absolute authority, deriving from the traditions of a collective authority—"the Councils of the undivided Church" and the Apostolic Succession, the latter a supernatural community in which Peter and his descendants were only *primus inter pares*. It had restored the liturgy to not just "decency and order" but to dignity, beauty, and wonder. It had made the sacrament of Holy Communion central to the life of the Church and of the individual Christian. It had restored the rites of passage, birth, death, puberty, vocation, eating and drinking, conversion, sexual intercourse as moments when transcendence, through the community, suffused and glorified human life.

The sacramental life is the essence of Catholicism, and holds people to the Church long after they have ceased to believe in its more undigestible dogmas. After 1845 the sacramental life was available to any member of the Anglican Church who wished to seek it. Most specially, the Tractarians, but above all the now so boring Pusey, brought together their leading principles and merged them in one vision—the life of faith as lived in, as in air, a transformed world. The Incarnation, the Atonement, the communion of the saints, the sacramental system, they were all one being—the living Body of Christ. They presented the Church as itself a Eucharist. To put it mildly, this was not a common notion elsewhere, least of all at Rome, in those days, as Newman would find out. Time would come when with Teilhard and others its full implications would be drawn out—being is prayer. "If I be lifted up, I will draw all things to Me."

The movement made prayer central to the daily life of the devout Anglican in a different way than the evangelical movement had done. Prayer was not founded on conversion and did not culminate in pentecostal possession. It began in penance and moved from petition to contemplation, and with daily practice left the orant in an habitude of abiding meditation. This was the state of soul that the doing of Catholic religion had produced in Nicholas Ferrer's community at Little Gidding, in the household of St. Thomas More, and in the lives of the medieval secular mystics. In other words it had restored to the treasury of the English Church its own special talent, distinguished by its lineaments, and marked with its values.

Incidentally it had purged Catholic belief and practice of non-essentials—whether "Romish" or "corrupt following of the Apostles" or not. It demonstrated that Catholic life was possible with collective authority, with a married clergy, alongside of voluntary celibacy and monasticism, with communion in both kinds, with a national vernacular liturgy, and without grossly superstitious practices. Considering the state of affairs in the Church in 1830, this was a tremendous accomplishment —considering the state of society in 1845 on the brink of famine, economic crisis, social breakdown, revolution, in the heyday of Liberal economics and moral hypocrisy. Yet how-

250 &~ *The Elastic Retort*

ever deep the prayer life of the Catholic revival, it was still narrow and isolated.

As with so many other institutions and movements it was 1848, the year of revolution everywhere, that was to break the shell of Tractarian Anglo-Catholicism. The new force was to come from the most unexpected quarter, the leaders to be men whom Newman had looked upon as hopelessly benighted or willfully malevolent. The first edition of the *Apologia pro Vita Sua* started off with an attack on Charles Kingsley, the Broad Churchman and Christian Socialist, so uncharitable that Newman, little given in his Anglican days to mercy to his theological opponents, later suppressed it. Kingsley was a young associate of Frederick D. Maurice and the Quaker John M. Ludlow, founders of Christian Socialism and English disciples of Lamenais. Maurice was also the greatest of the descendants of Coleridge and may have been the leading Anglican theologian of the nineteenth century after Newman's departure. Even more than Newman he spent his life at the turmoil center of the most violent controversy, with the significant difference that his controversies, unlike Newman's, were always foci of ever widening issues, whose ramifications extended out into, and permeated, the secular society. It is from Maurice that twentieth century English Catholic modernism stems, quite as much as from the Oxford Movement.

John Frederick Denison Maurice, the son of a Unitarian minister, was raised in a religious environment of radical Dissent. His early years were spent with Quakers and Unitarians and he had friends amongst the founders of the Irvingite "Catholic Apostolic Church," all three properly called anti-Protestant Dissent. Ordained in 1834, by 1837 he had become a sacramentalist, but of his own special kind, and was looked upon as one of the leaders of the Tractarian movement at Cambridge. As the Oxford men embodied their university's authoritarianism, so did Maurice the empiricism of Cambridge. He was possibly the first Englishman to believe that Catholicism might justify itself empirically as a way of life without the support of absolute conviction in the existence of God or the future life or a revealed Scripture. He himself of course believed, but at least he openly and consciously admitted religious pragmatism as a reasonable argument. Newman was of the same opinion, but he so disguised and confused it in his own mind that it emerges only in the writings of his more radical followers. From Pascal to the present, those who admit the argument of a purely pragmatic, "agnostic Catholicism" seem always to have been those whose own direct mystical awareness of God was most intense.

To Maurice, Catholicism was a way of life, lived in the world but over against it, as witness and catalyst. He took Catholicism as he found it, largely in a purged Roman practice. He was little interested in an historical continuity with the liturgics and dogmatic theology imagined for the Apostles. John Mason Neale had made the study of the great Cappadocian theologian poets popular in Cambridge religious circles. It is remarkable how much Maurice's fundamental conception of the sacramental life resembles that of the Russian Orthodoxy which descends from the Cappadocians. For him the sacrifice of the Mass was a temporal appearance of the eternal sacrifice of Calvary. The cross is central, not in an actuarial way, but in a metaphysical one not unlike that of the crux and *flagrat* of Jakob Boehme and his descendants, St. Martin and von Baader. For Maurice the actual rite, as he said it in a church in a poor slum, was more immediately symbolized, as it was in Russian Orthodoxy, by the phyloxeny of Abraham. We offer to God his creatures, and through them ourselves, and He enters the offering and makes it Himself the embodiment of the absolute act of love. The three Persons of the Trinity partake of the nourishment offered by a herdsman, "just a wandering Aramaean," under a shade tree at the edge of the desert, before a tent that smells of camels and sheep and garlic, and of hard-worked men and women, and the herdsmen partake of Them.

"The world is charged with the glory of God," "Turn but a stone and start a wing/ Tis you tis your estranged faces that miss the many splendored thing." Maurice saw the glory of the supernatural all about him, not least, hovering like the Shekinah over the tabernacle in the desert, over the slum parishes into which he led the third generation of young Anglo-Catholic priests, and for which he fought so passionately. Pusey inspired respect; Keble, affection; Newman, in his Anglican years, the love of disciples for a master; Maurice inspired simply love, which, when it is so simple, is supernatural love. We can feel it glowing through the Victorian prose of his sermons and theological works to this day. His followers could say with the Psalmist, "Lo my cup runneth over," for he opened them up with his own love, to be filled with the honey and oil and wine of charity, hope, and faith.

Faith—faith for Maurice was the Catholic life of supernatural love. He was very little troubled by the dilemmas of credal belief. For him the mysteries of Scripture or the Church were images embodying its wonder. Everything was miraculous to his eyes, most of all the orders of nature and supernature which converge and cross in the soul of man. So he welcomed the discoveries of science, whether geology, paleontology, or biology, or the application of the methods of science to the criticism of the Bible, and was fond in sermons of holding up Darwin as a model of patience and humility in the devotion to truth. Early in his career he was deprived of his professorships at Cambridge for advocating a modified universalism, for expressing the hope that the souls in hell would eventually cease to be punished and would come to enjoy, not the glory of heaven, but happiness according to their own lights. Far more than the evolution controversy and the literal inspiration of scripture, this was the touchstone of nineteenth-century orthodoxy. Disbelief in a deity, less moral than most men, who would condemn weak and fallible souls to eternal fire, made one a Broad Churchman. From then on, his life was a series of controversies and the root of his trouble was always the same —the catholicity of his life and concern, the all inclusiveness of his ideal of Christlike responsibility. For this reason the main body of the Catholic movement fought shy of him. His popularity was largely amongst Broad Churchmen until the last years of the century saw the growth of a conscious Catholic Modernism. He parted with his early Christian Socialist associates because they were making their movement an exclusive, intolerant sect.

Stewart Duckworth Headlam and the group of extreme Ritualist slum priests around him on one hand, and on the other Charles Gore, head of Pusey House, and then Bishop of Oxford, with the other contributors to the theological symposium *Lux Mundi,* represent the two wings of development of a modern Catholic faith and practice out of the teaching and example of Maurice. Headlam was certainly an *enfant terrible.* In the days when priests were being sent to jail for putting candles and crucifixes on the altar and wearing chasubles, Headlam, in a series of churches, St. John's Drury Lane, St. Matthew's Bethnal Green, St. Michael's Shoreditch, introduced immediately a full assortment of contemporary Roman Catholic devotions—rosaries, stations of the cross, eventually benediction of the Blessed Sacrament. Even far more outrageous to the Establishment, he founded the Church and Stage Guild, welcomed actors and actresses at communion, and got himself temporarily refused a license by the archbishop for his pains. He not only introduced public devotions to the Blessed Virgin and high Masses on her feasts, including the Assumption and Immaculate Conception, he founded and sheltered in his parish halls the Guild of St. Matthew, the first organized socialist group in England. Fully as much as Teilhard de Chardin in a later day, Headlam and the group of priests associated with

him welcomed not only the discoveries of physical and biological science, the immense age of the earth and the evolution
of man, but the destruction by the Higher Criticism of the
literal truth of an infallible Bible. Headlam saw nineteenth-
century science as freeing man for a pure religion suffused by
the divine power of Jesus Christ—the Word of God inspiriting
all scientific study, the wisdom in Lyell or in Darwin, the same
wisdom which danced in the Solomonic hymns—the Truth.
This was bourgeois-baiting with a vengeance and helps to explain the irrational malignancy of Parliament's persecution
of the parochial Anglo-Catholic clergy. God was good to Stewart Headlam and rewarded him with the opportunity to strike a
Christian blow of charity at the Establishment. In old age he
went bail for Oscar Wilde.

It's a wonderfully moving experience to contemplate the
activities of these passionate priests, incense pot in one hand
and red flag in the other, awakening the souls of men in the
smoky, filthy slums of late Victorian London and subverting
the Establishment. Their type of course still exists, and has
spread across the world, but they are the first, and are un-
deservedly too little known today.

Lux Mundi was the testament of another world altogether,
although it is significant that most of these Oxford theologians
and scholars were Socialists. The old High Toryism of the
Tractarians had withered away. Under the influence of German Higher Criticism, Broad Church theologians in England
had evolved a liberal theology of the sort that was to find its
final statement in Harnack best represented for us by Matthew
Arnold's *Literature and Dogma.* The miraculous and the eschatological passages were shorn from the New Testament.
Jesus was called the "greatest ethical teacher who ever lived."
This of course was not the historic Jesus but the Jesus of the
liberal historians. Nor was the Church at any time an association for making men good. An attentive and unprejudiced
reading of the Gospels would convince any outsider that the

preaching of the historic Jesus was saturated with eschatology and that he was emphatically not, in the Liberal sense, a great ethical teacher. His ethics, based on the imminence of the Kingdom, would destroy not only Victorian society, but even the noblest Victorian utopias, altogether. But an eschatological Christ raises the question immediately of the limitations of his human knowledge. He said he did not know the hour of the coming of the Kingdom. He quotes from the Pentateuch and the Psalms and the Book of Daniel with the assumption that they are by their traditional authors. He apparently believes that the Queen of Sheba really visited Solomon, and that Jonah and the whale really happened. Reacting to the blows of the Higher Criticism, the orthodox position, especially the Roman Catholic, became more and more docetic. The humanity of Jesus became more and more phantasmal. The suspension of the omniscience and omnipotence of God in the God-Man became a kind of pretense or even hoax—a position morally intolerable. We forget that devotion to the Sacred Heart was introduced to restore the humanity of Jesus to a central place. The devotion increased in popularity directly in proportion to the mythologizing of its object, until the Sacred Heart became a Gnostic statue representing a mysterious and inhuman minor deity.

The essays in *Lux Mundi* group themselves naturally around Charles Gore's "The Holy Spirit and Inspiration." Gore accepts the Higher Criticism of the mid-century Cambridge theologians Wescott, Lightfoot and Hort, who had turned the rationalistic criticism of the Germans against them and had demonstrated conclusively that the Old and New Testaments were inspired, not literally, but by the guidance of the Holy Spirit of the fallible and slowly evolving religious capacities of men, to culminate in the messianic evangel not only of the Gospels and the Epistles but of Acts—of the life and faith of the infant Church. The message of Scripture was supernatural, or it was nothing. As presented by Gore, this was not new, although more radically stated. The novel and still controversial element enters when he applies the same concepts of evolutionary revelation to the career of the historic Jesus as the Incarnate Lord. Gore takes over from the Danish Lutheran Martenson's *Christian Dogmatics,* and from A. J. Mason, the disciple of Wescott and Lightfoot, the notion that God in the Incarnation emptied himself of omnipotence and omniscience to become man, in all things like unto us. The term, *kenosis,* emptying, is derived from Second Philippians where the kenotic doctrine of the Incarnation is stated most clearly. What Gore did was to substitute for an irrelevant logical puzzle a new and believable mystery, the self-limitation of the divine love in incarnation for the redemption of mankind. No doubt St. Paul believed something very like this, but the tradition of the Church gives it little support. It is the doctrine of Origen, but Origen was a semi-heretic.

Bishop Martenson was relatively unknown in England and the kenotic implications of the Cambridge theologians had not been noticed. *Lux Mundi* struck the Church as a revolutionary document. Its mythological treatment of the Fall and of Original Sin, its communitarian theory of baptism, and Gore's *kenosis* created disturbances which are still resounding. At the same time they implied an entirely new cosmogony and theophany, fundamentally both mystical, and collective in inspiration. In the kenotic theology God empties Himself out of omniscience, omnipotence, eternity and infinity into Time, into His humanity, which is *our* humanity. In response the Christian soul empties itself into Him, empties itself into timelessness and so is emptied of contingency. The spiritual maturity of such a conception moves Christian theology up alongside the discoveries of the great Christian mystics with whom hitherto orthodoxy had always been unable to cope. After Charles Gore, who was to develop his ideas in a succession of books and his mystical vision in sermons and devotion, Anglo-Catholic theology grows largely around its doctrines of the Incarnation and the Atonement, defining one in the terms of the other, so that Atonement is read at-one-ment. Eventually and independently this would become the background presupposition of the most influential modern theology, whether Frank or Berdyaev, Schweitzer or Teilhard de Chardin, or for that matter the syncretists who came into prominence during the Second War and who first popularized in non-occultist and scholarly terms, the mystical theologies of the Orient. (Alan Watts is still an Anglo-Catholic priest. "Holy Orders is a sacrament conferring indelible grace.")

The contributors to *Lux Mundi* overlapped the turn of the century and the emergence of Catholic modernism, and the next influential Anglican symposium, *Essays Catholic and Critical,* is really a comprehensive statement of the Modernist position, better organized and more at home in the Anglican than the Roman Church. The rise of Catholic Modernism, its condemnation and its underground existence and its eventual emergence, greatly transformed, is another story. By 1890 the foundations had been laid in Anglo-Catholicism.

Some Notes on Newman

It would be as easy to write an essay on Newman as the leader of reaction, both political and religious, as it would be to write one claiming him as one of the fathers of Liberal Catholicism or Modernism in Great Britain.

Newman was an anomaly in so many ways. He occupied a position not unlike that Paul Tillich attributed to himself, suspended between contradictions in religion, in politics, in philosophy, in race, in family background, and not least in personal temperament. There is nothing unusual in the bare facts of his own intellectual development and his influence. He went from counterrevolution and *Restauration* to a position that could be claimed plausibly as ancestral by the first Modernists. But this is true of the Romantics generally. The medievalism of Chateaubriand becomes the socialism of William Morris. Sir Walter Scott becomes the favorite reading matter of revolutionary nationalists in Italy and the Balkans. Out of Schelling come Wagner and Nietzsche. Lamennais embodies the whole process in himself. What is consistent in Romanticism is what is consistent in Newman—anti-rationalism. Today in popular speech that term has become blurred and confused with "irrationalism" with which, in the final decadence of Romanticism, it does in fact merge. In 1830 Rationalism meant not Euclid or Aristotle or Aquinas, but Diderot, Voltaire, Condorcet, Condillac, even ironically enough, Rousseau—the whole Enlightenment lumped together.

The Romantics in their time were right. After the fall of Napoleon the *philosophes* were wrong, not for political reasons but for technological ones. Locke or Hume or Kant are

philosophers, if not for all time, for a very considerable length
of time, because they deal with problems that lie deep under
the technological changes of ten generations. The men of the
Enlightenment do not seem to us to be philosophers at all,
because they accept the picture of the world provided by the
tools and instruments of the eighteenth century as not just
adequate, but final. This is true in medicine or astronomy.
It is even more true in Biblical criticism, anthropology, comparative religion, of the subjects that bore on contemporary
religious development, some of which acquired names only
in the nineteenth century, and the sociology and histories of
religion and ideas. In little more than two generations the
simplistic picture of the world, which seemed profound on the
eve of the Revolution, had become simply vulgar.

By the time of Newman's youth the secular world was well-
embarked on a new scientific revolution that would eventually find the place for a sensibility such as his. In those days
his opponents were too busy in practical, non-ideological
activities to manage more than a kind of man-in-the-street
positivism. For Newman, and all those like him, this was not
enough. It's not that he could not reason, or that his reason
was affronted. It's that the entire world view of the "other
side" was totally irrelevant to his sensibility.

John Stuart Mill could go a long way toward understanding
Newman, but to Newman, Mill belonged to another species,
with a radically different nervous organization. One of the
things that makes Newman so baffling is the purely personal,
individual aspect of his sensibility. Thinkers who arise out of
a hot spot in a highly polarized force field are usually aggressive, even violent, personalities. The metaphor is chosen
to emphasize the appropriateness of the term "dynamic." Like
Paul Tillich, Newman was generated at a point where contra-
dictories and contraries cross, but unlike others so placed,
Newman after youth seems to be passive, uncombative, anything but dynamic, once he has found his home in the Roman

Church. Recent critics have called him a masochist, justly or not, but certainly, like masochists, his submissiveness was illusory, most of all to himself. Nothing is more domineering than indomitable submission. Geoffrey Faber is the best known of the critics who have subjected Newman and his comrades of the Oxford Movement to amateur psychoanalysis. This is another case where science and its instruments have outgrown a popular synthesis in two generations. I find his psychologizing as dated as Newman must have found Condorcet.

Nevertheless in Newman's case it is impossible to avoid personalities. That's what Newman's religion, and out of his religion, his philosophy, is—the posture of an irreducible reality—a personality—in the face of a worn-out mechanism. The story of the Oxford Movement has been told countless times, and almost always the tale has been centered on Newman. But Newman was the leader of the Oxford Movement not because he was its greatest theologian or Biblical critic or historian of religion, but because he was its leading personality. He was its spokesman because he spoke so well. He was in fact the only one of his colleagues who did not write abominably. Newman was the master of a great style. Style is the man. In the final analysis the Catholic Revival, Anglican, Roman, Russian, or French, is a matter of persons, not of doctrine or ritual or even "faith and morals." What Newman says is what Nietzsche or William Morris say, or what Blake at the very beginning says, or Kierkegaard, or Chaadayev—"There is no room for a whole person in the nineteenth century synthesis." Since there is even less in the twentieth-century synthesis, they are all still relevant.

So those critics who have either accepted and tried to trace, or who have denied, Newman's influence on Liberal Catholicism *and* Catholic Modernism have operated on a false assumption. There is nothing Liberal about Catholic Modernism. Historically it took its rise in a thorough-going attack on Liberal Protestantism, and specifically on Adolph Harnack.

The only reason the Modernists did not attack the tradition of Lord Acton and his friends directly was that they needed all the allies they could get. The situation is analogous to those anti-Liberal movements in our time who, when they get in trouble, call on the American Civil Liberties Union to defend them from the Liberal State. The comparison is not unjust. Those who link Blake, Kierkegaard, Newman, Baudelaire with Lenin, Mussolini, William Butler Yeats and Ezra Pound are perfectly correct. All are in revolt against the commercial industrial civilization, and in that civilization even the most humane Liberalism has its roots in the Liberalism, properly and first so-called, of the Manchester School, as those apostles of the satanic mills had their roots in the Enlightenment with its new moral and intellectual virtues that found their apotheosis in those heroic bourgeois, *le bon Franklin* and Goethe. This is the real reason why Newman is still influential. In detail much of his writing is absurd. His influence is really confined to three or four leading ideas, most especially the illative sense, the development of doctrine, the apologia to the doubting, and to his symbolic role. It's not true that "the Pope declared war on the nineteenth century with the Syllabus and the First Vatican Council." He just wanted it to be *his* nineteenth century. Newman stood against the world and the times absolutely. Yet in the end they had to make him a Cardinal. He had outlived most of his enemies. With the changing times the world was beginning to lose faith in the worldly syntheses so carefully put together, whether by Pope or Positivist.

To the Pope the doctrine of infallibility was true and proved by both logic and history. To Lord Acton and Döllinger it was false, illogical, unhistorical. To Newman it was a mystical experience. To Newman, as to Tertullian, the direct experience of Christ was primary. If that experience was incompatible with reason, so much the worse for reason. It simply showed that the world was not in that sense rational.

Sacrificium intellectus, what Aldous Huxley with consummate irony called the *philosophia perennis,* the visionary tradition, agrees with one voice that the abandonment of the rational intellect is the first portal of illumination, the first veil of Isis. Lord Acton knew this too, but he kept it to himself behind the facade of the other *philosophia perennis,* the rationalist tradition that begins with Aristotle. Only once in a great while Acton would drop a waspish remark that was revealing only to those who already knew—"I have never in my life had an intellectual doubt."

Newman doubted every day—intellectually—and came to think of himself as the Apostle of the Doubters. This alone was enough to outrage the entire establishment from Pope to catechist. It is not permitted to doubt your reason because it is reason that supports the Magisterium. If reason can be made to support the Magisterium, Newman implies it can be made to support anything, and so reason is always inadequate. Revelation is only something that happened in history, and so submits itself to reason, says both the Magisterium and the infidel.

In Newman's day the idea that revelation was immanent in all life and time, that it was the experience of reality itself, was unheard of in the Church, except here and there by obscure scholars and contemplatives, lost in the study of forgotten medieval and patristic semi-heretics, or lost in prayer. Here lies the explanation for Newman's devotional writing so shocking to Catholic intellectuals who discover it today. He learned early from Hurrell Froude to assault and subject the intellect with absurdities and impossibilities. Bleeding and nodding statues, holy napkins and every fragment of that thirty-ton "True Cross"—Newman accepted them all as he accepted the Holy House of Our Lady of Loreto, Patroness of Aviators.

Newman was a compulsive writer. Even in old age his output was enormous, yet when he was not sleeping or eating or playing the violin or counseling others he seems to have spent practically all of his time in prayer. There are few authentic portraits in all history so totally formed by the *"Sculpte, lime, cisèle!"* of the torch of prayer, yet his devotions are most of them the routine parochial performances you could find in a Birmingham parish of illiterate Irish working women, from his day to ours. They may shock intellectuals who go to them seeking a Liberal San Juan de la Cruz and find a more simple-minded Saint Alphonsus Liguori. They are purely disciplinary, like the rosary or *Om Mani Padme Om*. Is there any concrete evidence that Newman was really a contemplative? Very little, except the accounts of the proportion of his time he spent in prayer and meditation. His age, even, or especially, in the Church, did not give him the language or the audience. His intellectual background did not provide the tools, and finally his personality was secretive of its deepest experiences, but his entire career and everything he wrote is understandable on no other hypothesis.

Is Newman then one of the Fathers of Aggiornamento? It all depends. He is the father of one *aggiornamento*, but there are two; and the one he heralds is still largely outside the Church. If modern or Modernist Catholicism means social activism, de-mythologization, rationalization of the Gospel narrative, the liturgy in Kiwanis Club English, and sermons lifted from Norman Thomas, the ancestors of this *aggiornamento* are Newman's enemies—the elder Bishop Wilberforce, leader of the anti-slavery crusade, Charles Kingsley, founder of Muscular Christianity, and, ironically enough, the Ultramontane, but passionately rational, and tirelessly socially active, Cardinal Manning. If *aggiornamento* means a total challenge to the predatory technological society of post-capitalist Western civilization, Newman was an ancestor. At this moment when most of the progressive elements in the Church are just discovering Charles Kingsley, and are engaged in a rationalistic struggle with the rationalistic Magisterium, Newman's children are the young fellows and girls who quietly elbow

their way to the front rank of peace marches, chanting Hare
Krishna, who sit at the gates of army posts in the lotus posture
doing *zazen,* or who have worked out detailed astrological
prophecies of the fall of capitalism that supersede Marx. Before Vatican II there were large numbers of young people
like this in the Church, but today the liberal and enlightened
secularizers have pushed them aside. Where are the young
Catholic Workers who once sat up all night in Greenwich
Village bars arguing about St. Bonaventura and Dionysius the
Areopagite, who sang Abelard and Venantius Fortunatus instead of Woody Guthrie and Pete Seeger, and marched against
the atom bomb chanting *Media Vitae*?

His latter-day descendants, whether Bernard Lonergan, the
young Catholic Workers, or the Dutch Bishops, would have
horrified Newman and thrown him into paroxysms of penitence. He would not have believed that he had raised heretics,
but that he had raised devils. Like Matteo Ricci, Newman
was caught in his mission. You cannot appoint yourself Apostle to the Doubting without infecting yourself with their germs.
It's the kind of inoculation that produces the disease itself in
a non-virulent form by the injection of half-dead bacteria. It
does no good to say that by the phrase "development of doctrine" you mean the unfolding in history of the seamless cloak
given once for all to the Apostles. Your descendants will take
the term literally. Newman, Keble, Pusey, but not Froude, always spoke of the Oxford Movement as apostolic. Their apologetic moved back and forth through the conciliar period, the
Alexandrine, Cappadocian, and Syrian Fathers, the Apostolic
Fathers, always back to the Descent of the Holy Ghost, and
then forward—but to where? With such a hypertrophied notion of the Sacrament of Orders, Newman finally could make
no sense of the House of Bishops of the Established Church.
He had to find an absolute authority, because he had to believe that Holy Orders was not just a sacrament conferring an
indelible grace, but an absolute one. With the body and blood

of Christ it is all or nothing. If the body and blood of omniscience, omnipotence, eternity, infinity, flows through the dual flame symbolized by the cloven bishop's mitre—with it flows infallibility. All the terms of what is communicated in Holy Communion imply it, either the collective infallibility of the Council of Apostles or the guaranteed infallibility of their chairman's successor. The white and gold thread of the Papacy must go back clear through the unfolding, seamless robe to "Feed my sheep. Feed my lambs," because it obviously did not go back through the collective Anglican Episcopacy.

There is only one answer for Newman to the technique of systematic doubt, and that is infallibility. His descendants would find systematic doubt in itself sufficient as a foundation for faith. They would say, "In the sub-Apostolic period, where you are seeking evidences for infallible authority, there is no evidence for belief in the Trinity, much less for the primacy of Peter's descendants, or even evidence that anyone believed he had any descendants as such." It is significant that doctrinally Newman chose to agitate himself with the finest-drawn definitions of the conciliar period, Monothelitism and semi-Pelagianism. Newman, as he said of himself, was shaped early by Gibbon. Where Gibbon said in a sarcastic footnote that when the Pope read the Athanasian Creed, he threw up, Newman clutched it to his breast like the arrow of St. Theresa. Pascal, Kierkegaard, Newman—doubt, the instrument of ecstasy. Later generations would simply accept doubt as the normal environment of the soul, just as the most spiritually developed amongst them would accept the habitude of illumination as birds accept air, and fish, water. Eventually the mystic consciousness that Newman kept so carefully hidden would come to recognize doubt and illumination as two faces of the same coin, on one: the owl of Athena, on the other: In God We Trust.

Here is the source of Newman's "illative" sense. Illumination precedes thought. Vision precedes knowing. There is, in the actual fact, no epistemological problem. When the words "actual fact" are used in their etymological sense, they produce nothing resembling the process described by all the fathers of the epistemological dilemma, from Aristotle to Locke, Hume and Kant. In Newman's guide to the doubting, the illative sense sometimes sounds like a childish or even vulgar and sentimental conception, but it subverts the entire structure of epistemology, so carefully founded on tiny blocks of blue and green, salt and sour, loud and quiet, soft and hard, foetid and perfumed. His is the epistemology of mysticism. In the heyday of scholastic rationalism it was the epistemology of the Victorines and behind them of Arabo-Jewish mysticism, as it would later be the epistemology of the post-nominalist mystics, of Wilhelm Meister, Henry Suso, and Nicholas Cusanus. Here was the source of authority, not the Chair of Peter. Newman could never be content with it. He lived in England in the nineteenth century under Queen Victoria. His most fundamental experiences were socially disgraceful. There was nothing in his intellectual environment to provide him with the means to understand, much less express, his position at the center of the X which marks the spot where all contradictions and contraries cross. The time would come when his Catholic followers would read the Diamond Sutra with comprehension, but it was a hundred years away, a hundred years even from the old, gentle, gracious man refined by all the fires of prayer, who would soon be made a prince of the Church, a courtier of that Papal State at last reduced to a walled palace.

We must realize that always for Newman, poverty, chastity, and obedience were not only great virtues but they were very close to being sacraments—and most especially obedience. Newman carried over into the Roman Church his Anglican ultra-Episcopalianism. This explains his seemingly perverse masochism in crises like the Irish university, the translation of the Bible, the Oxford chaplaincy. Bishops were channels of grace. Submission was a door into prayer, but it's a strange grace the act of obedience confers, for its distinguishing virtue is *contemptu mundi*—not in the final analysis very complementary to its "matter," a bunch of politically motivated Irish-American bishops, for example.

Had Newman remained an Anglican, he too would probably have ended up a highly skilled political bishop. Certainly his role in the Oxford Movement was primarily that of publicist and political boss, or of course, he might have dribbled himself away, an ill-tempered neurotic, like Kierkegaard, blasted in quarrels with fools. Rome made a saint of him because it enabled his techniques of achieving sanctity.

Newman's Copernican revolution was not faith founded on skepticism, as in Tertullian, or de Maistre, but the shifting of the grounds of apologetic to ultimately purely psychological evidence, an immanent and continuous, rather than sudden, pentecostal Evangelicanism. Newman's opponents could not understand what he was doing but they could feel it. In those years there may have been no profound intellectual activity in the Roman Catholic Church in England except Newman's, but there was enough intelligence and experience, both in Westminster and in the Vatican, to recognize the gravity of the threat. Newman, far more than Pascal, is the religious empiricist par excellence. Pascal leads to Kierkegaard and thence to Barth and thence through Scheler to secular existentialism. Newman, as has been remarked countless times, and each time angrily denied, leads to Father Tyrrell. Father Tyrrell leads to Evelyn Underhill, who leads to—where? Aldous Huxley? Alan Watts? Simon L. Frank?

The rock of Newman's epistemology is purely and simply experiential—the fact of dialogue—the echo of the Word of the Person speaking to me is the essential principle and sanction of the Christian life, and of the Church—from *I and Thou* to Mounier, to Father Perrin. Newman's apologetic was like the hormones that kill weeds by overstimulating their growth. What was so important in the nineteenth century was the resistance he generated. Now that the resistance is almost impotent, what remains of Newman's apologetic is the sacramental life, the apostolic life, Pentecost. The progression, skepticism, empiricism, experientialism, existentialism falls away as only a patina of polysyllables. What remains is the sacramentalization of the world and the divinization of man. This was the Patristic progression as it must have been in real life, lived day by day, the apostolic progression in the actual lives of the Apostles. What was going on underground in Newman's apologetic was the same development that was going on in Russian Orthodox theology or philosophy. The Magisterium was at least philosophically astute enough to strike this new growth at its roots. To a theology of doubt it answers, "No doubt about it!" To the illative sense, a quiver full of quotations from St. Thomas on *De Anima*; to the development of doctrine, the flat statement that the brothers of the Son of Miriamne the Mother of the Lord believed in her immaculate conception and stood with faces uplifted while she rose bodily from the tomb fluttering into the clouds. Charges such as this can only be answered with obedience considered as a sacrament. *Contemptu mundi.*

The Surprising Journey of Father Lonergan

During Easter Week of 1970 I participated in a most remarkable and moving experience in the most unlikely circumstances. It was a theological conference, called "Ongoing Collaboration," held at tiny St. Leo College in Florida in honor of Bernard Lonergan, S.J., and intended for both further explication of his philosophy and for the most radical criticism of it. It was a living *Festschrift* with some 77 participants, among them many of the leading philosophers, theologians, religious and philosophical critics of the world. Due to the careful organization of Joseph Collins, the young man who financed this scholarly spectacular out of his own pocket, Bernard Tyrrell, David Tracy, Eric O'Connor, Cathleen Going and others, it was a unique event in philosophy, theology, ecumenicity, and plain human relationships, all at once. As everyone who took part and even the most cynical observers from the press recognized, it was a landmark: the achievement of a profoundly collaborative dialogue in regions of thought where men customarily talk only of themselves and nobody listens.

But it might be wise to first explain briefly who Bernard Lonergan, S.J., is. For even the well informed public has scarcely heard of him. To quote *Time* magazine:

Canadian Jesuit Bernard J. F. Lonergan is considered by many intellectuals to be the finest philosophical thinker of the 20th century. Easter Week 77 of the best minds in Europe and the Americas —critics and admirers, Protestants, Roman Catholics, and agnostics —gathered to examine Lonergan's profoundly challenging work at rural St. Leo College near Tampa, Fla.

He is a philosopher's philosopher and a theologian's theologian. To quote *Newsweek*:

269

Yet in the dozen years since it was published, *Insight* has become a philosophic classic comparable in scope to Hume's "Inquiry Concerning Human Understanding" and Lonergan's students have returned home to universities in Western Europe [and Latin America] and the U.S. to spread his influence far beyond the confines of the Catholic Church.

Bernard Lonergan was a professor of theology, first in Montreal, then in Toronto, then for twelve years at the Gregorian Institute in Rome, and now is back in Canada. Over the years a slowly increasing number of students have come to him from all over the world. By no means have all of them been Roman Catholics. Many have left his courses not even agreeing with him, but all have felt that their ability to, in Wittgenstein's best phrase, "do philosophy," has been vastly improved, precisely in "insight," in broadening of "horizons," "multiple dimensions," and in method, four of his favorite terms.

His major work, *Insight,* is highly technical and written in the technical language of three different modern schools of philosophy at once—the special German existentialism and phenomenology that stems from Heidegger and Husserl, themselves almost completely incomprehensible to the layman; the English epistemologists and linguistic analysts who descend from Wittgenstein; and the very special "transcendental" Neo-Thomism of Maréchal, who was one of Lonergan's teachers. The last is the principal influence, and the word transcendental is of key importance, because it is used in the technical sense of the neo-Kantians, with almost exactly the opposite meaning it has in vulgar discourse—a not uncommon peculiarity of technical philosophizing since Kant. What Maréchal did was to re-establish the Aristotelianism of St. Thomas against the devastating critical philosophy of Kant—not as hard a trick as one might imagine. As Wittgenstein might have pointed out, all one has to do to subvert and convert a philosophical opponent is to take over his language.

What Bernard Lonergan did was to humanize Maréchal and

to vastly broaden the horizons of his philosophy by taking account of more complex, subtle or simply up to date philosophical developments.

Now, the traditional objection to Aristotle or Aquinas, or Maréchal, or Lonergan, or Kant, or for that matter, Hegel, is that their philosophies lack interiority. They are sorting devices, tools to order an impersonal universe and so, in the long run, are reducible to the operations of those expensive binomial sorting machines that are *not* going to replace the human mind except on science fiction inter-galactic spaceships. Metaphysics, yes; but still physics, meta or no. They provide no meaningful account of the fundamental experiences of life which precede the epistemological problem with its sorting of percepts into concepts, concepts into judgments, and judgments into actions. In other words, they have no really valid explanation for the most real "fact of life," the experience of (to talk jargon) intra- and infra-subjectivity. For St. Thomas, in spite of his disclaimers, the mode of apprehension of the beatific vision, as of the self, and of the other, is knowledge. In Western Catholic philosophy, and even more amongst the Orthodox, there is a counter-tradition in which love is the primary and the ultimate mode of realization and being comes at us with what Whitehead called "presentational immediacy."

I came to the conference as a "critical respondent," not as a Lonerganite. In fact I should say that Lonergan interested me less than almost any recent religious or philosophical thinker. I shall quote extensively from my paper because it is a succinct enough presentation of one form of the opposition to Lonergan's philosophy, as it stood on the eve of the conference for those who did not know him personally, or in other words, as it was available in print up to, and including, his most recent publications.

A generation ago when I was young and given to the excited reading of philosophy I would have found books like *Insight, Verbum, The Subject,* very stimulating indeed. Today I find them entertaining but irrelevant, that over-abused abusive word. There is a certain pleasure to be derived from reading them and a sectarian admiration that "one of ours" has mastered the mysterious language habits of fashionable interbellum and immediate pre-contemporary philosophical writing—that a Catholic philosopher can be as cocksure as Wittgenstein, as amorphous as Husserl, as ambiguous as Jaspers, and as summary as Alec Mace. It's one form of updating Catholicism, of *aggiornamento*. But is it?

Is epistemological speculation fruitful in the latter years of the twentieth century? Was it ever? Perhaps the Marxists are right. Perhaps the long, drawn out epistemological agony of modern philosophy is due to the peculiar alienation fostered by the capitalist mode of production, and the resulting abstract, inapprehensible character of value and power in life, and in the State, and in class relations, and the final fragmentation of agent-action-act-result, in what had once been one dense reality. Epistemology was not an important concern of Aristotle or St. Thomas. They solved it with the simple syntactical arrangements of the realism that has come to be known by their name, and they passed on to what they considered more important matters.

Furthermore, those problems of classical and scholastic philosophy that we look on as epistemological were not, at least not in the psychological sense. The contrary or contradictory worlds of Parmenides and Heraclitus, Plato and Aristotle, were theoretical models of ways of being, not primarily of ways of knowing. Scholastic philosophy was, as everybody but neo-scholastics agrees, fundamentally syntactical or topological. It was concerned with ways of sorting a known being that was really taken for granted—"what makes a horse a horse is horseness." Capitalist philosophy has turned these concerns into the sausage grinder of its epistemological worry and dilemma. It has even done this with classical Chinese and Indian philosophy where arguments about knowing, naming, and the knower and the known are not epistemological in our sense at all, but a kind of transcendent lexicography. So the dilemma of Thomism which Father Lonergan resolves in *Insight* is not the fault of St. Thomas, but of Locke and Hume.

Furthermore, Father Lonergan's concept of insight as the first and final term of the epistemological process dates back to before St. Thomas, to Richard of St. Victor, who in addition, and even more profoundly, realized that in the final analysis epistemology is moral. And it survives, enfeebled by a hostile environment, in Cardinal Newman's "illative sense." Of course it's true that it is the whole man who knows he knows. The atomistic Newtonian machine that manufactures knowledge in the English empiricists of course cannot know it knows. So the system of production which came to birth with it cannot know what or why it is producing. Maritain realized this and it was his improvement on the Thomistic theory of knowing, an improvement he always insisted was orthodox Thomism. As I recall it was always the theory of Father Harper, S.J., the now forgotten and quietly discouraged author of the unfinished *Metaphysics of the Schools.* The intactness of the response of the whole human being to being itself was a favorite notion of the anti-Thomists of the nineteenth and early twentieth century—the Modernist Transcendentalists—and even, I suppose in their way, of their opponents, the Immanentists.

Still it is good that the issue should be raised again, forcefully, at least for those who can read with pleasure and can understand the peculiar language of twentieth-century philosophy which Father Lonergan has introduced into the Catholic universe of discourse. It's not just that we need to know how we know and how knowing in its most exact form builds up exact knowledge which is the vesture of truth. What is most important is that implicit of the kind the clergy pejoratively call mystical. Knowledge begins with the beatific vision and knowledge ends with the beatific vision. For Father Lonergan and St. Thomas this is truth, the sum total of knowledge. But to know all, is as the proverb says, to forgive all, which means,

274 &* *The Elastic Retort*

to love all. I think the anti-Thomist tradition would say that knowledge is the process of the soul realizing itself in the world and with the world. This can be called knowing when faith means primarily belief and assent to propositions, but it is better called love. Consciousness begins with love, the *scintilla animae,* and ends in love, the beatific vision. And so faith becomes a habitude, a kind and a state of being. We no longer know we know; we no longer know we love, as fish do not know they swim in water or birds that they fly in the air. This is what Zen Buddhism is all about, and other kinds of Buddhism too, less familiar to Westerners. It was what St. Thomas meant, when dying, he looked back on his career, and said that the best thing he had done was the Office of Corpus Christi.

If Father Lonergan was saying that all the ultimate terms of meaning are one meaning, and that meaning is vision, and that vision is love, he would be very contemporary, very relevant. Hidden under his shifting, cobwebby style, that is what Newman is saying, which is why the Integrists and Maximalists amongst his colleagues considered him a heretic and a father of heretics. It is why all the anti-Thomists from Blondel to Tyrrell could turn to him for encouragement. A hierarchy of love is not authoritarian in the same sense as a hierarchy of knowledge. So Laberthonnière, who owed so much to Newman, who could say in a letter to von Hügel:

St. Thomas . . . appears to stand doctrinally for a radical anti-Christianity. In place of the Gospel's God of love he put an ego-centric form. His metaphysic justifies the Inquisition and slavery. In a word he is the theologian par excellence of theocracy. For him the Church consists essentially in the ecclesiastical organization regarded as a *domination* that is to be exercised under the direction and to the advantage of the theologians . . . I have found that Buchez had a way of characterizing him that seems to me perfectly just. In St. Thomas, says Buchez, all the questions are asked in Christian language, but all the answers are given with a pagan meaning.

It's all interconnected. Is Lonergan's insight the overseer of an authoritarian epistemological process? I think it is. Is Lonergan's neo-Thomism a highly complicated revival of the imperial Papalism inherent in the very metaphysics of St. Thomas? I think it is. Lonergan has a long and characteristically ambiguous discussion of the development of doctrine, more ambiguous even than Newman himself. Does Lonergan believe in the evolution of doctrine accompanied with radical mutations and the failure of certain species to survive? Does he believe in the organic growth of doctrine from a genetic code programmed in the seed, or does he believe in the umbrella theory, the unfolding cloak whose pattern was already there and just becomes more apparent to our eyes as we, not the doctrine, develop? I think he believes in the latter. His turgid apology for the infallible declaration of the Doctrine of the Assumption of the BVM would certainly indicate that he was as maximalist as any parish de Maistre could wish. Here we are back with the Syllabus of Errors and a deliberate defiance of the twentieth century, and of course of the sixteenth and the first four centuries as well. This is the heart of the matter. When Lonergan is discussing, not faith and morals, but behavior and belief, it is only too obvious what his philosophy adds up to. Doubtless its conclusions in ethics or politics or dogma can be rejected and its more etherial reaches retained even by the most radical. But why bother? What we need is what the Orthodox philosophers and theologians have always said the Roman, and in fact the whole Western Church (except for groups like the Quakers and Mennonites) so conspicuously lacks—a life philosophy, and ultimately a philosophy of being and meaning, of which Christianity is not an appended conclusion, ultimately unprovable, but of which Christianity is the primary substance, the body and blood. Life lived in the eye of Apocalypse, in the arms of the abiding experience of God—there is such a thing as an eschatological epistemology —but it is not to be found in the rationalistic system of Father Lonergan.

So I for one do not find Father Lonergan relevant. Jules Feiffer's man says to his little boy, "Relevance means about black and white." An Apocalyptic revolution is going on all about us, lit by burning buildings. Outside the Church people who read about *aggiornamento,* Vatican II, and the last Saint John, assume that a revolution is still going on inside the Church. Maybe. As far as the magisterium is concerned, what is going on is a counterrevolution. Father Lonergan defends the Pope when he invokes his own infallibility to proclaim a doctrine which is intrinsically unbelievable. When he, Lonergan, should be explaining the profound, mythic meaning of the Assumption, a symbol in the same class as "and sitteth on the right hand of God the Father Almighty." Meanwhile other people are shouting from the housetops or at least from the underground passages, "Depose Montini!" Similarly there is an eschatological politics. There was no room in the coming Kingdom for unconverted scribes and Pharisees, although there were Zealots amongst the Twelve. Except for cutting off an ear or two, they were not Zealots of the sword, but of the spirit. So today it behooves the Christian, and most especially the Catholic, to be far more, not less, revolutionary, than the followers of Che Guevara. Read the Gospels, St. Paul, the early Fathers, even the Cappadocian and Syrian Fathers. No organized society in history could survive a thoroughgoing Christianity. Certainly a putatively Christian philosophy which justifies a State and an economic system which can stay alive, or rather, artificially be animated, by continuous war, economic exploitation, emotional repression and perversion, and rabid hatred of the young and of other races, can only be called neo-Catholic now that we are really living in the Fire and the Judgment. But then the Church has always been neo-Catholic since the Donation of Constantine—another myth and symbol like "sitteth at the right hand," but less beneficent.

I would like to see a profound and profoundly Catholic philosopher whose thought prepared one to grapple with the real issues facing the Church: not superficialities like a married clergy and communion in both kinds, but the admission of women to the priesthood, the destruction of the financial empire of the Church and of course the private enterprise of the Vatican; not divorce and birth control but the right of homosexuals to marry; not mini skirts for nuns but the revival within the Church of the lay monasticism that secular youth are reviving all around us; not the rediscovery of Charles Kingsley and muscular social Christianity, but the revival of what the hidden Church has always had, a flaming social action which comes out of the most profound contemplative realization; not Mass and the Scriptures in the flabby jargon of a Kiwanis club luncheon, but a restoration of liturgy as *tremendum*. How silly it is for the Church to start mimicking the long dead Norman Thomas, when placard-carrying nuns and priests march in demonstrations, and around them weave young people in oriental robes chanting "Hare Krishna." I think some of the questions besetting the Church are unanswerable. But I think the philosophy of Berdyaev, Soloviev or Simon Lyudvigovich Frank amongst the Orthodox, or Blondel or Marcel or Mounier amongst the French, or Ernst Bloch amongst the Germans, comes nearer than Father Lonergan's to underwriting that Church which we remember from only a few years back— young lovers of the Catholic Worker group marching arm in arm in demonstrations chanting *"In media vitae, in morte sumus."*

> He who is near to me is near to the Fire.
> He who is far from me is far from the Judgment.
> He who is near to me is near to the Judgment.
> He who is far from me is far from the Fire.

In his talks at the conference, Bernard Lonergan made it very clear that he thought of his present thinking, as he would say, in these latter terms, terms of "inter- and infra-subjectivity," of social responsibility, esthetic realization, and the dynamism required by the contemporary apocalypse. He promises his new and major work will be a "theology of love." True, he spoke of the basic discussion of *Insight*—"What do we know when we know we know"—as leading on to and being subsumed into the book he has been working on for several years now. This is doubtless true. Only the individual can see clearly his own present in his past or vice versa, but for the rest of us Lonergan's talks at the conference represented movement into a new dimension, a shift into another universe of discourse. Naturally such a radical shift of direction took all the wind out of the sails of his opponents. There was nothing left to do but to agree with him.

The changes in philosophical orientation seem to have been accompanied by political changes as well. Opponents have abused Lonergan in the past as "the metaphysician of the Magisterium," in other words as a fancy apologist for Papal absolutism and the Roman Curia. His newly richer and broader and more human philosophy seems to be accompanied by a certain estrangement from the Montini counterreformation. This is apparent in the statement of the Canadian bishops on the birth control encyclical and in the recently developing very radical ecclesiastical and social positions of many of Lonergan's most devoted followers. It is no longer possible to say that Lonergan's philosophy has no place for a true interiority, no place for the contemplation of love, no place for deep wisdom in human relations. Today he says these are the foundations of his philosophy, not the epistemological sorting of billiard balls of color, sound, smell, taste, and touch.

I think the change in Lonergan is a reflection of the change in the Church and in the whole meaning given to life by those at the growing point of contemporary society. Lonergan would say that of course there is no change at all, simply the development into ever widening horizons. This may be true of Lonergan himself, and it may be true that the Church has only developed implicits that have been there since the beginning.

But certainly these implicits have been deeply buried for a long time under the virtues of organized Christianity—formalism, bigotry, cruelty, egocentricity, anger, pride, and the lust for power. Organized Christianity is the only world religion all of whose operative principles have been the exact opposite of those of its founders (at least until November, 1917). Then one day there came along a very ordinary pious man, much given to contemplative prayer, who put on the triple crown, and said, "Let's try acting like Our Blessed Lord."

The papers said that the Lonergan conference may well have been the most important religious event since Vatican II and that it was the first high level international attempt to realize the principles laid down in Vatican II. It was in fact much more than that. It was a realization of the spirit of Pope John, an "infra- and inter-subjective" noumenous happening, ultimately unanalyzable into any taxonomy. This was the big event, the important thing.

I have been to other philosophical and theological conferences and they have been markedly less distinguished by wisdom and more secular than any conference taken at random, say of apiarists or plumbers. And they have been filled with contention, where people only listened to themselves. The organizers of "Ongoing Collaboration" moved in some mysterious way to select participants and set up modes of discussion which created an atmosphere not unlike that of an ideal Quaker ashram or Benedictine retreat: where theologians from the Gregorian institute sang "Ciao Ciao Bambina" in a very rocky rhythm while people danced in the evening and Senators and abbots and students from St. Leo's and biblical exegetes sat on the grass and discussed the Church and revolution—what does the responsible spiritual man do as a civilization dies around him, or is it already dead? The all-pervasive atmosphere of a creative community, of agapé, of affection, respect, realization, contact, was unparalleled in my experience except precisely at Pendle Hill, the Quaker ashram near Philadelphia, or once at a retreat at the Community of the Resurrection in Mirfield, England.

At the beginning of the first day of seminars I thought at first it was going to be Bishop Dom Butler of Westminster, the Dutch theologian, Henri Nouwen, Eugene McCarthy and myself against the other participants in our little group who seemed much more secular, but as in every one of the seminars, and in all the sessions, the technical papers which we had submitted and which, tactically very important, were read beforehand, not delivered, were forgotten, and the meetings turned into conversations "unprogrammed" as Quakers say, a sharing of concern in the face of worldwide chronic catastrophe. The conversations were lively enough, but their foundations were no longer contention but contemplation. The seventy-odd participants were moving severally and together in the same paths as Lonergan's philosophy itself in the most recent years of its development. The atmosphere of comradeship and joy was an outward visible sign of an inner spiritual reality. It was a meeting in interiority. It was not necessary finally to argue about "infra- and inter-subjectivity." The meeting of persons was apparent. If the conference was the most important thing since Vatican II, this is why it was. Ecumenicity has characteristically been founded on platitudes exchanged with middle class gentility. If persons who presume to speak for the deepest meanings of life and the deepest responsibilities of man actually make contact in depth, perhaps theology and philosophy can once again justify themselves. Somewhere in these regions lies wisdom, and we need above all else a new, more profound wisdom philosophy. For here in the eye of Apocalypse who would not prefer Marcus Aurelius to Rudolph Carnap. . . . ?